The Musicology of Record Production

Recorded music is as different to live music as film is to theatre. In this book, Simon Zagorski-Thomas employs current theories from psychology and sociology to examine how recorded music is made and how we listen to it. Setting out a framework for the study of recorded music and record production, he explains how recorded music is fundamentally different to live performance, how record production influences our interpretation of musical meaning and how the various participants in the process interact with technology to produce recorded music. He combines ideas from the ecological approach to perception, embodied cognition and the social construction of technological systems to provide a summary of theoretical approaches that are applied to the sound of the music and the creative activity of production. A wide range of examples from Zagorski-Thomas' professional experience reveal these ideas in action.

SIMON ZAGORSKI-THOMAS is a Reader at the London College of Music, University of West London. He is a director of the annual Art of Record Production Conference, a co-founder of the *Journal on the Art of Record Production* and co-chairman of the Association for the Study of the Art of Record Production (www.artofrecordproduction.com). His publications include *The Art of Record Production* (co-edited with Simon Frith, 2012). Before becoming an academic he worked for twenty-five years as a composer, sound engineer and producer with artists as varied as Phil Collins, Mica Paris, London Community Gospel Choir, Bill Bruford, The Mock Turtles, Courtney Pine and the Balanescu Quartet. He continues to compose and record music and is currently conducting research into the musicology of record production, popular music analysis and performance practice in the recording process.

The Musicology of Record Production

SIMON ZAGORSKI-THOMAS

CAMBRIDGE
UNIVERSITY PRESS

CAMBRIDGE
UNIVERSITY PRESS

University Printing House, Cambridge CB2 8BS, United Kingdom

Cambridge University Press is part of the University of Cambridge.

It furthers the University's mission by disseminating knowledge in the pursuit of education, learning and research at the highest international levels of excellence.

www.cambridge.org
Information on this title: www.cambridge.org/9781107428348

First published 2014
First paperback edition 2016

A catalogue record for this publication is available from the British Library

ISBN 978-1-107-07564-1 Hardback
ISBN 978-1-107-42834-8 Paperback

Contents

Acknowledgements

This book is, for me, an important milestone in the Art of Record Production project: the conferences, the association, the journal and the edited book. The ideas have been brewing for more or less the entire decade that I've been working on the Art of Record Production. The many discussions that I've had with the various conference organisers, paper presenters, keynote and panel speakers, journal editors and other participants have been crucial in shaping my ideas, and a great many of them have been accompanied by wonderful food and drink. In particular, I'd like to thank Katia Isakoff and the respective hosts of all the conferences for making the Art of Record Production work and being such a delight to be involved with. A few other special mentions should go to Sam Bennett, Steve D'Agostino, Anne Danielsen, Simon Frith, Mike and Been Howlett, Allan Moore, Steve Savage, Alan Williams, Paula Wolfe and Albin Zak.

Another group of people who I owe a debt of gratitude to for helping me (and putting up with me) while I learned my craft as a sound engineer are all the engineers, producers, musicians and others from my days at Thomas Crooke Musical Services, The Premises Studio, Da Studio and Southwark College, and my freelance work. And, of course, my colleagues at the London College of Music, University of West London have been very helpful and supportive. I particularly appreciate the discussions I've had over the years about various aspects of recording and production with Paul Borg, Andrew Bourbon, Richard Liggins, Larry Whelan and Pip Williams and the support that 'the boss', Sara Raybould, has given me to develop my research activities. In addition, the students on the MA in Record Production and others I've had the pleasure of teaching have all helped to shape these ideas in various ways.

This is a very interdisciplinary project and it has led me to a whole range of conferences that have introduced me to new ideas and new people that have inspired me to strike out in various different directions: several IASPM conferences, the 2004 BFE conference, various CHARM events, the 2012 CMPCP Performance Studies Network conference, the 2012 SHOT conference, the 2011 Osnabrück summer school on Methods for Popular Music Analysis, the 2011 Sound in Media Culture research network meeting in London, the 2006 Music and Gesture conference, the 2005 Conference on Interdisiplinary Musicology, the 2010 Black Box Pop conference in Mannheim and the University of Oslo's Rhythm in the Age of Digital Reproduction research network meetings.

I also need to thank Paul Borg, Anne Danielsen, Anthony Meynell, Liz Pipe and Alan Williams for having a look at my early draft and offering opinions and very useful and supportive criticism.

And Natalia and Alex for everything.

1 Introduction

What do I want to do with this book?

In 2007 I wrote an article for *Twentieth-Century Music* with the same title as this monograph, in which I laid out an earlier version of my thoughts and therein lies the rub. Having been involved in the Art of Record Production conference, journal and association for over eight years now, I have observed several problems that others involved in the study of music have been wrestling with. These problems lie broadly in two areas. The first is that, despite the fact that the academic study of music has really developed in tandem with the development of recording and recorded music, it hasn't sufficiently addressed the ontological question of how recording changed music and how that change needs to be incorporated into its study. The second is a broader question and one of which perhaps the first question is a symptom. Why are there such chasms between the studies of different types of music? Why, for example, do popular music scholars so rarely talk to classical music scholars? This seems to be a much deeper problem than for the visual arts or literature, and yet also coincides with a period of unprecedented cross-fertilisation in musical practice.

The first question is really the subtext of the whole book and I'll start to get to grips with that in the next chapter. The second, though, informs my approach to writing this book and, as such, although I hope the detail will emerge as the book progresses, I will lay out some of my thoughts on the subject in this introduction. As for the question of what I'm trying to achieve with this book, although in one sense it is a personal manifesto about an important direction I believe musicology needs to cover, it is also intended as a spur for discussion. In a specific sense I am trying to establish a broad framework for the subject area that combines my ideas about some issues with a survey of how I think other existing work fits within this framework. As Anne Danielsen suggested when she was reading through a draft chapter of the book, it is a meta-text: a book that seeks to elaborate the nature of the academic subject itself rather than one that provides an in-depth analysis of any specific features. By using examples to illuminate some particular theoretical points it does, of course, enter into that territory, but my primary purpose is to draw a rough large-scale map of the disciplinary landscape and to suggest a strategy for filling in the detail.

In a more general sense, I am aligning myself with what I see as a larger trend in musicology, an agenda that flows out of ideas from psychology and sociology. In psychology, this is the ecological approach to perception and the ideas of embodied cognition. In sociology (and cultural theory) it involves the constructionist approach to the sociology of technology, the systems approach to creativity and other ideas from the sociology of culture and anthropology. I'll expand on these shortly (and throughout the book) but first I should explain something about the structure and organisation of the book.

The structure of the book

The structure of this book has evolved out of three layers of categorisation. The first is concerned with the issue of the dichotomy between production- and reception-based approaches to musical analysis. By analysing the connection between the composer/performer/producer and the audience/listener, I want to examine areas of compatibility between them and the potential for common tools. There is quite a major structural divide within the academic study of music that has its roots in the historical division between what might crudely be described as learning how to do and learning how to listen. On the one hand, musical analysis has tended to be predicated on the idea that the 'text', the object of musical analysis, should be treated as a standalone object. The intentions of the composer or performer, the historical or cultural context in which the work was created, and the influence of the technologies of musical instruments and other aspects of the creative process have, in the ideology of 'pure music', been considered irrelevant, or at least given. The way that the musical text creates meaning is inherent in the music itself. In recent years, the ideology of analysis has shifted to include the historical and cultural context and, for example in historically informed performance practice, the influence of instrument technology. This shift has involved the notion that musical meaning is a result of interpretation and that different listeners will produce different interpretations. These are fundamentally reception-based approaches to musical analysis: they focus on how music produces musical meaning for a listener. The production-based approach that examines the creative process rather than the creative output lies in a fundamentally different and pragmatic tradition.

In the ideological context of higher education where the status of a subject is related almost directly to its practical applicability, pure mathematics, theoretical physics and philosophy are at the top of the tree, while mechanical engineering, nursing and sports science are at the bottom. This traditional hierarchy is to a certain extent self-perpetuating, in that the inertia in the older, more established and prestigious universities means that they tend to be less concerned with vocational subjects. The more established and prestigious researchers therefore tend not to be attracted to the analysis of the practical creative process. Recently, commercial pressure and the politics of the research impact agenda have started to put pressure on this hierarchy and there have also been certain historical anomalies. For example, research into the process of creating medicines has a higher status than other practical applications of scientific theory. In the academic world of music practice, composition, performance and record production have tended to follow a traditional model of the vocational subject: the teaching of good practice in terms of a framework of rules and guidelines. Some are rules per se and some are rules that are learned so that they can be creatively broken from a position of knowledge. Research in these areas is far less common than on the reception side, and has tended to be about the identification and formulation of these rules and guidelines. Of course, ethnomusicology has been engaged in the study of the processes of music creation in a parallel but largely separate discipline. It is only in recent years that performance studies, the study of the record production process and ethnomusicology have started to infiltrate music departments and to bring the tools of psychology, sociology and anthropology to bear on the creative process. This distinction between the production- and reception- based approaches to analysis exists within the book's structure mostly through the attempt to build bridges between them. Certain chapters cover areas that lend themselves to one approach more than another, and the commentary in Chapters 2 and 3 will make this clear as well as explaining how I intend to reconcile them.

The second layer of structure is the relatively obvious formal process of typology that I've engaged in with my chapter headings. While this introduction and the following two chapters address some of the methodological questions, there follow eight chapters that, I argue, constitute a functional typology of the key issues that need to be addressed if recorded music and record production are to be integrated into musicology. There are, of course, areas of overlap, but this typology has been useful to me in developing my research ideas and the curriculum for the Master's in Record Production I wrote for the London College of Music, University of West London. This typology is based around an analysis of the agents and activities involved in the production and reception of recorded music. On the reception side I start with two chapters (4 and 5) that deal with the psychology of listening to recorded music, while Chapter 10 deals with the sociology of audience reception and Chapter 11 deals with that halfway house between production and reception: the recording industry. On the production side, Chapter 6 examines the technology: the non-human 'participants' in the recording process. Chapter 7 deals with how humans engage with that technology, and Chapters 8 and 9 examine how the participants on the recording and performance sides work together and interact. I should reiterate, though, that my aim here is not to attempt an explanation of all these phenomena but to lay out a map of how I believe they can be explained and to provide a few examples along the way.

The third layer relates to the way in which the underlying theoretical framework unfolds throughout the book, and the four interludes that intersperse the eight chapters of the typology provide brief explanations and introductions to this. After some initial explanations in this chapter and the following two, Chapters 4 and 5 involve some further expansion of the ideas around ecological perception and embodied cognition. This forms the basis of my ideas about the psychology of listening to recorded music. Chapters 6 and 7 introduce some ways in which actor-network theory (ANT), the social construction of technology (SCOT) and the systems approach to creativity can be applied to various aspects of record production. This allows us to discuss both the technology and the ways in which humans engage with it. Chapters 8 and 9 then start the process of integrating these psychological and sociological approaches from a practice/production perspective. This happens through the prism of the collective creative practice, communication and interaction of the recording process. Chapters 10 and 11 do the same from a reception/audience perspective by discussing the way audiences engage with production on a collective level and the way the business combines the role of fan/audience with that of motivational driver of the production process.

The structure of the book reflects my rather pragmatic philosophy, a recursive idea that my knowledge is schematic and the features I'm interested in determine the schematic representation that I use. Although the eight categories were a decision that predated the book and grew out of the article for *Twentieth-Century Music* (Zagorski-Thomas 2007), the other layers have been an emergent property of the writing process.

Music and reification

Christopher Small's (1998) lasting legacy in both ethnomusicology and performance studies was to coin the term 'musicking' to describe music as a process rather than a thing. I'll explore the relationship between recorded music and business in more depth in Chapter 11, but three fundamental changes in the nature of music have occurred because of the development of technologies that allowed its reification. The development of sheet music publishing made a durable consumer product out of music for the first time. Before then, the only potential for commercial exploitation lay in the ephemera of performance. Sheet music afforded a physical product from the composer's output that could be sold. It was the key driving force that propelled the European art music tradition to privilege composition over performance, and it did this in two ways. First, and most obviously, it provided a vehicle for durability, legacy and the estimation of value through the process of widespread dissemination and the potential to put a numerical or financial value on popularity. But it went further than the comparable simplicity of sales figures. Beyond the boundary of their lifetime their work could continue to sell. Not only could their work live on, but its popularity could be measured. Of course, sales are not the only criterion for assessing a legacy, but if any cultural capital that might accrue from gatekeepers and academics extolling a composer's value is not subsequently reflected in audience approval then it is likely to be short-lived. I'm not suggesting that an assessment of whether Bach is superior to Mozart or Beethoven should be made on cumulative sheet music sales, just that it is unthinkable that a composer who was lauded as great could retain that position as a legacy without widespread dissemination.

The second way in which sheet music led to the privileging of composition over performance was that it provided a mechanism for the analysis of composition that wasn't available in relation to performance. This provided composers with a way of representing the rules of composition in a much more straightforward manner than was possible for performance. That representation also allowed those rules to be extended, altered and expanded in a much more systematic manner than those of performance. Further to that, it led to the academic study of the score becoming a cipher for the study of music.

The next technological change that led to a fundamental shift in the nature of music was the development of recording. The wax cylinder, disc, tape and CD provided a century-long range of technologies that allowed a similar process of reification for performance that sheet music provided for composition. Nellie Melba, Ella Fitzgerald and Elvis Presley have a legacy as performers in a way that Adriana Ferrarese, Hans von Bülow and Jenny Hill[1] can never have because they were never recorded. The analysis of recordings has had a similar effect on performance practice to that the analysis of scores had on composition, particularly in jazz and popular music styles. Practitioners have used the detail of their heroes' recorded performances as a starting point for learning to play and improvise, and this has led to a similar extension, alteration and expansion of the rules of performance practice.

The last of these technological changes is the shift from recorded music as hardware to software: from a physical product to a digital file. Of course the main way that this change is discussed is in relation to economics and distribution: the revolution in the market for recorded music. Equally important, though, is the fact that recorded sound has become something that consumers can manipulate themselves. While the physical product of music embodied in a disc or CD allowed repeated plays, the digital audio file allows a further level of analysis that affords the visual representation of recorded sound. I can see the amplitude, dynamics and frequency spectrum of an audio file as easily as I can see melody and harmony on sheet music. This kind of representational system will surely lead to as significant a change in the way we think about music as the development of musical notation did. Not only does it afford these new types of visual representation, it also affords an expansion in both the scope and availability of audio processing. Not only can the consumer have access to the types of audio processing that were previously only available to the semi-professional and professional sound engineer, there are also an increasing number of new techniques for processing being developed all the time.

These forms of reification also point to another key theme in this book that I will expand upon in Chapter 4: the nature of recorded music. I argue that recorded music is as different from live performance as photography, film and even painting are from the objects they seek to represent. Indeed, representation is the key word for me. Recorded music is a representational form of art. It may be the result of Small's (1998) process of musicking, but what is produced is a schematic representation of some real or constructed performance. The representation may be relatively realistic, like a photograph or an unedited section of a film, but the 'two-dimensional' nature

[1] Adriana Ferrarese was a famous eighteenth-century soprano who sang in Mozart operas at the Burgtheater in Vienna. Hans von Bülow was a nineteenth-century German conductor and pianist and Jenny Hill was a nineteenth-century British music hall performer.

of recorded music will ensure that we can tell the difference between the representation and the 'real thing'. Of course, the representation need not be realistic, like an edited film where close-ups tell us where to focus our intention. We may, for example, mix a whispering voice to be louder than a drum kit in a recorded song.

How music works

Earlier in this chapter I suggested that this book is a personal manifesto about the direction I believe musicology needs to be taking. Defining that direction has to be based on an ideological position about the nature of music and the process of music-making. I say it is an ideological position because I believe it is a case of the evidence suggesting rather than proving anything about the neurology, psychology or sociology of music. I'm therefore going to start with an outline of how I see ecological perception and embodied cognition relating to the interpretation of music. This is intended as a brief overview so that the flow of the book isn't interrupted by having to systematically elaborate these ideas as they crop up in various chapters.

Ecological perception

The ecological approach to perception was developed by James Gibson (1979) and has been applied to music by Eric Clarke (2005), among others. The foundation of this approach is that perception emerges from a system comprising both an animal and its environment. The properties of the physical and cultural environment produce a richness of perceptual data that can produce direct forms of interpretation that don't require the kinds of mediating cognitive activity required by other theories of perception and cognition. Particular rich patterns of stimulation such as optical flow (the rate of change of size and shape of light patterns on the retina) produce direct forms of interpretation. For example, the way light reflects off objects in the environment means that forward locomotion, either by the animal or by an object in the environment, generates a pattern of expansion on the retina. When I move towards a rock or it moves towards me, the particular pattern of light that is reflected off it will get larger on my retina. I don't need to know about rocks or even travelling to develop a mental connection between this type of optical flow and the painful sensation of something hard hitting my face. The connectionist approach to perceptual learning (Clarke 2005, pp. 22–32) suggests that patterns of stimulation and action that are encountered frequently become entrained into the structure of the brain. This is not a form of learning in the cognitive sense of creating a mental representation of some aspect of the world that includes logical and causal connections: it is about the creation of a frequently trodden pathway in the brain, which includes the expectation about how a particular pattern of stimulation might continue and what it normally leads to, including bodily action.

As the physical experiences that lead to the creation of these well-trodden pathways are not exactly the same each time, the process is based on the identification of certain aspects of experience that remain the same while the details may differ. Gibson calls these 'invariant properties' (1979, pp. 310–12). The connectionist approach to perceptual learning would involve the brain activity associated with these invariant aspects of experience being reinforced as pathways with repeated experiences, while the detail that differs each time would not be reinforced. This, for me, is the basis for the schematic nature of mental representations: certain common features are established as invariant properties of different categories of events or objects through the reinforcement of certain paths and the revealed irrelevance (non-reinforcement) of others. Thus, the relative pitch differences within a scale might become established as invariant properties, while the vocal or instrumental timbre, absolute pitch and rhythmic pattern may vary. The idea that perception and action cannot be separated and that the connectionist structures of invariant properties that become entrained in the brain involve both the stimulus and the bodily responses leads to another crucial idea in Gibson's work: 'affordances'. Put simply, an affordance is the potential for future activity that perception suggests. The frequently trodden pathways of perception are associated with and lead to previous forms of activity (affordances) that may or may not be followed. Stoffregen and Bardy (2001) have suggested that the perception of invariants and affordances happens at a global level rather than within the individual modal systems (vision, audition, touch, etc). Under this system the structures of perceptual learning would be multi-modal.[2] The sound of a drum being hit would be part of a mental structure that also involved an invariant visual pattern of a hitting gesture and, bringing us neatly to the notion of embodied cognition, to the sensorimotor experience of performing a hitting gesture.

2 See also Tagg's notion of composite anaphones for a different perspective on multi-modal perception through his prism of semiotics (2012, pp. 509–13).

Embodied cognition

George Lakoff and Mark Johnson have, in a series of books (Lakoff 1990; Lakoff and Johnson 1999 and 2003), been at the forefront of the development of the notion of embodied cognition. One of their key concepts is the 'image schema'. This is a schematic representation of a familiar, repeatedly experienced activity. For me there is a very clear mapping between this and the structures of perceptual learning that I've just been discussing in relation to ecological perception. Johnson and Rohrer have characterised the image schema as:

1. recurrent patterns of bodily experience;
2. 'image'-like, in that they preserve the topological structure of the perceptual whole, as evidenced by pattern-completion;
3. operating dynamically in and across time;
4. realized as activation patterns (or 'contours') in and between topologic neural maps;
5. structures which link sensorimotor experience to conceptualization and language;
6. structures which afford 'normal' pattern completions that can serve as a basis for inference.

(2007, p. 30)

Both Lakoff and Johnson and others have developed extensive lists of image schemata that range from containment to axis balance and from full–empty to part–whole. Many of these imply the next step that is referred to in points 5 and 6 of Johnson and Rohrer's list: the creation of metaphorical relationships between our bodily experience and phenomena we perceive in our environment. Rohrer has examined the neurological evidence for image schemata and outlines the following example in relation to the image schema for grasping an object:

When one monkey observes another monkey perform a grasping task with their hands, the mirror neurons will activate the motor-planning regions in the monkey's own hand cortex . . . experience in one modality must cross over into another. In this example, the visual perception of grasping crosses into the somatomotor cortices, activating the same sensorimotor schemata that would be activated by the monkey grasping something on its own . . . The monkey needs only experience a small portion of the motor movement to complete the entire plan . . . Such patterns can serve to integrate sensory input across modalities; a monkey's grasping mirror neurons can fire, for instance, when the monkey hears a sound correlated with the grasping motion, such as tearing open a package. This suggests that even when

> triggered from another modality, the brain tends to complete the entire perceptual contour of an image schema . . .
>
> The perceptual and motor imagery performed by certain regions of the brain subserve at least some processes of language comprehension: we understand an action sentence because we are subconsciously imagining performing the action. (2005, pp. 170–2)

How then does this relate to the perception and interpretation of music? I'm going to return to my example of the sound of a drum and the image schema of hitting that it is associated with. The richness of the information that is encoded in a sound like that provides much more information than the simple fact of a hitting gesture. My past experience of things being hit in the world, whether by myself or by others, will allow me to glean a lot of contextual information. What kind of object is being hit in terms of size, shape, the materials it might be made of, etc? Is it being hit with a hand or with an implement of some kind? How close to or far from me is the hitting taking place, and in what kind of environment? What kind of energy is being expended in the hitting process?

Cross-domain mapping

This brings me back to the idea of metaphor, but more generally to the notion of cross-domain mapping. Fauconnier and Turner (2003) describe conceptual blending – the mapping of features from two mental spaces onto a third, blended space – as fundamental to the way we think. Hearing a particular type of snare drum playing a march rhythm might suggest a blend between the musical content of a track like 'Travelin' Soldier' (Dixie Chicks 2002) and the military theme of the lyrics. The death of the soldier mentioned in the lyrics and the military snare rhythm of the outro evoke a blended space that combines the military theme with a funeral march. However, this high-level interpretation is built upon a whole sequence of more basic mappings between the sound of the drum and various other domains that contribute to our interpretation. Although few of us would know that the sound of a military snare drum is characterised by a second set of metal snares on the underside of the top skin as well as one on the bottom skin, the metallic sound and the lack of resonance will be familiar to many. In addition, the feeling of distance and space in the outro changes from the more intimate space of the song to a more public and formal distance for the ending. This simple trope of transporting the song to a different space and adjusting our positional relationship to it is achieved through our intimate understanding of spatial sound: something that emerges from our lifelong perceptual learning in conjunction with our environment. Lastly, the highly controlled marching pattern that incorporates the buzz roll suggests the regimented gestures of military drumming. Although most of us couldn't reproduce the performance of this drum pattern, we still understand the sound in terms of the possible physical movements that would produce it and understand those movements in terms of the kinds of cultural context in which they might occur. The solemnity and control of these gestures can evoke both the physical/emotional mood that these types of activity would be associated with and mappings to broader cultural associations like a military funeral or a commemoration service.

Metaphor involves a different type of mapping: from a source domain to provide a structure for a target domain. Lawrence Zbikowski has explored this notion of conceptual blending between lyrics and music in relation to multi-modal metaphor (2009, pp. 370–6). In an analysis of Jerome Kern's 'The Way You Look Tonight' performed by Fred Astaire in the movie *Swing Time* (Stevens 1936), Zbikowski makes the metaphorical connection between aspects of focused attention in the lyrics and the music and the suggestion of intimacy they invoke. More generally, expectations about pitch movement, rhythm and timbre are based on embodied and cultural metaphors about the type of activity that might have made them. Downward pitch movement generally suggests a lowering of energy expenditure, while upward pitch movement suggests the opposite. Large upward leaps suggest a sudden surge of energy and large leaps downwards suggest the opposite. I've already discussed how rhythm reflects gestural activity and timbre has a similar close relation to the suggestion of types of activity. These are not interpreted as separate features but are cross-modal and multi-dimensional. We do not, for example, interpret pitch or harmony in isolation from rhythm or timbre.

As important as the direct visceral connection between certain sounds and certain gestural activities are the more indirect connections and mappings that are made between sounds that have no direct embodied correlation. Of course, this is a continuum rather than a dichotomy. At one end of the continuum are sounds that can be made by the body without tools: singing, hand claps, etc. Moving away from that extreme are instruments with a straightforward connection to a tool such as a drum or a kazoo. As the tool becomes more complicated, the sound becomes less human and more machine-like. Instruments such as the trumpet, the violin and the piano rely on us being able to create some cross-modal mapping with a particular form of gesture: blowing, stroking or finger movements. Those of us who don't play those instruments hear their sounds in terms of more generic gestural shapes. Even further along the continuum are the sounds of machines and electronics that don't have a necessarily human gestural correlate to their sounds but which, nonetheless, we understand by how they stand in relation to gesture. For example, a synthesiser sound might have a timbre and a morphology reminiscent of a brass sound but, through its consistency, be obviously artificial. The conceptual blend of different mental spaces that we employ to represent this will suggest a further blend of metaphorical relationships through which we can generate a musical interpretation. Another dimension in relation to this continuum relates to sounds that are obviously non-human. Human vocal range extends from around 80Hz to around 1100Hz, and within that range there are limits to the kinds of sounds that can be made – loud volumes aren't possible at very low frequencies, for example – and thus sounds that lie outside this range or are somehow 'inhuman' within this range create supernatural or other-worldly associations. The extreme high- and low-frequency sounds of church organs and the use of high- and low-frequency sounds in science fiction and supernatural film soundtracks are both examples of this kind of evocation.

However, this is just the tip of the iceberg and, although I'm convinced that this is the right theoretical model, it is far from complete and there are a great many problems as well as areas that have yet to be examined. The nature of a theory about tonal and harmonic systems that fits within this framework is a big gap that needs addressing in the future, but I think it offers an opportunity to address a problem that has exercised me for several years: the idea that the interpretation of harmony shouldn't happen without simultaneous recourse to rhythm, timbre and gestural shape. However, as sketchy and incomplete as this may be for a universal theory of musical meaning, it provides the basis for the analysis of musical interpretation in this book. The use of the word 'universal' might be seen as controversial, but the intention is to suggest that there are series of underlying universal processes rather than a single universal way of interpreting any given piece of music. From this exposition it should be clear that there are certain fundamentals about the nature of being human within our environment in the most general sense that affect our interpretation of sound and music, such as having arms that move in a certain way, being subject to gravity and having ears that respond to acoustic signals in a particular way. These fundamentals may give rise to certain universally human forms of interpretation such as the perception of gentle, energetic, simple, complex and other forms of activity within music, which afford some types of interpretation but not others. However, these basic types of affordance are then filtered through the complexity of cultural and personal experience to ensure that we share some aspects of our interpretation with some communities and yet some remain highly personal and individual.

Representational structures in the brain

Before I move on to the next section, I want to take a short diversion to explain my thoughts on the nature of knowledge structures in the brain. There are only five claims that I believe need to be made about the specific nature of these structures to support the theoretical framework that I'm using.

1. All these structures, from the simplest to the most complex, are schematic in nature. Certain features are represented, the invariant properties, and need to be perceived (either directly or through some form of mapping) for the structure to be triggered.
2. These structures all involve direct links between perception and action. Whether the action is carried out or not is not important. If a structure is triggered, the affordance of the connected action is also triggered.
3. All these structures, from the simplest to the most complex, are initially created and subsequently maintained through a process of reinforcement.
4. The connectivity between these structures is recursive and can be bi-directional. The complex structures involve multiple iterations of simpler structures, and mapping involves one structure (A) that is triggered from within two or more other structures (X and Y) and through which, if A triggers X, Y can be triggered by A. This is the process by which features from X can be mapped onto features from Y.
5. The more complex structures can be created and maintained voluntarily.

Outlining the detailed structure of this complex network of cognitive structures is beyond me and beyond the scope of this book. Within the theoretical models that I will use and discuss in this book there is a bewildering array of terms used by different authors. I consider image schema (see Lakoff 1990; Johnson 1990), neural networks (see Feldman 2008) and the establishment of invariant properties and affordances through the process of reinforcement in ecological perception (see Gibson 1979) as being broadly equivalent and the simplest forms of structure. Feldman (2008) uses the terms 'frames' and 'scripts' for higher-level structures. Schank and Abelson (1977) also use the term 'scripts' and incorporate the notion of 'goals'. Fauconnier and Turner (2003) use the much less specific term 'mental spaces' in relation to conceptual blending and cross-space or cross-domain mapping. Lakoff's

(1990) term 'idealised cognitive models' relates to more detailed and specific notions that include prototypes, metonymy and metaphor in cognitive structures. As we shall see shortly, several theorists in the constructionist approach to the sociology of technology use the terms 'script' and 'program' in a more abstract way but with a similar connection to a learned or prescribed sequence of perceptions, responses and activity. I will endeavour to use the authors' own terms for these types of representational structures when referring to their theories and will also aim to make it clear when I am drawing comparisons between the different ideas and terminology.

How musicians work

If the previous section reflects the reception-based approach to musical analysis that I discussed earlier, this section examines the production-based approach. Latour asserts that 'the social' is not a material or a domain but is something that exists only in as much as it is performed (2005, pp. 1–16). This is reminiscent of Small's (1998) assertion that music is a process and not a thing. Indeed, the notion that musical activity should be analysed as a social process involving people, technology and their environment is also a central tenet of this book. If the theory of ecological perception is concerned with how an animal and its environment act as a perceptual system that incorporates both stimulus and action, the theoretical basis I'm using for how musicians and other participants work together in the creative practices of music-making is also an interactive system involving information transfer and activity. At the same time, just as the mental representations of knowledge and action in the perceptual and cognitive models involve feature-based schematic representations, so too are the representations of social activity schematic. In both instances the messy physical reality – of neurobiology and chemistry on the one hand and groups of individuals with complex webs of motivations, knowledge and capabilities on the other – is described in a schematic, representational way to make it easier to understand. Also in both instances the theoretical structures that combine stimulus/information transfer and activity therefore also provide the potential to bridge production- and reception-based approaches to analysis. One of the key attractions for me of this theoretical combination is this coherence between the individual and the social.

Pinch, Bijker and Hughes, in the twenty-fifth-anniversary edition of their 1987 edited collection on the *Social Construction of Technological Systems*

(2012), described three main areas in their constructionist approach to the sociology of technology: ANT, the systems approach and SCOT. Interestingly, although the initial ideas focused on the production side of technology, the other important theme they describe is that of various feminist writers who addressed the users of technology: the reception-based approach. In some ways this agenda from the sociology of technology forms the basis of my approach to creative practice in music. Of course, the notion of applying these ideas to music technology is not new (see, for example, Pinch and Trocco 2004), but their application to musical activity in more general terms is more recent.

My approach to ANT is based around the performance of social activity and relationships through the construction and alteration of schematic mental representations within the individuals involved in the network. One of the thornier issues with Latour's (2005) definition of the theory involved the inclusion of inanimate objects as well as people as actors within the network. The idea was that, while the designers of these objects weren't explicitly members of the network, the inherent scripts for usage that were built into the design meant that the technology configured the activity of the human members of the network. In fact, Latour specifically references Gibson's notion of affordances (Latour 2005, p. 301) in relation to the way the design of technology configures its use and therefore its users. The fact that there are usually multiple affordances but only one 'correct' script designed into technology, has led Akrich and Latour (1992) to identify the notions of the program and the antiprogram. This notion of a user repurposing an object, rejecting or redefining a design script is also apparent in Hirsch and Silverstone's (2004) process of the domestication of technology. For the purposes of representing the social activity of a network, the specific nature of the neural or cognitive structures is less important than the kind of schematic information that they represent. It is important to remember, however, that there are two potential processes involved: the involuntary process of perceptual learning, whereby experience reinforces certain connections and inhibits others; and the voluntary process that can occur in the more complex structures, whereby the choice to reconfigure a mental representation is made as a result of the processing of evidence or persuasion. The social process of interaction involves all the human actors in the network reconfiguring their mental representations of the activity, the music and each other in response to their engagement with the other actors (human and inanimate). The inclusion of musical instruments and notation as well as recording technology as actors in a creative musical network allows this approach to be applied to all forms of music-making and not just record production.

Within the constructionist agenda in the sociology of technology, the systems approach has tended to be about analysing the design and structure of the technological system. Csikszentmihalyi's (1997) systems approach to creativity, on the other hand, is focused on reception, on the usage of the system. This is because both Csikszentmihalyi and McIntyre (2012) – who has applied the systems approach to recording – have tended to take the technology as given and focus on the development of the knowledge systems and the processes for judging the quality of the creative output. Under this model, the individual engaged in creative activity interacts with two other elements in the system. The first is the cultural domain, which consists of the conventions, traditions, rules and habits that shape the creative activity of the individual. The second is the social field, which is the range of experts, gatekeepers and audiences that pass judgement on the creative output of the individual. My reason for using this in addition to ANT is that, while ANT allows an examination at a high level of detail that is useful for delving into the nitty-gritty of specific situations, the systems approach can be better for discussing more general attributes.

The third string to this methodological bow that I have borrowed from the constructionist approach to technology is SCOT (Pinch and Bijker 1987). A key term in this approach is the technological frame, which refers to the way in which different groups view and define a particular technological question. For a musical example we could look at whether recording technology is designed from the musician's perspective, focusing on features that make performing with technology easier, or from the editing perspective, focusing on the post-production of audio. Different frames may be mutually exclusive or may overlap in various ways but they help to define the ways in which technology progresses. Within any given frame, the participants and stakeholders will have varying levels of inclusion – the extent to which they are committed to that particular frame. This level of inclusion will be influenced by a whole range of factors: cultural, psychological, economic, etc. Related to both the technological frame and the level of inclusion of the participants is the interpretive flexibility of technological artefacts, ideas and processes within a frame. As ideas within a frame become more and more established, the willingness and ability of the participants to question certain basic principles or characteristics reduces: their interpretation becomes more fixed. SCOT provides a perspective from the production rather than reception side and it too can be better for discussing more general attributes than ANT.

Other ideas inside and outside musicology

Drawing from psychology and sociology might seem an odd starting point to a discussion of how to incorporate record production into musicology. However, this is part of a broader move within certain areas of musicology to provide a more coherent basis for the study of music. In my view, this perspective would work equally well if used to explain the possible interpretations of a Beethoven score, the development of the musical and social subculture of UK Dubstep or the design, decoration and social meaning of drums in Western Africa. The decision lies not in the types of music, people, objects or social activity that it studies but in the type of information that is being sought. The aim of musicology for me is to understand how and why we make and listen to music. The 'what, where and who', the subjects of the study, will necessarily be elucidated by these aims. And the how and why of human activity is the stuff of psychology and sociology. If this fusion of ecological perception and embodied cognition with the constructionist approach to the sociology of technology and the systems approach to creativity forms the theoretical basis of the book, there are a great many other ideas used to provide clarity and nuance. Indeed, part of the project of this book is to demonstrate how existing academic work can be accommodated into this framework. Having said that, it is a book on the musicology of record production and so existing academic work will only be addressed that relates to that aspect of musicology. I do intend, in the future, to explore further applications of these ideas but they are beyond the scope of this current book.

There are certain aspects of popular music studies that I have referenced because of the ways in which they relate to these ideas. The notion of the persona in popular music (Frith 1998, pp. 203–25; A.F. Moore 2012b, pp. 179–214) is, of course, crucial to understanding the interpretation of recorded music as well as to its production. The way that a listener creates a schematic mental representation of the performer as part of the listening process is central to the type of interpretation they will develop for a piece of music. In a similar vein is the distinction between different performance types and the cultural resonances associated with particular approaches. Peterson (1997) distinguishes between soft shell and hard core performance styles in the development of country music, relating the performance styles to the introverted and domestic in the former and the declamatory and public in the latter. Once again, these types of category are based on schematic mental representations that the listener builds on the basis of sonic characteristics. Closely aligned to these ideas are the ways in which the notion of authenticity is constructed (see, for example, A.F. Moore 2002), something that seems based on the comparison of a specific example to some prototype of authenticity. Lakoff's idealised cognitive models are one proposed structure of schematic mental representations of knowledge that allow the comparison of prototypes with specific examples (1990, pp. 68–76). Different types of authenticity might be represented as a set of features that characterise certain forms of practice or sound as more appropriate than others.

There are also a number of ideas drawn from the study of recorded music, recording arts and electronic and electroacoustic music that are relevant. Eisenberg's revision of his 1987 book *The Recording Angel* (2005) was an important spur in the development of my ideas about sound as a representational art form and of sonic cartoons.[3] This has been further informed by various theoretical approaches to spatial sound that can broadly be characterised as staging (Moylan 1992; Lacasse 2000), the sound box (A.F. Moore 2002) and the landscape (Wishart 1986). For me, these theoretical models all lend themselves to the idea of a feature-based representation of space. They also work with theories about the social construction of space and place such as Hall's (1966) theory of proxemics and Auslander's (1999) work on liveness. This feature-based approach to metaphorical meaning in sound is also central to Smalley's (1986) notion of spectromorphology in electroacoustic music.

Moving outside the discipline of music, I have used a range of ideas that originate in areas such as cultural studies, literary theory and anthropology but have already been employed by academics in the study of music and musical practice. Bakhtin's (1982) concept of heteroglossia, Bourdieu's (1986; 1993) work on forms of capital, the field of cultural production and habitus, and Born's (2005) adaption of Gell's (1998) work on retentions and protentions in communal creativity are all ideas that can be used to enrich the social constructionist approach that I've adopted. Also, outside musicology, although there is a great deal of work in the area of neuroscience that supports some aspects of the psychology used here (for example, Rohrer 2005), there are only a very few occasions when I look at research at this level for support. One such example is Iyer's (1998) work on microtiming and another is Feldman's (2008) work on linguistics and

[3] The term 'sonic cartoon' is explained in more detail in Chapter 4, but it refers to the schematic, feature-based and, in some instances, exaggerated nature of the representation rather than anything to do with comic animations. It relates more to the Da Vinci cartoon sense of the word rather than to Bugs Bunny or Donald Duck.

metaphor. An approach that helps bridge the gap between the psychological and the sociological levels is Clark's (1996) joint action theory that Kaastra (2008) has applied to performance practice in music. The relationship of role-playing to schematic mental representations of persona and behaviour has also been explored through Goffman's (1956) work on dramaturgy in human interaction. And this examination of interaction and the ways in which collaborative activity can be initiated is also discussed through Long Lingo and O'Mahony's (2010) work on brokerage in the music industry and record production.

2 Why study record production?

In a posting on the Musical Performance on Record discussion list in December 2004 Robert Philip described a demonstration by Gidi Boss, in which a group of academics was asked to evaluate two recordings of the same performance, one on contemporary digital equipment and the other on a 1940s system:

> The modern stereo recording, compared with the mono 40s-style, put the audience in a much less comfortable relationship with the singer. Because of its clarity and impact – qualities characteristic of modern recordings – the singer seemed somewhat overbearing, right there just in front of us, and yet still singing as if we were a more distant audience in a concert hall. The 'old' recording seemed to place the singer at a more appropriate distance (though we were told that the microphones were very close together). The relationship seemed more 'natural'. One could relax and enjoy the performance, instead of cowering from somebody who was singing insistently in one's face.[1]

I'm not going to examine this quotation in too much detail now, although I will revisit it briefly in Chapter 10. Instead, I want to use it as a stimulus to ask a few pertinent questions. If the design of recording technology is a science and audio quality can be judged by the objective measurement of certain features, then how could an older technology produce a more 'natural' and more pleasant sound? How could it be that microphone design or the recording medium can change our spatial perception and make something appear closer or further away? How can recording technology affect the relationship between a performer and a listener? How is it that a recording can make a piece of music sound wrong?

Specific answers to these questions will emerge later in the book but they also pose a deeper ontological question about the nature of recorded music. What is the relationship between a performance and a recording of that performance?

[1] See the Musical Performance on Record discussion list (MUS-PERF-REC@JISCMAIL.AC.UK) for December 2004. The demonstration described was part of the paper given by Gidi Boss at Record Time: an International Conference on Recording and the Record (1998).

How recording changed music

Eisenberg wrote that 'one of the paradoxes of the recording situation, namely that the audience is not there ... [is] the flip side of the fact that, for the listener, the performer is not there' (2005, p. 157). This captures one of the critical issues in understanding the nature of recordings: a fundamental alteration of the performer/listener relationship. However, that frames the question in a way that is akin to saying that photography alters the relationship between the viewer and the view. This is true, of course, and a great many interesting insights can be gained from framing the question in that way, but there are other frames. Just what is it that is captured by an audio recording?[2] The 'reality' of a sound in a space is that we perceive it through a multi-modal perceptual system and we interpret it as part of the whole. Even if I shut my eyes while I listen to something, I have a whole other range of sensory information about my environment. When I listen to a recording I am adding a displaced set of information into the environment in which I listen: hearing the ambience that was recorded in the performance space bouncing around in the ambience of the listening space. As discussed in Chapter 1 perception is not a passive process, and just as any slight movement of my eyes reveals the two-dimensional nature of a photograph in contrast to the rest of my environment, any slight movement of my head will reveal the speaker/point source nature of the recorded sound in contrast to the rest of my environment. In short, I can tell when I am listening to a recording because it is a simplified, schematic representation of the complex, multi-modal experience of a live performance.

There's an analogy here with the relationship between speech and writing. Speech is a transient, performative process and writing allows the storage of some aspects of the information that can be represented through speech. The storage of information aspect of both writing and recording (and other media) is one of the fundamental achievements of human activity, but all representation systems involve the selection of certain features and the loss of others. In the case of writing, the words are represented but the tempo and rhythm, accents and stresses, pitch and tone of voice are all lost. Recording is a representational system for musical events and we recognise that it is not a linear, first-hand experience. There's also a fundamental difference between recorded sound and musical notation, in that a recording is a representation of a performance while notation provides a set of instructions for how to

[2] I'm going to avoid the complications of multi-tracking, overdubbing or electronic music for the time being.

create one. Like writing, music notation represents certain features and not others, although there are usually some forms of performance instructions that are not present in writing. These conventions relate to its function. Writing that is intended to be performed, like a script for a play or a film, will be annotated with performance instructions much like music notation. In a similar vein, when music notation or writing is used to create a transcript of a real event, the system is often altered and added to so that the inflections of performance can be represented in some schematic form. In all these instances, our understanding of an example's representational nature stems from our recognition that it doesn't provide the kind of fully coherent, multi-modal experience that the global interpretation of invariants and affordances of the ecological theory of perception requires.

Authors such as Katz (2004), Chanan (1995), myself (Zagorski-Thomas 2010a) and others have written about various examples of the way in which performers have adapted their performance practice to recording. One of the general factors that has influenced this is the affordance of critical reflection and post-performance editorial decisions. This means there is a fundamental shift in the nature of agency from the single performer in linear performance to the collaborative construction of a composite and partially transformed non-linear performance. It also means that there is a shift in responsibility for the performers. They no longer simply do their best in a performance situation. They may have to listen back to that performance and make an assessment – or at least participate in a collaborative assessment – of which aspects are acceptable and which, given the technical possibilities of the available technology, need to be improved in some way. This not only changes the psychology of performance but also changes the social dynamic of the performance situation through both a different type of performance anxiety and a different type of positive reinforcement.

As Simon Frith and I said in the introduction to our recent book, *The Art of Record Production*: 'to study recording is . . . to raise questions about two of the shibboleths of everyday musical understanding: the importance of the individual musical creator and the sacred nature of "the musical work"' (Zagorski-Thomas and Frith 2012, p. 3). In relation to the question of the individual musical creator, one of the key changes in musical practice that has emerged from the development of recording is also part of a larger shift in emphasis, perception and practice within modern forms of art, particularly during the second half of the twentieth century. The notion of creative authorship has expanded to include creative management and editing or the supervision of a creative performance or production process in the definition of 'artist'. This reflects the fact that many forms of artistic practice have moved from a solitary craft-based activity towards technologically complex manufacturing processes. Thus, a film director essentially manages the collaborative creative practice of manufacture, and the same is true of record production. In the visual arts, figures such as Andy Warhol and Damien Hirst developed forms of practice that involve designing an artistic product and managing a manufacturing process undertaken by others.

In relation to the question of the musical work, many scholars have pointed out that a recording can be the musical work as well as being an instantiation of one. Frequently cited examples of musical works that only exist as recordings include Schaeffer's *Etude aux Chemin de Fer* (1948) and the Beatles' *Sgt. Pepper's Lonely Hearts Club Band* (1967). However, there exist similar ontological issues that plague different editions and versions of score-based works, in that mono and stereo versions, different applications of mastering on different releases and different mixes of the same multi-tracks may compete for the status of the 'original' work. Indeed, it is perhaps ironic, given the supposedly fixed nature of an audio recording, that the development of the technology is undermining the notion of the work. It could be argued about the way in which recording and video technology have become so closely integrated with each other and with live performance that the notion of the work is often replaced by the notion of a project with many and varied forms of output: remixes, videos and the sound, lighting and stage design of live concerts (and the DVD releases of the live events).

This idea of outputs, of course, relates to both the production and the reception side of things: to the difference recording has made to the listener as well as to performers and the rest of the production team. Since musicians first developed mechanisms and social conventions for being paid for their performances, through to the development of the music publishing industry that created income streams for composers, there has been a steady process of commodification in music and recording contributed further to this. The critical thrust of this process is related to Benjamin's (1969 translation of the 1936 essay) argument about mechanical reproduction's removal of the aura of an original work of art. However, a unique aura is only applicable to something with a single instantiation such as a performance. Aside from the process of recreating it as a schematic representation, the recording process removes a performance from its original context and allows it to be reproduced elsewhere. As technology developed throughout the twentieth century this portability increased, and recorded music started to be used increasingly as background to other forms of activity (see, for example, DeNora 2000; Bull 2005). Indeed, the development of audio playback technologies has been at least as much concerned with widening and expanding the opportunities for consuming recorded music as it has with improving quality. This agenda of making recorded music accessible at every turn must surely have contributed to lowering the listener's valuation of it: the more commonplace it becomes, the less value it must have. It seems no coincidence that the cost of recorded music has declined in relation to the cost of attending live performances, which are marketed more and more in relation to the aura of the occasion.

As Gracyk has noted, composition (like a book or a poem) is an allographic form, a work that should be considered without reference to the specific nature of its representation, as opposed to an autographic form that constitutes the unique object of study (1996, pp. 31–6). A recording, even if it does constitute the musical work itself as opposed to a performance of a composition, is never an autographic work. There may be an original master recording just as there may be an original manuscript of a novel but, in terms of someone engaging with the work of art, there should be no difference between that original and a reproduced instance. It is notable that allographic forms of art are the areas where income streams have been hit hardest. The technologies of reproduction – starting with audio tapes, videos and cassettes and moving through CD-R and DVD-R to digital file formats – have become consumer products in themselves, allowing the process of reproduction to become a cottage industry or a hobby, undermining and bypassing the laws on intellectual property.

Another key aspect of how recording changed music, and one which is central to the ethos of this book, is the various ways in which recording technology has become a creative tool in itself. Recording allowed the manipulation of many parameters that were previously fixed. Some, like the relative amplitude of musical components, were part of the broader technological change of microphones and amplifiers that also affected concert performance. Others, like double tracking the voice and editing, allowed occurrences that were impossible in performance.

How recorded music is different

In both Chapter 1 and the previous section, I have described recorded music as being a schematic representation of a real or constructed performance. Building on the ecological approach, whereby perception involves a heuristic process that attempts to interpret the data from the senses in terms of schematic mental representations, it is a continual process of guesswork based on the available evidence and the available cognitive models. In the instance of a representational form, though, there need to be two simultaneous interpretations: what the reality is (such as a canvas with paint on it or a CD player and a pair of speakers) and what is being represented (such as a bunch of flowers or a musical performance). We construct meaning through a process of conceptual blending between the representation and the reality. Within the interpretation of the representation, however, there can also be several further layers of interpretation. There are questions of which instruments are being played, what kind of music is being played, what kinds of personae are engaged in the performance, where (and perhaps when) it is happening, as well as what kinds of emotional, gestural and intellectual meaning the music might suggest.

The more abstract or incompetent the representation is, the more the interpreter may struggle to come up with a specific interpretation. The reality usually isn't in question. There is seldom an ambiguity as to whether we are in the presence of performers or a playback system, but that is certainly possible. Once we recognise we're in the presence of recorded music then the questions of instruments, personae, place and time need to be hypothesised from the sonic output alone. In many instances this is either unproblematic (e.g. it is a piano) or unimportant (e.g. I don't care if it is an acoustic or a digital piano) but we may, for example, be interested in disambiguating complex ensemble textures. The absence of visual cues in particular can make this process difficult and result in ambiguous or generic categorisations of sounds. Although these kinds of ambiguity can sometimes be a production objective, they have also stimulated the creation of even more schematic versions of performances to achieve greater clarity. As we shall discuss in more detail in later chapters, this can be seen as the aural equivalent of drawing diagrams that represent and exaggerate certain features and avoid or de-emphasise others.

The history of recorded music is supposedly a story of improved 'realism', of high fidelity, and yet studio designers and sound engineers have – in parallel with the technical challenge of achieving full frequency response and full dynamic range in a recording – sought to reduce the muddiness caused by low-frequency reverberation and increase perceived clarity by using multiple microphones in close proximity to instruments and spreading them across the stereo image. All of which creates a simplified or schematic version of reality: a cartoon of sound.

Fitting in with existing musicology

In Chapter 1 I discussed certain aspects of musicology that I have explicitly incorporated into my theoretical framework. In this section I want to start to examine why musicology should be interested in record production. The first reason is that certain intellectual trends within musicology both afford it and would be improved by it. Within the UK, in particular in recent years, there has been a general move to include performance practice and non-score-based music into the academic study of music. There has also, since the 1980s, been a further move to examine the context of musical practice and its influence on that musical activity. Both of these trends need to be inflected by the study of the recording process and its impact on both performance and listening.

Studies of performance practice and non-score-based music both tend to use recordings of various types – commercial releases and field recordings – without much in-depth examination of the way the recording process may have involved different forms of compositional and performance activity than the norms of concert performance.

Small's (1998) notion of musicking, as discussed in Chapter 1, becomes problematic when dealing with the various ways in which music has become a commodity. Recording has intensified the process of conceptual separation of production and consumption involved in the incorporation of music in the capitalist system. The study of recorded music in relation to the concert hall therefore becomes analogous to the study of cinema in relation to theatre: a product constructed in a non-linear process as opposed to a linear process of performance. Despite the problems that recordings as a reification of music introduce to Small's approach to musicology, it is still possible to examine recording as a process, as well as treating recordings as a text. Record production as a non-linear form of musicking therefore needs to be absorbed into the academic mainstream as part of this agenda of widening musicology to include the process-focused approaches of ethnomusicology.

Allan Moore (A.F. Moore 2012a) makes the point that there cannot be a separate musicology of record production any more than there can be a musicology of harmony or of singing. Recorded music and the process of producing it need to be examined in relation to all the other aspects of music creation and reception that have to exist within musicology. My aim in this book is to incorporate record production into the body of musicology rather than to establish it as a separate subject.

Production or reception?

I've already outlined in Chapter 1 that I intend to examine both production-based and reception-based approaches to record production, but another part of the 'why' question is what we wish to learn from the study of record production. The starting point for the academic study of music was learning the musical arts of performance and composition. It was only later that musicology developed to incorporate a reception-based approach with historical and analytical musicology. In the early part of the twentieth century this was in some part due to the spread of the notion that the appreciation of classical music improved the mind; that one learned to be a better listener by understanding more about the techniques and intentions of composition and, to a much lesser extent, performance. Any form of analysis or study will, in some way, tell us how to listen or how to perform, compose or otherwise produce music. This imposes an ideological slant and it is the duty of academics within musicology to recognise these ideologies and to describe and balance them as part of their considerations. Clarke and Cook provide a summary of various applications of empirical methods that their edited collection brings together (2004, pp. 3–14). Among these different approaches, part of their agenda is to call upon musicologists to utilise the methods of the perceptual and cognitive sciences to test their hypotheses where possible. It will be appreciated from Chapter 1 and the rest of the book that this project is a step in that direction. Currently, it mainly consists of the outline of a theoretical model that requires both further elaboration and further testing, but the model is built on a good deal of empirical musicology of various sorts.

Allan Moore's *Song Means* shares a lot of theoretical ground with this book, particularly the mixture of ecological perception and embodied cognition, but he points out that he is 'concerned here with only ... the making sense of specific listening experiences' (A.F. Moore 2012b, p. 3). The performance and production of the music is only of concern to the extent that they might be audible in the musical output. Philip Tagg (2012) has also discussed how the ideology of an analytical method based on the technical tools of performance (musical notation) excludes the listener who doesn't read music from the majority of the theoretical discussion. One of my concerns is to examine how production and reception are related. From a pragmatic perspective, producers and musicians must surely benefit if they understand the effect of their actions and listeners will add a further dimension to their understanding if they have some knowledge about the mode of production and the creators' intentions. From an academic perspective it seems an important question to answer: how similar to the process of listening for someone involved in producing the sound of music is that of an audience member? Referring to Feldman and neural networks (2008), Moore states:

> As we know from the discovery of the operation of motor neurons in the brain, [a trumpeter's] neurological response to trumpet music differs from her or his neurological response to piano music, a response she or he can't control, by virtue of the fact that she or he has intimate physiological knowledge of what it takes to produce music from a trumpet. This is because the same body of neurons fires whether the action (e.g. playing the trumpet) is being undertaken, or is being perceived and hence simulated. (A.F. Moore 2012b, p. 4)

However, the question goes further than this. I learned how to play the trumpet as a boy but I certainly wouldn't describe myself as a trumpeter. That does mean, though, that I hear trumpet music differently from either a trumpeter or someone with no knowledge of how to produce music from a trumpet. Indeed, while we may have certain basic universal understandings of some actions or environments,[3] the kinds of cross-domain mapping and metaphorical connections that we make are not only all different but are also in a continual state of flux. As a trivial example, the first time I heard Patti Smith's (1975) *Horses* I was at my schoolfriend Ian's house and his mother gave us some chocolate-covered shortbread. Several years later I was surprised to discover, in one of those Proust moments, that when I heard a track from that album I could taste the shortbread. I've just tried the experiment again, nearly forty years after the initial connection was made, and the association is gone. These random connections that are sometimes made become highly noticeable because of their strangeness, but the huge majority of perceptual learning becomes 'invisible' because it forms part of the seamless norms of conceptual mapping. What it does suggest to me, though, is that this process of the neural mirroring of perception and action creates a philosophical link between production and reception. If interpretation is based on a subconscious hypothetical model of what kind of activity might be making that sound, it is also about the attribution of intention and motivation. Of course, the less we know about the musical tradition and circumstances in which the sound was made, the less likely it is that our hypothetical model will have much in common with the actual activity, intentions and motivation of the music maker.

There are thus two aspects of this bridging between a production-based and a reception-based approach. The pragmatic aspect is based on the idea that knowledge about reception will help producers work more effectively and that knowledge about production will afford a richer listening experience for an audience. The academic aspect is a logical progression from

[3] For example, the rhythmic experience of breathing or walking and the acoustic characteristics of larger and smaller spaces.

ecological perception and embodied cognition, and is concerned with building a more complete understanding of both the production and reception processes.

To do it better or to understand it better?

These two aspects of the production/reception relationship can be seen as part of a larger question about the motivation for studying record production in particular and music in general: to do it better or to understand it better? One of the main divisions at the Art of Record Production conferences is between those seeking to improve their technique and those seeking to improve their understanding. Of course many are seeking to do both, but there is usually an implicit agenda relating to one or the other in every paper. I think it is quite unusual at a music conference to find the two under the same roof, or at least to find that the balance between them is relatively even. There are frequently gulfs of understanding between them, but it is also remarkable when the two sides do get together and learn from each other. In the grand scheme of things neither can exist without the other. There can be no doing of something, especially something as complicated as record production, without an understanding of how the something works. Equally, there can be no analysis of a creative process unless there are people 'doing' the creative process to study.

The problems lie in building connections and effective communication. There is also, of course, the question of status and value. In the professional world of performance and recording there is only value in theoretical understanding if there is an immediate and direct benefit to practice, and obviously, in that world, practical ability has a higher status than theoretical knowledge. In the academic world the attribution of value and status are the other way round. Building connections needs to be done on neutral ground and in an atmosphere of mutual respect. In the past there hasn't been much motivation for either side to make this effort. The current situation, in the UK at least and seemingly – from my lesser experience – in other countries, has seen two changes that are increasing this motivation. In a move that in some ways mirrors the fact that more musicians are including teaching in their portfolio careers,[4] the reduction of financial opportunities in the field of record production has seen more producers moving into teaching

[4] A career that includes a variety of activities: see https://jobs.telegraph.co.uk/article/what-is-portfolio-working-and-why-is-it-growing-/ [accessed 23 August 2013].

and more aspiring producers using a teaching job as a way of financing their production 'habit'. The other change is that recent ideological shifts in research funding have put theoreticians under more pressure to point to the practical impact of their research and practitioners working in academic institutions coming under pressure to characterise their work as practice-led research or practice as research. Although these changes may not have been welcomed with open arms by the participants themselves, they have had the effect of bringing the two communities closer together, which has resulted in more debate and more collaboration.

Critical theory and the role of music in our society

One topic that is almost guaranteed to make eyes roll among the industry practitioners who sit in the 'to do it better' school of thought is the application of critical theory[5] to record production. A key aspect of this is the identification, analysis and critique of the ideological position inherent in any interpretation of a text. Our motivation for studying music will also determine what we consider a worthwhile topic for study. We study what we think is good and important, and our ideology determines what we think is good and important. One aspect of the ideology that informs this book is the belief that an important part of our understanding of music should come from knowledge about how the brain works. The increasing influence of this ideology can be seen in books such as Clarke and Cook's (2004) *Empirical Musicology* and Moore's (A.F. Moore 2012b) *Song Means*, but it can also be seen as part of the recent rapid expansion and development of neuroscience. Whereas postmodernism might be seen as based on an ideology that grew out of the notion of relativity, we seem to be in the midst of a stage in the social sciences where they are informed by psychology and neuroscience. Indeed, critical theory itself is also now inflected with the ideology of embodied cognition and neuroscience. As with all intellectual trends, there are some avenues that have proved to be highly constructive and useful and others that appear less so. Tallis (2011) has written about the twin evils that he recognises as neuromania and Darwinitis, which involve quite arbitrary and ill-thought-out theories about potential applications of neuroscience and evolutionary theory in economics, for example.

[5] The definition of critical theory I'm using here relates to literary criticism and the humanities rather than to sociology. It relates to a raft of theoretical positions about the interpretation and explanation of various types of 'text' rather than to the explicitly transformational sociology of scholars such as Adorno in the neo-Marxist Frankfurt School.

A musicology of record production that seeks to incorporate these aspects of contemporary musicology would need to encompass the methodologies and theoretical approaches of critical theory as well. These new directions in thought about music need to be examined fully and in a way that incorporates the sound thinking from previous paradigms but avoids any pitfalls that can be identified in the new. Which brings us to the question of how.

3 How should we study record production?

The research paradigm

In his book *The Structure of Scientific Revolutions*, Thomas Kuhn makes the point that Aristotle and Galileo would interpret the sight of a stone swinging on the end of a piece of string in very different ways because of the theoretical paradigms about motion that they were born into (1962, pp. 121–5). Aristotle would view it as a constrained form of falling and Galileo would see it as a pendulum. They could receive the same retinal image projected onto their eyes and yet both see something different. Kuhn also cites a fascinating experiment:

> An experimental subject who puts on goggles fitted with inverting lenses initially sees the entire world upside down... after the subject has begun to learn to deal with his new world, his entire visual field flips over, usually after an intervening period in which vision is simply confused. Thereafter, objects are again seen as they had been before the goggles were put on. (1962, p. 112)

This experiment, therefore, raises the prospect that two people could receive different retinal images projected onto their eyes (i.e. the normal and the inverted) and yet both see the same thing. In very crude terms, what you believe about the nature of the world determines what you see and, therefore, how you study it.

What does this mean for our musicology of record production? The theoretical paradigm used here stems from a confluence of our psychological and sociological approaches with ethnomusicology, popular music studies and what in the 1990s was labelled the 'new musicology'. Perhaps the major difference of the 'new' from traditional musicology is the perception that the cultural context of a musical experience is as important as its sonic structure in determining musical meaning. Thus, although there may be a nominal text such as a score or a recording, the musical meaning should be explored through how it emerged from a production system and how it is interpreted through a reception system. These in turn need to be examined from within their cultural context. These reception and production perspectives might be seen by some, and in particular ethnomusicologists, as referring to a particular model of music-making that involves a performer/audience split and takes no account of communal and participatory forms. Indeed, Small proposes the notion of musicking as:

> to take part, in any capacity, in a musical performance, whether by performing, by listening, by rehearsing or practicing, by providing material for performances (what is called composing), or by dancing. (1998, p. 9)

Obviously, when we include recorded music as well as performance in the musicking model we have to allow that taking part doesn't have to happen at the same time or in the same place. We also have to allow for another set of participatory types such as editors, sound engineers, samplers, remixers, DJs and record producers. There's no reason, however, why the overarching notion of musicking is incompatible with an analysis that involves the twin perspectives of production and reception. The reception/production dichotomy is an analytical tool and not a descriptive one: it provides a way of explaining and interpreting musical activity rather than simply characterising it. There may be some forms of participatory musical activity where it ceases to be a useful analytical tool but recorded music, by its very nature, isn't one of them: production and reception don't happen at the same time.

Reception, production and cultural context

The systems of musical reception and production and the need to examine and analyse them within their cultural context form the basis of this study and, indeed, of my approach to musicology in general. In the most basic terms this can be distilled down to how the listener interprets a musical event or experience, how it was produced and how the technology, history, geography and sociology of the culture surrounding it have influenced both its creation and interpretation. These are, however, not discrete or autonomous subject areas. There is a continuous interaction and intermingling between audience/critical reception and the rules and conventions of what constitutes good or authentic performance and production practice. This approach might also be seen to imply that there is an identifiable and quantifiable audience and either that the rules and conventions apply to all or that we can identify and quantify different musical communities through genre, historical period, geographical area or some other criteria. In reality, though, there are no fixed genres and there are no fixed rules: there is a complex mass of individuals and there is no 'system' – just an unholy mess.

The point of a study like this is to provide a theoretical model that simplifies reality: that allows us to test its reliability by undertaking a kind of musicological Turing Test. In his 1950 article, Alan Turing proposed that the only meaningful test for successful computer intelligence was whether someone interacting with the machine could differentiate between the computer's responses and another human's (1950). In the musicology example, the more accurately a theoretical model predicted the behaviour of a notional system's participants, the more successful the model. In other words, the musical meaning generated for a particular participant (or group of them) happened *as if* they were part of a particular theoretical production/reception system (or network).

The design of this kind of theoretical model should, therefore, make it easier to think about the complexities of reality, but at the same time should also seek to be 'upwardly compatible' with more generalised theories in the field. In fact, I would contend that this compatibility reflects a contemporary consensus, which has grown out of a mid- to late-twentieth-century paradigm shift that understands human creativity as being more complex than the work of an isolated creative genius. This shift flows from the growing sophistication and importance of the humanities and social sciences in modern culture and the broader influence that these developments have had on philosophy and the ontology of works of art and creativity. Historians and analysts in all areas of the arts have incorporated ideas from disciplines such as psychology, sociology, anthropology and economics into their work and this, in a very general sense, involves theoretical models that seek to explain the worlds of art and culture *as if* they were a mechanical, causal or computational system. Yet at the same time this theoretical model is also broad enough to encompass approaches from parallel disciplines such as literary theory (e.g. Bakhtin 1982), cultural studies (Bourdieu 1986) or architecture (Hall 1966). And equally importantly, the model aims to provide a framework that can include important existing work within its subject area such as Porcello and Greene (2004), McIntyre (2012), Moore (A.F. Moore 2012b), Moylan (1992), Théberge (1997) and Zak (2001).

How then should this broader model of creative systems be applied to the specifics of record production? If we start with reception, a question that has dogged musicological analysis throughout the twentieth century in one form or another has been the definition of the listener or the audience. How can a musicologist propose a single way of interpreting a piece of music when we all have such individual sensibilities? Is such an interpretation only to be assessed statistically: by how many people agree with it? Or should musicologists attempt to find objective, quantifiable features in the music itself and leave the interpretation of these features to their readers? Of course the latter, by the very act of selecting which features to study (for example, by looking at harmony and form rather than rhythm or timbre), makes implicit value judgements about a piece.

An approach that seeks to understand how listeners interpret recordings in order to generate musical meaning must both identify the audience and theorise the process. This can be undertaken on the level of the individual listener through psychology, psychoacoustics and perceptual theory (Clarke 2005) or through an analysis of the types of social groupings that have, and help to form, opinions (Walser 1993). I will also further break this down into two categories:

1. studies that examine the musical 'text', the recorded sound in this instance, to investigate how the participants interpret it;
2. studies that examine the audience members and the purveyors of critical opinion either as individuals or as social formations.

In the first category we might, for example, examine how the multiple edits with which Teo Macero pieced together Miles Davis' 'Pharoah's Dance' for the *Bitches Brew* album (Davis 1970) created a structural coherence that wasn't in the original improvisations. Or we might explore how 'spot' microphones[1] changed the typical experience of space in orchestral recordings during the 1970s in relation to earlier recordings. In the second category we might examine how the importance of live performance in Irish traditional music in comparison to Detroit Techno is reflected in notions of what constitutes an authentic-sounding production to those communities. Or we might consider what influence the historical and social construction of who constitutes a valid creative agent had on UK and US journalists' assessment that the Beatles were a more important creative and cultural phenomenon than Motown in the 1960s.

One of the section headings in the last chapter was 'To do it better or to understand it better?' and, as we've discussed, vocational studies are considered less academic than theoretical ones. One of the aims of this theoretical framework is to help put them on an equal footing. In both aspects of the study of production systems for recorded music the same kinds of categories are applicable as in reception systems: to distinguish between individuals and groups and between participants and processes.

[1] 'Spot' microphones are placed close to specific instruments in an ensemble to allow the recordist to bring them forward in the mix in relation to the ambient (more distant) microphones that would provide a normal concert listening experience.

An added factor that is much more important from the production than the reception perspective is the nature, role and development of the technology. In traditional musicology, with its focus on the composer rather than the performer, organology is a rather minor tributary of the academic stream, but the academic study of record production often seems to be headed in the opposite direction: foregrounding technology over the study of the creative process.

So alongside the study of this technology we need to look at how the technicians and the musicians work, train, communicate, interact with the technology and engage with the social and economic structures involved. Thus, on the technical side, we might look at how the historical and geographical spread of multi-track recording technology affected production techniques in South Africa compared to Argentina. We might also investigate how the change from VU meters[2] to computer screens has affected how technicians conceptualise recorded sound. On the participant side, we might look at how the informal 'do it yourself' training system in small independent studios such as Norman Petty's studio in Clovis, New Mexico, may have engendered a different attitude to 'breaking the rules' among sound engineers than the unionised systems in studios such as Decca Records' Pythian Temple Studios in New York. We might also research whether the introduction of headphones in the mid-1960s was resisted or embraced by session musicians and how they might have thought it affected their performance and communication.

As we have seen, the cultural context of any musical event must inform its study from either of these perspectives. The character of a listener or the social structure of an audience or community in a reception-based study will be a function of their gender, race, education and experience, historical, geographical and socio-economic position and many other factors. And the nature of the participants in a production system will be similarly determined. Of course, some of the studies in the field of recorded music, especially from the production perspective but also in relation to audio perception, will be scientific in nature. So, for example, we may undertake a spectral and dynamic analysis to compare the audio effect of analogue tape saturation with a digital signal processing emulation of the same effect. We may even go so far as to try the analysis on a variety of musical examples and even on broad band noise examples. In the end, though, any such evaluation is based on a presupposed audience aesthetic that is likely to differ between musical communities. It may nonetheless be useful to particular musical and

[2] Voltage meters that use a needle on a gauge to show the volume of the signal in decibels.

economic communities in choosing between products or developing new ones. For the most part, however, musicology is concerned with elucidating musical meaning, both in terms of how a sound or technique produces it and how an individual or audience interprets it; and that requires some understanding and analysis of its cultural context.

Eight categories

In addition to the production/reception dichotomy, I have also outlined how the psychological and sociological theory will unfold progressively throughout the book. Both of these structuring principles occur in the context of the eight typological categories that I am proposing as the broad constituent parts of this musicology of record production. It should be remembered, however, that these categories are conceptual tools rather than an attempt at description, and that the relationships and interactions between them are as important as the nature of their contents. This process should be seen as a developmental tool in the evolution of this academic field: a way to elucidate many of the complexities of the subject by studying them in isolation, so that future scholars can get a better overview when it comes to putting them back together and finding their place in the wider study of musicology. The categorisation is thus not meant to 'ghetto-ise' these disciplinary approaches but to provide an overarching framework that facilitates interdisciplinary work by providing a conceptual system that outlines their inter-relationship and connectivity.

As with any such project, the devil is in the detail and the rest of the book takes each category, a chapter at a time, and examines some of that detail. Before that, I will provide a short sketch of each of the categories.

Sonic cartoons

The first of the eight proposed categories involves the analysis of music in relation to recorded sound and the difference it makes to musicology. On the one hand, we have the emerging discipline of performance studies examining the recorded (and edited and mediated) performance as opposed to the score. On the other hand, we have an expanded notion of composition such as that expounded by Zak (2001, pp. 24–47), in which the precise characteristics of the recorded and mediated sound become part of the compositional process. One of the key issues here, then, is the question of how to analyse musical sound as opposed to the musical score, and the solution is obviously determined by the nature of the source material. Recorded sound, by allowing multiple repetitions of the listening experience, permits a detailed and considered exploration of a piece in a way that the concert experience doesn't. Indeed, the phenomenon of repeated listening has had a complex effect on music. It has altered our perception of what constitutes a musical work and at the same time, by providing a storage medium for performance practice as well as composition, it changes the nature of our culturally constructed notion of lasting musical creativity. While eighteenth-century performers could not compete in terms of posterity with composers, John Coltrane has left 'texts' that allow his art to be experienced by those born after his death.

Recorded music provides a different type of musical text from a score, though. The score, like the text of a play, provides a particular type of text that consists of a set of instructions for creating an instance of the work of art. A recording is a unique instance: complete and the same every time it is reproduced. Much as the study of a painting might include the specifics of the brush strokes, the techniques of layering and even the chemistry of the paint mixing, as well as the broader notions of form, style and the conceptual approach, recorded music allows a similar focus. The specifics of the sonic product allow us to study the sound of a particular performer's gestures and any metaphorical or other meaning they may elicit. I will also argue that a recording allows us to think about music in different ways than a score does. In addition, it allows us to study the impact of the technological mediation of the recording process in its various forms. This may relate to the 'perfection' or otherwise of a performance that stems from editing or processing, or it may relate to the timbral and dynamic shaping that techniques such as equalisation or compression can provide. And all these factors can contribute to a more generalised understanding of how various 'sonic signatures' may have evolved that are associated with particular record producers, recording studios, record labels, musical styles, geographic locations or historical periods.

Staging

Although it may not always be possible or desirable to differentiate clearly between the two, the distinction between a performance and its staging is a useful analytical tool. This question of staging goes to the heart of the issue of differentiating between concert-based music and recorded music in the same way that we differentiate between the theatre and the cinema – i.e. that they are related but separate and different art forms. Closely allied to this question is the notion of 'realism' and what the 'real' experience that a recording might be seeking to represent is. However, in much the same way that the venue, set design, costumes and lighting can alter the meaning of a dramatic performance, the staging of a musical performance can also affect its meaning. And just as the cinema both removes some of the more visceral perceptual experiences of the theatre and yet allows mediatory manipulations such as multiple perspectives and close-ups, recorded music stands in the same sort of relation to the concert hall.

Perhaps the most obvious, and certainly the most widely studied, aspect of staging in recorded music has been the creation of the impression of real and imaginary space through the production process. Perceptions of intimacy, scale and atmosphere that suggest or reinforce particular interpretations of a performance have become the common currency of recorded music. Likewise, levels of realism and cartoon versions of sonic space have developed in relation to particular musical styles and their associated musical cultures. However, just as theatrical and cinematic staging goes beyond the choice and design of the performance space, the staging of recorded music can be used to alter the timbre of a performance through techniques such as equalisation, distortion, phasing, flanging and others. And just like camera angles, costume and lighting, these techniques can suggest mood, atmosphere, relationships between performers, priorities or points of focus and historical or cultural references. Also, with recorded music the mode of consumption is often something other than listening with fixed attention, and the function of the music – for example, dancing or mood creation – can have an impact on the way it is staged.

The development of audio technology

When examining recorded music from a production perspective, the aspect that tends to dominate the academic curriculum for prospective sound engineers and record producers is the nature of the technology. Questions such as 'what is a compressor?' and 'what are the control parameters that can be varied and what effect do they have on the audio output?' tend to predominate at the expense of less 'scientific' factors such as the social interaction between musicians and technicians. The nature of this technology is, of course, very important, and its development over the past century has had a huge impact on the sound of recorded music. On the one hand, the technology for capturing the sounds of performance includes microphones, cabling, mixing consoles, monitoring systems, pre-amplifiers, analogue to digital signal converters and, of course, the storage media: wax cylinders, direct to disc recorders, various formats of analogue and digital tape and the various 'audio engines' that allow the storage of digital audio on hard discs. On the other, the technology for processing and manipulating those recorded signals to prepare them for mass production and distribution includes equalisation, dynamic compression, noise gates, delay, reverberation, phasing, flanging, chorusing and the myriad of hardware and software plug-ins that has proliferated in recent decades. In addition to these two aspects of audio technology is the vast range of acoustic spaces, isolation screens and other architectural hardware that has a strong impact on the sound of a recorded signal. Aside from describing what these technologies are, work in this category details their chronological development and how these changes altered the sound of recorded music.

We can detail the chronological development of audio technology purely in terms of when it first emerged. However, the geographical distribution of this technology and even its distribution between different companies in the same country was determined by logistics, patent law, economics, trade restrictions, political affiliations, prejudices and a host of other, perhaps less tangible, factors. Further, the factors that determined which problems were addressed in the research and development of these new products can be seen to be equally haphazard, or at least determined by factors other than musical reasons. Thus, for example, the cost of real estate in high-density Western city conurbations such as London and New York may have influenced the development of mechanical and electronic reverberation simulators and, in turn, have influenced the sound of music made in locations without such financial restraints on acoustic ambience.

Using technology

The next category deals with the interaction between the technicians and the technologies outlined in the previous category. How do developments and trends in product design affect working practice and thence sound in record production? A particular form of interface design will make certain tasks easier and certain tasks more difficult. The simple principle that the well-worn path is easier to follow will make particular forms of practice – and therefore particular sonic results – more ubiquitous. While it is evident that the interfaces with technology have changed enormously over the years, there is still a tendency to refer to the design of outdated technology in newer products. Thus, the software controls for recording and mixing technology maintained a strong flavour of tape machine transport and mixing console design in their visual displays. This was despite the apparent redundancy of rewind and fast forward controls on a hard-disc system and the bad ergonomics of using a computer mouse to alter a visual graphic of a rotary knob. Or do these features simply reflect a consumer demand for interfaces that are already firmly established and familiar?

On the subject of consumer demand, there has been a highly trumpeted democratisation of production technology since the 1980s. This has reduced both the cost and the training required to produce decent-quality audio productions, and yet has transferred much of the creative control to the product designers by relying on presets and automatic settings. The producers of recorded music have been turned into the consumers of production technology. Despite this, there exists a tradition of 'creative abuse' that involves the deliberate misuse – or, perhaps more accurately, the non-standard use – of technology, and this in turn has led product designers to standardise this non-standard usage.

Parallel to and connected with the notion that product design affects practice is the perhaps deeper notion that it affects both the perception and the conceptualisation of music in the process of production. Thus, the visual stimulus in the recording and playback process has altered. With tape storage, the flickering needle on a VU meter provided an instantaneous, real-time representation of the audio level. With disc storage there is a graphic representation of the audio level of the whole file over time, with a moving line to show the current playback position in relation to the graphic. This fundamental change has influenced the way that both technicians and musicians think about music and the recording process, and has also altered the notion of what the musical 'object' is for product designers (i.e. to being a 'thing' instead of a 'stream').

Training, communication and practice

One of the side effects of the organic and collaborative nature of record production is the lack of any clear definition of the role of the record producer. It has changed historically and with the differing approaches to production in different styles of music. Yet there is also a great deal of individual negotiation about various tasks in any given project between the record company executives, the artists, the sound engineers and the producer, and this can be further complicated when individuals have multiple roles. This category looks at the various types of management and organisational structures that have developed to run the logistics, human resources, creative decision-making and technical detail of the production process. These structures exist in both the formal (contract-based business sector) and informal (semi-professional and amateur) spheres, and their analysis needs to take account of historical, geographical, socio-economic, stylistic and cultural factors as well.

This category also includes the training and education of sound engineers and record producers – from apprentices in white coats to music technology students. It is only relatively recently that training and learning in this field has become formalised, and there is still a great deal of – often heated – debate about what the structure and content of such courses should be. There is also the study of historical apprentice systems in various companies and geographical regions, of the self-education of small-scale entrepreneurs in the industry, of the development of trade, hobby and other magazines and, of course, of the huge explosion of internet resources, interviews and discussion forums.

There are also the related questions of the relationships and power structures in the studio and of the technical language and communication. While the distribution of tasks and the decision-making hierarchy may vary from case to case, a number of economic, technical and psychological factors can certainly be studied. The often necessary physical structure of the studio, with the musicians separated from the technicians 'behind the glass', can create a psychological divide as well as a physical one. Also, the fact that the technicians tend to control the means of communication, the talkback button, can often make matters worse. Issues of communication and language can often have an impact on the power relationships in the studio. Both musicians and technicians can use the jargon of their specialism as a way to demonstrate their expert status and to exclude others from the discussion of particular aspects of the process. Of course, the establishment of common language can also do the opposite and allow more frank and universal discussions of the collaborative process to take place.

Performance in the studio

The next category deals with one of the enduring dilemmas of recording: the tensions between the ideal performing environment and the ideal recording environment. Prior to recording, musicians always worked face to face and in real time, and yet the development of recording technology has involved spatial isolation, editing, headphones, overdubbing and a host of other techniques that have undermined this process. There are many areas in which there can be a straightforward conflict of interests between what is best for the musician and what is best for the recordist. Some of these are relatively simple, such as a performer wanting to move while playing and the recordist wanting them to stay in the same position relative to the microphone. Others are more complicated, such as finding a balance between generating some atmosphere to compensate for the lack of an audience stimulus and avoiding the pressure of 'red light fear': the stage fright relating to creating a permanent record of a performance. There are also the problems of hearing, such as listening through headphones or playing along to a pre-recorded track that can't respond to fluctuations in your playing.

Possibly the biggest difference between the concert hall and the recording studio for musicians is the fact that one can edit. While some performers consider it a matter of professional pride to be able to play a piece through from start to finish, others engage with the editing process as allowing a different form of performance: one that has its own markers of professional excellence. In the recording studio, the construction of the final composite take is often a complex collaborative process including performer, editor and producer in the decision-making process. This has far-reaching ramifications for issues of performance authenticity, ownership and creative agency, and has been further complicated by the way in which simplified versions of production software have been targeted at composers and performers: a democratisation of sorts, but that simplification also involves a reduction of options and the homogenising effects of presets and automation.

Aesthetics and consumer influence

This category examines how musical communities and cultures have influenced the sound of recorded music. It is still relatively unusual for record production to be considered directly as an issue by audiences, although exactly how unusual is a function of the musical styles and the types of audience member. In some instances any such consideration is predominantly negative – i.e. aspects of production only tend to be mentioned when they are considered to have intruded on the music. In others it has been absorbed into the panoply of appropriate creative practice and is sometimes discussed as such. These two opposites on a notional continuum of audience responses can also be seen to relate to the perceived norms of creative practice in various musical communities. In styles where unmediated (and therefore usually acoustic and unamplified) concert performance is the norm, the notion of record production as creative practice, or indeed of it having any aspiration other than complete transparency, has historically been frowned upon. On the other hand, various styles in popular music have evolved where the creative practice of the artists involved has become perceived to be based more in the recording studio than the concert hall. While this may have started with producers such as Joe Meek and Phil Spector in the early 1960s, it became much more visible when performing artists such as the Beatles, the Beach Boys and later Pink Floyd and Queen were seen to be using the recording studio as part of their creative palette. In parallel to the notion of how audiences perceived their artists, we can also see the development of a culturally constructed aesthetic of what constituted a good-quality recording. There are empirical measures of parameters such as the frequency range and the dynamic range that can be seen to have improved gradually throughout most of the twentieth century (albeit with an interesting reduction in those ranges in recent decades). Yet we can also see that, from the 1960s onwards, distortion in the form of exaggerated high- and low-frequency content came to be regarded as a signifier of high fidelity.

One key feature affecting the influence of audiences is the notion of perceived authenticity and how it relates to different styles of music. In some areas a performer who engages creatively with editing together multiple performed fragments can be perceived as a cheat; in others this can be seen as the norm. In fact, as computers and DJs have become more involved in record production the idea of what constitutes authentic musical creative practice has expanded beyond composition and performance. This has caused an interesting tension in contemporary ideas about agency: artistic agency in the industrial and post-industrial periods being predominantly perceived as being individual rather than collaborative. Even a process as obviously collaborative as film-making, where script-writing, visual design, editing and acting might all compete to be considered the primary creative input, has adopted the convention of crediting the director as overall auteur: a convention that's even reflected in academic referencing. Recorded music, however, generally only affords that accolade to a record producer when they are either the composer or the artist as well.

Another issue that affects the way audiences perceive the authenticity of a production relates to ideology and economics. On the one hand, there are characteristics of recorded music that have become associated with expensive studio technology and that may be seen by some audiences as a 'classy' production. On the other, there are audiences who have embraced the sound of 'lo-fi', a deliberate use of low-quality recording techniques, to reflect a rejection of – or rebellion against – the large-scale corporate interests of the record industry.

The business of record production

The last of the eight categories examines the issue of how the business practices in the music industry have an impact on the production of music. As the role of the record producer grew out of artist and repertoire (A&R) departments in the 1940s and 1950s, and as many of the entrepreneurs that started small labels from that period onwards have acted as producers, production and business practices in the music industry are inextricably entwined. The various business models and contractual relationships between artists, record companies and record producers are almost as disparate as the companies themselves, and the budgets and other commercial restraints placed upon recording projects can have a major impact on the sound of recorded music.

How to study these categories

The main theoretical ideas that can be used to create a methodology for this musicology of record production were outlined in Chapter 1. One crucial point about the structure of this book is that in order to gradually introduce these ideas over the length of the book, certain simplifications have been made. These are addressed more extensively and consistently in the Afterword, as they will make more sense in the context of rest of the book, but a few important points will be outlined now.

The typology has been arranged in a sequence that fits broadly with the progression of the theoretical work from psychology to sociology and, more specifically, from the individual through the small scale to the larger scale of social activity. Although this is broadly true, there are aspects of each of the categories that don't fit so neatly into this progression; these aspects have received less attention than those that fit the structure of the book. That's not to say that I consider these factors to be less important than others, but the problem is that there is a dual agenda to this book – the subject area and the methodology – and that has resulted in these sorts of compromise.

As I pointed out in Chapter 1, another aim of this book is to stimulate debate about the theoretical study of record production and recorded music, and its place in musicology. These omissions and distortions that flow from the structural considerations are certainly something that I'm sure many readers will pick up on. I've outlined some in the Afterword and I look forward to reading and hearing about more. Probably the largest imbalance, which is due to the analytical focus and the desire to establish a map of the theoretical landscape, is the lack of explicit discussion of how this theory should inform the practicalities of production. I would hope that academics and students will see the implicit connections for themselves and, hopefully, engage in further exploration and understanding of the ways in which practice suggests interpretation and vice versa.

Theoretical interlude 1

Chapters 4 and 5 relate primarily to the ways in which the theories of ecological perception and embodied cognition can be applied to the interpretation of recorded music. Although this is examined primarily from a reception-based approach, the way the specific techniques employed encourage a particular interpretation, or at least afford a range of possible interpretations, is also discussed. The theoretical substrate of these two chapters is concerned with the way that we, as listeners and/or producers, perceive and interpret the schematic representations of real or constructed performances in recorded music and how the techniques of production can frame or stage them in ways that contribute to or affect that interpretation.

As a brief summary of how these specific issues relate to the more general exposition of the theory in Chapter 1, the ecological nature of the perceptual process is crucial to the understanding of recorded music as a schematic representation of performance. Our perceptual system is built around the recognition of patterns of connectivity between stimulus and action, but this is a multi-modal system and any incongruence between different modes affords a recognition that something is 'wrong'. No matter how good the audio quality of a recording is, if the other modes of my perception are telling me that I am not in the presence of musical performers I will recognise it as a representation rather than as the 'real thing'. Although it may be obvious that this approach has much in common with Tagg's (2012) interpretation of semiotics applied to musical analysis, there is a fundamental difference. The basic premise of semiotics, that in representational systems like language or music there is a message for which there is a transmitter and one or more receivers who interpret the signs in the message, is a schematic representation of the nature of human thought and communication that is too much of a distortion of the messy reality. That said, Tagg's work provides a theoretical framework that allows a wide range of powerful insights into the ways we interpret music.

The way that the framing or staging of a recorded sound affects our interpretation is similarly based on our theories of perception and cognition. Various forms of activity and environment will become associated, through the reinforcement-based process of perceptual learning, with invariant properties. Thus, for example, particular acoustic changes will be associated with being inside particular forms of enclosed space. The invariant property in this instance will not be a particular sound or type of sound but a particular way in which sounds change. Hearing some prototypical form of musical activity inflected with that invariant property will then suggest the interpretation that the activity is happening within that particular form of enclosed space. If that form of enclosed space is not recognised as somewhere that we currently are, that's another compelling piece of evidence that we are experiencing recorded music.

4 | Sonic cartoons

Cartoons of sound

In the vocal performance of Britney Spears' (2000) single 'Oops! . . . I Did It Again' there's a pronounced vocal rasp on many of the vowel sounds that is a common signifier of emotional angst. The 'creaky voice' has this emotional significance because it is the result of tightening the neck and throat muscles in a way that restricts the passage of air through the vocal cords and, of course, this type of muscular tension is associated with stress of various sorts: it is a fairly universal characteristic of angst-ridden vocalisations. During the recording of this single the Swedish producer, Max Martin, decided that the natural rasp in Ms Spears' voice didn't convey the sense of angst effectively enough and hit upon a novel way of exaggerating it. He took a short recording of a guiro scrape[1] that was provided in the percussion set on a Yamaha keyboard and positioned multiple copies of this sample in the recording at many of the moments when the creak occurred in Ms Spears' vocal performance. These were then processed to blend in with the vocal sound but to provide a pronounced emotional creak.[2] As soon as you listen to the track with this in mind it becomes obvious, but without knowing about this 'trick' it sounds like an exaggerated performance technique. I've mentioned the notion of sonic cartoons earlier in this book and elsewhere (Zagorski-Thomas 2015), and this example – the deliberate exaggeration of a single characteristic of a recording in order to influence the listener's interpretation in a particular direction – provides an extreme illustration of the concept.

As also mentioned earlier, recorded sound is a representational form. We hear musical sound as performance in the broad sense of the word, and recorded sound presents us with a representation of a performance. And just as visual representations can be more or less figurative and more or less abstract, so too can recorded music. When I hear a good-quality

[1] A musical instrument with a serrated surface that gives a rasping sound when scraped with a stick, originally made from a gourd and used in Latin American music.

[2] This anecdote was recounted to me by Mark Gillespie at one of the Rhythm in the Age of Digital Reproduction research seminars hosted by Anne Danielsen in Oslo.

binaural[3] recording from a concert hall I may be impressed by the realism of the sound but I am not deluded into thinking I am in the presence of a performance. Ignoring any visual stimulus or contextual knowledge, even the slightest head movement reveals that the directional information and ambience doesn't change in the way that it would in a concert hall. I'm no more convinced than I would be that a photograph is a window onto the scene it portrays. I'll talk more about spatial sound in the next chapter on staging.

Just as we recognise the differences between a photograph of a house, a realistic painting of a house and a line drawing of a house, so too can we recognise levels of realism and artifice in recorded sound. Orchestral recordings usually involve multiple microphones. Alongside the general ambience that is used to create the impression of a concert hall, usually the actual ambience of the recording space, additional microphones that are closer to particular sections or soloists are mixed into the general stereo recording to provide greater clarity, depth of field and stereo separation. In the concert hall, with the added visual dimension, if I look at the cellists I can perceive them better: the multi-modal nature of perception makes them seem louder.[4] By using additional microphones to create greater but artificial clarity in a recording, the record producer is also creating a sonic cartoon: perhaps it is less of a caricature than the Britney Spears example but it is a distortion designed to influence our perception and interpretation nonetheless. Although this may not have been an explicit and conscious strategy on the part of record producers, the many ways that production techniques have gravitated towards greater and often artificial clarity seems like an obvious counterweight to the loss of other perceptual modes that recorded sound involves – most notably the visual mode.

Simon Frith (1998), Allan Moore (A.F. Moore 2012b) and others have applied the notion of persona to vocals in popular music to explore the way complex layers of perceived agency and character are assigned to the performed activity. As far as I know this is yet to be applied in the world of classical musicology, but I think it provides a powerful alternative to Scruton's (1999) notion of disembodied or abstract musical motion. Of course, when we listen to recorded music one of these complex layers of perceived personae is removed: the 'reality' of the performer's presence and

3 Binaural recordings involve a dummy head system with two microphones positioned within the artificial ears, which can provide very strong and realistic spatial information in a recording.

4 For an example that illustrates the multi-modal nature of perception, see the demonstration of the McGurk effect (McGurk and MacDonald 1976) at: www.youtube.com/watch?v=G-IN8vW-m3m0 [accessed 20 July 2013].

of the singer as a performer becomes less pronounced because we lose the visual aspect. The persona of the song's protagonist becomes that much stronger as a result – a cartoon-like distortion that makes the persona behind the music much less multi-dimensional and that encourages a form of interpretation very different from that of the concert hall.

There are many ways in which our interpretation of recorded sound can be affected by the types of distortion[5] and manipulation involved in the recording process. I shall explore some of the ways that these sonic cartoons work in the rest of this chapter and later in the book, but first I want to discuss another feature of recorded music that is a result of its representational nature.

Repeated listening

Leiber and Stoller, the songwriting/production duo who created a string of successful recordings for Atlantic Records in the late 1950s and early 1960s, are often quoted as having said 'we don't write songs, we write records', an acknowledgement that, for them, the creative process involved assembling the right performances, timbres and spatial effects as well as the lyrics, melody, harmony and arrangement. Until the advent of recording, composition had involved producing a set of instructions that allowed the musician to recreate the piece through performance. The development of recording technology allowed the creation of a new type of physical product. And physical products afford different types of scrutiny. A musical score allows the repeated study of the melody, harmony, rhythm and instrumentation, but only in an abstracted form. Whenever a piece is performed, the tempo, the precise tuning, the rhythmic microtiming and the instrumental and vocal timbres will always be different and the combination unique. A recording affords an altogether different form of scrutiny: repeated listening to a particular representation of a particular performance or set of performances.[6] A recording therefore allows the detailed examination of both the performance and the representational form. And just as music

[5] I'm using the term 'distortion' in the broadest sense. Although it includes the types of harmonic distortion that can be introduced by overdriven amplifiers, I mean distorted as in changed. This is problematic in that it implies a single original sound that can then be changed, while sound engineers are very aware that the same sound source will sound very different depending on how you position a microphone in relation to it.

[6] I am using the term 'performance' to include constructed performances such as step-time sequencing and sample loops.

notation as a representational system allowed musicians to think differently about melodic and harmonic structure and form, so too did recording as a representational system allow them to think about performance parameters and the detail of timbre and spatialisation in new and more complicated ways. Without music notation the complex thematic, harmonic and formal developments of Western art music would not have been possible. Without recorded music the complex spatial, timbral, dynamic and rhythmic developments that characterised both art music and popular music in the twentieth century would not have been possible.

On the one hand, there are the obvious connections. Musique concrète grew out of the ability to use the gramophone and later the tape recorder to focus in on the grain of timbre – partially through playing back recordings at incorrect speeds. Minimalism was at least in part inspired by Pierre Schaeffer's vinyl loops (with circular rather than spiral grooves[7]) and then more directly by Pauline Oliveros' tape loops.[8] However, we shouldn't fall into the trap of attributing all the kudos for the development of this new sonic aesthetic to a few iconic art music composers. The 'chipmunk' recordings of double speed vocals, the development of tape loop delay systems and the experiments in spatial sound documented by Peter Doyle (2006) in the world of popular music are equally part of this huge incremental change of mindset. The facility to listen repeatedly to the same recording, and indeed the consumerism-driven impulse to do so, was the primary force behind these new ways of thinking about sound. And it hasn't only had an impact on these technology-driven aspects of creativity and aesthetics: the twentieth century saw other aesthetic and cultural shifts that resulted from this new representational form. The role of the performer has risen to challenge that of the composer as the dominant artistic force in music. There's more resistance to this in art music than in popular music, but even in the classical music world (outside academia, anyway) it is the contemporary performers who are the dominant cultural figures rather than contemporary composers, and it is recording that has not only brought them to a wider audience but also allowed their artistry to persist beyond the brief span of their performing careers.

I would also argue that this shift in artistic sensibilities during the twentieth century has permeated the worlds of both composers for acoustic instruments and live performance in general. The representational system of recording afforded more complex and nuanced interpretations of the world of timbre both through the straightforward mechanism of repeated

[7] For example, Schaeffer's *Etude aux Chemin de Fer* (1948).
[8] For example, Oliveros' 1966 'I of IV' on the CD *Electronic Works 1965/66* (1997).

listening and through the evolving techniques of audio processing that this encouraged. This worked not just through the aesthetic processes of musical creativity – the technical process of recording also facilitated deeper understandings of the physics of sound and the complexities of timbre, and this has contributed to the more general ways in which the shape and texture of sound have come to be seen as part of the remit of composition. Thus, the twentieth century not only saw a major extension in the scope of score-based instructions to players (e.g. vibrato and timbral descriptors) but also saw the expansion of extended playing techniques to create a wider palette of timbres emanating from traditional acoustic instruments.

In the world of live performance, the technologies of sound reinforcement have not only been designed to make it possible to play to larger audiences but have also allowed the sonic cartoon distortions of the recording studio to be transplanted to concert venues. The example of popular music with close microphones on every instrument being amplified through a large stereo sound system is, perhaps, the most obvious and extreme sign that the aesthetic of recorded sound is now driving live sound. However, the use of sound reinforcement in opera houses and large concert halls is now fairly commonplace and reflects the trend for artificial clarity and detail mentioned above. It has also become noticeable in the last fifteen years that jazz venues are using sound reinforcement in ways that mimic the artificially boosted high-frequency content of influential record labels such as ECM. Indeed, as we shall see in Chapter 9, the whole notion of high fidelity has become characterised by exaggerated extremes of high- and low-frequency content, which creates sonic cartoons of exactly the same type as those that dominate popular music.

It can be no coincidence that these trends have coincided with the development of what Eisenberg has called 'phonography' (2005, pp. 89–131), and the accompanying changes in aesthetics. The ability to listen to the same performance many times allows the attention to focus on the minutiae of timbre, pitch and phrasing, and these lie at the heart of this performance- and timbre-led aesthetic. Indeed, the study of performance practice is wholly reliant on recording technology to enable the measurement and analysis of these factors.

Music and metaphor

As we saw in Chapter 1, Lakoff and Johnson's (2003) work on the metaphorical basis of thought and language is one of the foundations of this book. The idea of schema-based knowledge structures that is key to this theoretical work is property- or feature-centred, and the work of Fauconnier and Turner (2003) on conceptual blending between feature-based conceptual spaces also underpins the notion of sonic cartoons. Thus, for example, in the first sentence of this paragraph, I construct a blending-based connection between a building and this book by using the metaphor of a foundation. This relies on our shared schematic representation of a building having a foundation as one of its potential features – understood as the lowest element on which everything else is built – its crucial structural function being that if the foundation is in some way unsound, the whole structure becomes unstable. It also relies on a schematic representation of a book as a receptacle for knowledge, with that knowledge having a hierarchical structure. Thus, the progression of an argument that exhibits or explains knowledge can be represented (through another round of metaphorical conceptual blending) as a series of steps, each reliant on the soundness of the previous one, and this can be related to the structure of a building. The metaphor relies on a single property of the two mental representations – that of progressive stages of a 'construction' (building or argument) being reliant on the soundness of the earlier stages, and that of some fundamental starting point. The blending of the two conceptual spaces involves only a single property: there's no extension of the analogy to suggest, for example, that there might be a connection between rooms and ideas or that we might find some blending between the doors and windows of a building and the structure of knowledge.

The notion of a cartoon is, by definition, schematic and demonstrates that the way our brain works has determined the nature of human creativity. Cartoons in particular, and representational art and craft forms in general, rely on a mapping between a limited number of features or properties in a conceptual space and similar features or properties in its representation. Even on a very basic level in visual representations we have to create a metaphorical connection between two-dimensional lines and shapes on a flat surface and the richer (and constantly shifting) visual stimuli from the 'real' world. The very fact that we think of pictures as somehow not 'real' demonstrates their power as representational structures as opposed to material objects. According to this way of thinking about art, even abstract visual artwork can only be subject to interpretation through the metaphorical process of thought. We may make metaphorical connections with properties from multiple and disparate schemata or conceptual spaces that don't suggest any possible 'object' being represented but that provoke an interpretation relating to those schemata or conceptual spaces, which flows from the associations and connotations of those properties.

Thus, for example, when I look at a Mark Rothko painting, the large expanses of layered paint may suggest three-dimensional monoliths, the textures and colours may suggest something more organic and the proportions of the blocks may suggest certain features of commercial human fabrication. These, however, are very loose and tentative connections that are likely to vary from person to person. If, on the other hand, I draw a 'stick man', the kind used to represent a man on the doors of public toilets, this schematic representation is pretty universally interpreted as human (if not male). This type of cartoon is based on a very basic topology of the human form and suggests a great deal about the way we may represent that topology in our schemata. The details of faces, hands and feet and the different girths of limbs and torsos may add detail but are not required to make it any more recognisable as a human. However, the nature of those details can be used to help me create an interpretive back story about that figure. If I draw eyes that are either proportionately larger or more detailed than the other facial features I will assume they have greater significance and will use any hints I have to create a hypothesis about what that significance might be.

Similarly, in the domain of recorded sound, multiple microphone techniques create a sonic 'image' that exaggerates or distorts particular features. Very often this is done to enhance the attack transients of a sound[9] in relation to background ambience and sustaining sounds. As these aspects of sound are very important in the interpretation of musical meaning, enhancing them is usually interpreted as creating greater musical clarity. This type of decision to produce a representation of a performance that makes a certain feature more prominent in a way that encourages a particular type of interpretation is obviously analogous to the world of visual cartoons. The use of frequency shaping (filtering and equalisation) and dynamic control (compression and noise gates), two of the fundamental and most frequently used tools in the story of record production, similarly affects a single property in order to manipulate or influence the listener's interpretation. The manipulation of spatial cues through the use of reverberation and delay is another aspect of this and will be dealt with in the next chapter on staging.

Scholars such as Roger Scruton see the musical meaning we interpret in factors such as melody and harmony as being based on a disembodied or intellectual causality divorced from gesture and physical experience (Scruton 1999). For Lakoff and Johnson the conceptual blending between

[9] Attack transients, the sonic characteristics of a new sound starting, are important in musical sound not just because they are important in the determination of rhythm; they are also key indicators of timbre.

schemata attributes meaning to virtual causality and flows from metaphorical relationships with embodied experience (2003, pp. 97–105). The schema that associates particular forms of melodic movement with tension, release and flow, for example, does so because it is built on previous embodied experience. Those forms of melodic meaning can blend with rhythmic meaning (which has obvious metaphorical relationships with physical activity) and the perceived gestural energy that stems from the timbre. Whereas for Scruton this causality is an abstract and therefore ontologically different type of relationship, for Lakoff and Johnson the metaphorical meaning that stems from, for example, tonal relationships is just somehow more deeply buried than something more obvious such as how hard a piano key is being struck. It is not a different form of causality so much as one that is less accessible consciously.

This issue flows from a deeper ontological question regarding representation. Whereas Scruton characterises music as an abstract art form because it is not representational in the way that painting is, Lakoff and Johnson hold that abstract images and music only have meaning for us in so far as we can create metaphorical relationships between them and our previous experience, and that they are therefore representational. In fact, Lakoff and Johnson, Fauconnier and Turner, Eric Clarke and other scholars present a theory of perception and interpretation that challenges Scruton's idea of music as an abstract art form. According to them music is fundamentally representational, but the extent to which the representation is 'realistic' may vary considerably. Certain mappings between the characteristics of music or abstract art and our embodied experience occur at such an early stage in the interpretive process as to be subconscious or hard to dig down to in the substrate of consciousness.

Indeed, as this should make clear, I see music in general as being an abstract representational art form built on empathy and metaphorical relationships with our embodied experience. How melody, harmony and rhythm can be explained in these terms must wait for another book, but let us return to a discussion of how the process of record production can be seen in terms of creating sonic cartoons.

The sound of gesture

There is neurological evidence that 'a perceived beat is literally an imagined movement; it seems to involve the same neural facilities as motor activity, most notably motor-sequence planning. Hence, the act of listening to music involves the same mental processes that generate bodily motion' (Iyer 1998, p. 30). If, at a subconscious level, the interpretation of music involves hypothesising what it would feel like to produce that sound, even if that hypothesis is faulty or incomplete, then any manipulation of our propensity to perceive those gestures will influence that interpretation. Eric Clarke's work on ecological perception similarly builds on the idea that 'perception is primarily concerned with knowing about what is going on in the world and acting appropriately (adaptively) in relation to it' (2007, p. 48). Any electronic audio processing that enhances or inhibits our ability to recognise any attributes of human activity or gesture could have a profound effect on the way in which we interpret a sonic stimulus. In many ways, the history of record production is a history of the development of techniques and technologies that do exactly that. From the very beginning, recordists were positioning musicians in different spatial relationships to the recording cone to affect their relative volumes and prominence. That is, they were aiming to determine which aspects of this human activity or gesture should be enhanced and which should be inhibited.

Up close and personal

It is perhaps not surprising that by introducing the notion of listening to music in the intimacy of your own home, the recording process encouraged the cultivation of an intimate connection between the recording performer and the listener. Since microphone and speaker technology became better at picking up and reproducing high-frequency content in the 1920s and 1930s we can follow the well-documented development of crooning and other forms of intimate vocal and instrumental performances.[10] As Peterson (1995) has suggested, the other aspect of this was the ability to project domestic forms of music, music that was played at low volume in the home for a small (or non-existent) audience, through radio and recordings to mass audiences. The fact that microphones allowed mass audiences to hear the subtle and quiet gestural activity of these forms of music – finger-picked guitar accompanying soft-voiced singing, for example – created the same kinds of challenges and opportunities for musicians as the movie

[10] I recently gave a paper at the seventeenth IASPM Conference in Gijón, which I hope to expand into a journal article shortly, that explored the complexity of this process. Early speaker systems for live performance didn't allow the singers to monitor this type of intimate performance very clearly, and when they sang on radio or on record no monitoring either via speakers or headphones was available to them. Thus, the development of amplified quiet performance over a loud ensemble performance wasn't a straightforward or obvious progression.

camera created for actors. In the cinema close-up shots required actors to develop more natural, less exaggerated facial expressions in their acting and close microphones did a similar thing for musicians. Of course, both forms of media simultaneously allowed the continued use of the long shot, the more traditional, public and declamatory forms of performance that had developed in the theatre and the concert hall.

Hearing motion

We interpret sounds in terms of the type of activity that, given our past experience, might make that sort of noise. This is true in categorical terms – for example, distinguishing between car and train sounds. We might not have heard that exact sound before but will have experience of the types of sound that trains can make and the types of sound that cars can make. This is related to the type of energy being expended. Denis Smalley (1986) defined a complex typology of these spectromorphologies in relation to electroacoustic music, although he didn't extend this idea explicitly to explore the metaphorical meaning that these morphologies might suggest through association with our past experience. However, he does apply this idea of spectromorphology to motion and thus to energy expenditure (Smalley 1986, pp. 73–80), and the connection between timbral shape and energy expenditure is key to our interpretation of sound in terms of activity. Not only can I tell the difference between the voices of different people – the sonic imprints of their different bodies and the way they use them – but I can also hear the difference between them speaking softly and shouting. Obviously one of the differences is volume, but the major factor that helps me to distinguish between these sounds is the timbre: the spectromorphology. In fact, someone speaking softly near me and someone shouting from further away may be the same volume when they reach my ears, but there won't be any confusion as to which is which.

In a 'real life' situation of this sort there will be volume, timbre and spatial sound clues (such as the balance between direct and reverberant sound), providing me with a complex set of ecological and embodied information. In a recording such as, for example, 'Ironic' by Alanis Morissette (1996), dynamic compression and volume adjustment can be used to make the soft vocals in the verses and the more high-energy vocals of the chorus the same amplitude.[11] In this example, the volumes and ambience are

[11] If you look at some audio metering of the amplitude level while listening to this song (after the first verse, which has no drums) you will see that the verses and the choruses are the same level on the meters, despite the chorus seeming much louder.

pretty much the same, but in the verses the timbre is of a single voice singing with low-energy expenditure and in the choruses there are two voices singing with high-energy expenditure. This cartoon, a schematic representation of loudness based on the single parameter of timbre, takes us back to the example of Britney Spears at the start of the chapter, where a single aspect of timbre – the vocal creak – was exaggerated. The Alanis Morissette example is further complicated by the fact that some of the timbral attributes of high-energy singing have been filtered out – i.e. the bass and lower mid frequencies of the voice: even the single parameter of timbre is being represented in a schematic, reduced form. This schematic, reduced form of timbre, however, is enough to allow us to interpret the gestural performance through empathic and metaphorical association. We're given a sketch of a vocal performance, and through this process of mapping between sound and gesture, and gesture and emotional narrative, we arrive at an interpretation.

Noise reduction

I'll come back to these ideas at various points in the book as they are a crucial part of my hypothesis, but before we move away from this section on gesture I want to look at one other technique used in record production to accentuate and schematise the sound of musical gesture. We've looked at how, since the development of the microphone in the 1920s, the proximity of the sound source to the microphone has been used for this kind of accentuation. So far, we've thought of this purely in terms of how it allows us to hear the detail of that activity more clearly. The flip side is that it also makes other noises less clear. In any 'real life' performance situation there will be both desirable sound, the noise the musicians make, and undesirable sound, any unintended noise that nevertheless happens during the performance. That might be anything from the hum of the lighting system, the gurgle of the central heating, the rumble of a plane overhead or a train in the distance. Close microphone placement can reduce some of these sounds but can also make others worse: the musicians turning the pages of their music, their chairs creaking, the rustle of their clothing as they move or the sound of their breathing.

Aside from close microphone placement, many other strategies have been developed to remove the unwanted realism of these reminders of all the non-musical life that continues in the background of performance. Frequency equalisation and filtering is one such technique: if our instrument plays no notes lower than 100Hz we can filter out all the sound beneath that frequency and make the recording clearer. There are also various forms of frequency-banded volume control such as the de-esser, which can be used to reduce the volume of sibilance or breath noises.

Also, from around 1966 when the Dolby A system of tape noise reduction was first introduced, a variety of noise-reduction technologies that filter our analogue tape hiss were developed. Although the frequency of the tape hiss is generally above the pitch of the musical content, this kind of noise affects clarity for two reasons. First, it creates a noise 'floor', a constant background noise, and our perceptual system is built to respond to change and difference. If there is noise floor then a quiet sound played against that background will register as a smaller and less noticeable change than if there is no background noise. If 'silence' in a recording studio is about 20–25dB and my tape noise floor takes that up to about 35dB, if I record a quiet sound of about 50dB (about the level of normal conversation) then the perceived difference in levels will obviously be greater if there is no background noise. The second way that it affects clarity is by masking[12] the sounds in the recording that are at the same or a similar frequency to the noise. In the case of tape hiss, this will mask some of the high-frequency content of musical sounds, making them seem less bright. Noise-reduction systems therefore help to prevent this reduction of clarity and brightness. While these systems help to reduce noise problems introduced by the analogue tape recording system, there are also technologies that reduce the extraneous noise floor that exists in any room. The noise gate, a device that examines an audio signal and only opens to allow signals through when they rise above a preset threshold, was developed in the early 1970s. This, and later forms of technology that do the same for digital audio files (such as the 'strip silence' function on the ProTools Digital Audio Workstation), remove such ambient background noise, guitar amplifier hiss and hum, unwanted breathing sounds and so forth, to bring the sound of the musical gesture more to the fore.

The sound of perfection

The removal of breaths, rustles, creaks and similar can be done for two very closely aligned and yet subtly different reasons. The first, as we've just seen, is to highlight or exaggerate the sound of the musical gesture; the second is to render the sound less human and more abstract. In some ways, this is a logical extension of the notion of Western art music as a purely cerebral art form, a form created by the composer:

[12] Masking is a perceptual phenomenon where one sound inhibits the perception of another sound.

It was said in the nineteenth century of Hans von Bülow's playing of Beethoven's piano music that as a performer he effaced himself: when you listened, you were conscious only of Beethoven, not of Bülow... What is telling is that this was, and is, said by way of high praise, as if the best performers are the ones of whom you are not even aware. (Cook 2000, p. 25)

If this is the ideal, to hear the music and not the performance, then editing techniques that erase traces of the unwanted performer are surely a good thing: we don't want to be reminded that this frail human has to take breaths, move their arms and fingers or sit on a piano stool in order to reproduce the composer's art. In some forms of popular music there is a similar but slightly different aesthetic. On the one hand, the emotional expression of the artist is central to this aesthetic and therefore the storms and tempests of their performance – the sighs, growls, gasps and gulps – may be vital too. On the other hand, the art music tradition lives on in the vehicles for these storms and tempests: the arrangements. While we want to hear the individuality of the star's performance, we want to hear the music and not the performance of the accompanying arrangement.

Repeated takes and edits

If we take that a little further, we get to the idea of removing imperfections from the performance – assuming, of course, that we can agree on what a perfect performance might sound like. Right from the beginning of recording there was a technique that allowed musicians a greater chance of perfection, or – more realistically and less controversially – of creating a performance without unacceptable mistakes: the ability to have another go. Fletcher Henderson's release of 'Naughty Man' (1924) with Louis Armstrong on trumpet was the fifty-second take of the tune they recorded before they were satisfied. In fact, right up to 1945 and the advent of tape recording, that was the only technique available.

In 1947 Ampex produced their Model 200A tape machine, developed from a German Magnetophon made by Allgemeine Elektricitäts-Gesellschaft (AEG) and brought to the USA by Jack Mullin, a major in the US signal corps during the war. Bing Crosby had been looking for a high-quality recording system so that he didn't have to perform his radio show, 'Philco Radio Time', live twice for east coast and west coast audiences:

Starting in the 1947–8 season, Mullin became Crosby's chief engineer, recording Philco Radio Time on tape, both the dress rehearsal and the 'live-to-tape' show. The final mix, transferred to 16-inch ETs [electrical transcription discs] for airing, was often an edit of both performances. Mullin‘s skillful edits created the kind of program pacing that most live radio shows could not achieve. (Hammar 1999)

Very soon recording to tape took over in recording studios from disc lathes, and the potential to edit together different sections from different performances was available to all recording musicians. Rudy Van Gelder, one of the best-known sound engineers who worked in jazz (most famously for his Blue Note Records recordings) was an early adopter both of tape technology and of the creative possibilities of tape splicing:

The introduction of magnetic tape made possible another means of manipulating recorded material: editing by cutting apart and splicing together passages from two or more different takes. Van Gelder quickly developed extraordinary skill with a razor blade, making precise cuts on the diagonal to produce a smoother transition when the splice ran back over the play head. His adeptness at precision splicing would later stand him in good stead when editing tracks for many labels, for which he would frequently patch together the best sections of various takes to produce a more ‘perfect’ final performance. Although seemingly antithetical to jazz, an art form that prizes the uniqueness of each performance for its qualities of spontaneous improvisation, the practice of producing more polished recordings through splicing and other tape manipulations quickly became an accepted practice in many quarters of the jazz world. (Skea 2001, p. 64)

The advent of computer manipulation of digital audio files in the 1990s saw the start of a trend in editing techniques that has allowed progressively more control over not just the selection of phrases but also the timing, pitching and dynamics of the individual notes in those phrases. As an extension to the diagonal cuts of analogue tape editing, computer-based post-production techniques can offer much tighter control over cross-fading between edits, the ability to zoom in at a microscopic level to cut, erase and fade sound files, and the ability to let one sound – such as a cymbal crash – play to completion while another one starts. In addition to extending the scope of techniques that were already available on analogue (and digital) tape, alterations to the internal timing of recorded performances through time stretching and audio quantisation[13] were also introduced and gradually grew in sophistication.

[13] Time stretching is the process by which a digital audio file (or part of it) can have the speed of its playback (i.e. the tempo) altered without changing the pitch or vice versa. In the analogue world, if you play a tape faster, the pitch gets higher; if you play it slower, the pitch gets lower. Time stretching lets you adjust one without affecting the other and can only be achieved by digitising the signal. Audio quantisation compares an audio file against a tempo grid (such as the metronome pulse the performance was played to) and time stretches each beat or subdivision so that the audio file is in time with the grid. Ideally, this means that imperfect timing can be corrected.

Time stretching can also alter the pitch of an audio file, or a portion of it, without changing the length, and so it became possible to correct the pitch of out-of-tune notes. From a painstaking manual task that required complex editing and programming skills, a range of commercial features and plug-ins such as ProTools Elastic Audio and Antares Auto-Tune were developed. As long as the metronome and pitch were roughly adhered to in the performance, and the computer is provided with the tempo and scale required, the process can be automated and, if necessary, tweaked manually to achieve the desired results. Depending on your ideological position, this can either give the performer greater freedom – allowing them, for example, to keep a wonderfully expressive but technically imperfect performance – or it can destroy creative identity by making all performances conform to a single template of 'rightness'.

Human and inhuman

This brings us to the question of where 'the line' is. At what point does ever-increasing consistency in a performance cease to sound like an expert human and start to sound like a machine? There are two aspects of this: a recording can sound inhumanly[14] performed or inhumanly processed. Thus, a performance that is processed with audio quantising and Auto-Tune may sound inhumanly performed. It may also sound inhumanly performed because it has been processed to allow other 'impossible' features: the lack of breaths, rustles and squeaks mentioned above or something more extreme like a very long vocal line, too long to be sung without a breath, that has been edited together. On the other hand, a performance that has been heavily compressed – a process that will remove dynamic inconsistency in volume but retain the timbral signs of energy expenditure that suggest variations of dynamic – will sound inhumanly processed. So too, for example, does the extreme electronic sound of Auto-Tune applied to Cher's vocal on 'Believe' (1998) or the distortion added to Greg Lake's voice on King Crimson's '21st Century Schizoid Man' (1976).

Thus far, we've mostly been discussing vocal performances and, of course, as soon as we introduce a musical instrument we are dealing with a machine as well as a person: the sound is automatically, if only partially, inhumanly performed and processed. The extent and nature of this element of 'inhumanity' varies enormously. To give two examples, the harpsichord can be

[14] I use the term 'inhumanly' because although in most cases this would be 'mechanically', there may be examples that sound more superhuman or unworldly than machine-like.

seen to render a gesture machine-like because, whatever the weight and speed of the finger on the key, the mechanism will play the same timbre and volume,[15] while the sustain an overdriven amplifier can add to a guitar tone is not so much inhumanly processed but provides an un-string-like tone. Despite this, both harpsichords and electric guitars are considered expressive and presumably, therefore, human – although 'considered' is the operative word here. Notions such as expression and perfection are social constructs and we need to examine by whom, where, when, how and why they have been constructed.

I've already mentioned Csikszentmihalyi's (1988) systems approach to creativity, and will develop this idea and actor-network theory (ANT) and the social construction of technology (SCOT) in later chapters. For now, though, I want to mention that a fully fledged musicology, whether it is examining record production or any other musical practice, needs to interrogate how the value systems that underpin any aesthetics are constructed. In this instance, we need to think about the notions of agency, humanity and artificiality. The problem, of course, is that as soon as we start to try to define the limits or extent of a system or network we have to make simplifications and generalisations: we have to describe humanity and the world in schematic forms. For example, looking at this question of editing and perfection, is the technology of the piano less de-humanising than the technology of analogue tape editing? Or is the technology of analogue tape editing less de-humanising than that of Elastic Audio or Auto-Tune? If so, how do we define the communities for which this may be true? Obviously there were historical periods before the invention of the piano and analogue and digital recording for which this couldn't have been true, but is it also more true for audiences of classical music than for rock? And if we can start to answer questions about the ways that different communities and groupings think about technology, can we start to build a more general theory about humans and technology?

Whether we can or not, we can see that perfection in music is a term that requires us to value certain parameters above others: adherence to a temporal grid or tuning system above expressive deviation from it being an obvious example. Given that, we can therefore characterise the kinds of technique we've examined in this section as being aimed at creating a schematic representation of a performance – a sonic cartoon – that prioritises one set of parameters above another. This can be through highlighting one (and/or

[15] Although there are other mechanisms for changing the volume and timbre in harpsichord performance.

reducing the impact of the other) or by removing the unwanted elements altogether.

Timbre

In 1951 producer Mitch Miller recorded Johnny Ray's vocal for his hit single 'Cry' (Johnnie Ray and the Four Lads 1951) by placing him between two parabolic reflectors in the studio to create a very bright, detailed sound, to which he then added reverberation from a chamber (Schmidt-Horning 2012, p. 36). Almost thirty years later Vic Coppersmith-Heaven used a similar technique when producing 'The Eton Rifles' (The Jam 1979):

> 'The studio didn't quite have the sharp, metallic sound that I wanted for Paul's Vox amp', Vic remarks, 'so I went out and bought about 30 corrugated iron sheets and just lined them over the walls and on the floor and in front of the amp, deflecting sound into the microphone. We used a [AKG] D12 with a Neumann U67 – I put the D12 right on top of the Vox amp, smack on the speaker, and then used the 67 to pick up more of the studio acoustics, to help to create a live ambient effect.' (Buskin 2007)

This also illustrates the way in which timbre and ambience are inextricably entwined. We never hear sound without ambience,[16] and it is therefore impossible to disassociate the first, immediate reflections in a space, especially a small room, from the timbre of the sound source itself – another feature of ecological perception. In an interesting experiment, Mark Mynett (2013) recorded the same sounds through the same amplifiers with the same microphones in the same (close) positions in a small recording studio and a semi-anechoic chamber. The results were almost indistinguishable but the studio recording was fractionally brighter than the anechoic recording – i.e. the ambience wasn't noticeable as a reverb 'tail' making the sound longer or less defined, but the reflections did add to the high-frequency content.

In the earlier section on gesture, I mentioned that timbre is a function of the nature of the object making the sound as well as the nature of the type of activity. In this regard there are characteristics that can be used in a schematic way to reflect and take advantage of this in the suggestion of meaning. For example, both the Johnnie Ray and the Jam examples above

[16] With the exception of the very few people who work with anechoic chambers which, as far as possible, are rooms that are ambience free – i.e. their walls are specially (and expensively) constructed to absorb sound rather than to reflect it. Open outdoor spaces without nearby objects offer something like it except, of course, that the ground is a reflective surface.

rely on the fact that harder and more reflective objects make for brighter sound, but they also relate to the idea that higher-energy activities tend also to create more high-frequency sound. By using bright reflective surfaces in the recording, the schematic representations of the vocal and guitar timbres in these examples suggest a metaphorical, cross-domain interpretation of them as being more energetic. The gestural structure of the performance provides the basic emotional thrust – a semi-hysterical sorrow in the case of Johnnie Ray and an indignant rage in the case of the Jam – and the brightening of the timbre merely serves to ratchet up the energy level on either type of emotion.

Serge Lacasse (2000) has taken William Moylan's (1992) ideas on staging in the spatial sense (that I will explore in more detail in the next chapter) and examined the idea of timbral shaping as staging. While Lacasse was discussing this in relation to the production of voice, it can obviously be extended to any type of sound. Lacasse examines the meaning of these effects in terms of listener surveys but also relates some of the physical characteristics of the sound with emotional correlates – suggestive of the embodied cognition and metaphorical approaches outlined above.

Signature sounds

The terms 'sonic signature' and 'signature sound' are quite ambiguous. In one sense, the term relates to unambiguous connections between a sound and its cause. Thus, a 1974 paper 'Sonic Signature Analysis for Arc Furnace Diagnostics and Control' (Higgs 1974) uses the term to describe how a particular state of activity in a particular type of furnace produces recognisable types of vibration. The use of the term in music has been to describe the character of a particular individual or group's performance style and output (see, for example, Arn 1989), but can also relate to a record company or a producer (see, for example, Gillespie 2007). Thus, Tom Waits successfully sued a Spanish advertising company and Volkswagen-Audi in 2006 for using an impersonator to sing a rewritten version of one of his songs,[17] on the grounds that it violated his moral rights that protected his personality and reputation. In another example, Susan Schmidt-Horning describes how:

> [conductor Andre] Kostelanetz conducted the Coca Cola radio programme from Liederkranz Hall [in New York] for five years beginning in 1938, and claimed that

[17] See http://news.bbc.co.uk/1/hi/entertainment/4629274.stm [accessed 21 July 2013].

> his ear had grown so sensitive to the acoustical perfection of the room that after a while he could tell 'just by how the orchestra sounded on a given morning whether the floor had been swept the night before'. (Schmidt-Horning 2012, p. 33)

In these instances a signature sound isn't an exact sound as it would be in our arc furnace example. After all, the impersonator wasn't using Tom Waits' larynx, they were mimicking him; and Kostelanetz wasn't recognising a sound because the orchestra would be playing different notes on any of those given mornings. These were schematic mental representations of some of the characteristics of Tom Waits or the Liederkranz Hall that were being recognised. Mimics always state that they pick up certain characteristics to emulate, and in these instances they may have been a particular form of low growl combined with a slurred articulation for Tom Waits and a particular length and colouration of the reverberation for the Hall.

What, though, might be the sonic characteristics of a particular record producer? The ones that are often identified as having a signature sound tend to consistently do something dramatically different from 'common practice' in whatever period and genre they worked. Thus, John Culshaw and Phil Spector both used space in ways that were unusual in their field: Culshaw by creating dynamic theatrical staging of operas and Spector by creating dense spatial textures through microphone (and musician) placement. Joe Meek and Rudy Van Gelder, on the other hand, might be characterised more through their approach to processing: Meek by using dynamic compression in extreme and creative ways and Van Gelder by using microphone placement and mastering techniques to get such a strong sense of detail and presence on his recordings.

Another feature of Phil Spector's sonic signature might also be the fact that he used the same pool of musicians in a lot of his iconic projects. This is even more true of Motown, especially in the period up to 1970, when the Funk Brothers playing in the Snakepit[18] constituted a large part of the signature. With the advent of MIDI[19] and electronic and computer-based forms of production, the particular configurations of instrument technology and the way they were employed became an important element. For example, Trevor Horn's production, for a time in the 1980s, was closely associated with the sound of the Fairlight digital sampler and synthesiser

[18] The Funk Brothers were the rhythm section, or more accurately a small group of players who made up a variety of rhythm sections, that played on the vast majority of Motown's hits in the 1960s. The Snakepit was the name they gave to the relatively small but well-equipped studio in Detroit where the recordings were made.

[19] The Music Instrument Digital Interface (MIDI) is a digital protocol that allows the computer control of electronic music instruments.

with its own computer interface. Although they were expensive and rare instruments, they were being used by quite a range of well-known artists and producers at the time,[20] and the Trevor Horn sound differed from them both in the way that he and his programmer, J.J. Jeczalik, used the instrument and in the attention to detail that is revealed in the productions that emerged from his work during this period.

This also relates to the sound of particular forms of technology. Just as instrumentalists and others with a highly attuned sense of hearing can tell the difference between different manufacturers of instruments – whether it is Stradivarius and Stainer in violins or Fender and Gibson in electric guitars – so too can sound engineers and producers tell the difference between the technology in their world. The sound of analogue tape versus digital recording is one such example, but we could just as easily compare Neve and SSL mixing consoles, Fairchild and Urei compressors or Neumann and AKG microphones. And, of course, just as my choices of only two violin and guitar makers are incomplete and semi-arbitrary, so are the binary choices I listed for audio equipment. So entrenched is the fact and mythology about the sonic signatures of audio equipment that we have a growing industry based on the software emulation of 'vintage' hardware processing for the digital plug-in market.

It is clear from all this that a signature sound has to be defined in terms of its schematic nature: of how certain features are particularly pertinent and others are not. The 'signature' can relate to particular types of performance or programming characteristics that characterise the musical gestures, to spatial characteristics, to particular types of distortion, to the characteristics of particular types of sound sources or instruments or to the type of processing. All these things can be influenced by both the technology (including instrument technology) being used and the way the individual or group of individuals use them. The way their individuality or group identity is judged – by the social field of Csikszentmihalyi's systems model (1988) – relates to the perception of both conformity and rebellion in various features of their practice. In terms of Bakhtin's (1982) heteroglossia,[21]

[20] For example, Richard James Burgess, Peter Gabriel, Stevie Wonder, Kate Bush and Duran Duran.

[21] Bakhtin used the term in relation to language in the novel, suggesting that 'the novel can be defined as a diversity of social speech types . . . and a diversity of individual voices' (1982, p. 262). These individual voices have a relationship with the mainstream of language, and that can be characterised as conformist (centripetal) or non-conformist (centrifugal). Monson (1997) has applied this notion to music in relation to jazz improvisation and the way an individual's musical 'voice' will be conformist in some respects and non-conformist in others. This creates a tension, and the 'speaker' can be analysed both in the general way they tend to

Phil Spector may have been very centripetal (conformist) in terms of his use of melody, harmony and rhythm, and yet very centrifugal (rebellious) in terms of his instrumentation and use of ambience. Throughout this section I have referred to the fact that a sonic signature might relate to a group as well as to an individual, and that has been illustrated by using examples of production teams and even companies (such as Motown, Stax or PWL). The notion can and has also been applied to musical styles, national characteristics, historical periods[22] and so forth. This highlights one of the dangers of this approach: the categorisation of these types of schematic features relies on individual interpretation rather than empirical analysis, and any such analysis should only be measured by how useful it proves to be to our understanding rather than how 'true' it is.

use language (as in the Spector example above) or in the way that any specific utterance moves dynamically between different types of centrifugal and centripetal forces.

22 I, myself, have examined the question of the UK versus the US sound in rock music in the early 1970s (Zagorski-Thomas 2012b) – a study that engages all three of those criteria.

5 | Staging

Realism, artificiality and the idea of staging

Is it live or is it Memorex?

What's the connection between audio quality and the changing nature of perceived 'realism'? From the 1930s and 1940s onwards, the quest for this elusive realism established the notion of transparent mediation as a holy grail in the world of sound recording. But going back as far as 1915 the Edison Company organised a series of 'tone tests', in which audiences and critics were invited to try and tell the difference between the sound of the well-known opera singer Anna Case singing from a darkened stage and the new Edison Diamond Disc recordings of her voice. Ms Case alternated between singing along with the records and miming to them, which prevented the sound of surface noise and crackle being an issue and ensured a remarkably favourable response from audiences of the time.[1] This is more of a testament to the way in which human interpretation of sound can focus on salient features and both ignore 'noise' and cognitively 'construct' missing components than it is an endorsement of the sound quality of Edison's product.

Fifty-seven years later in 1972 the Memorex Corporation started an advertising campaign for its compact audio cassette products using the slogan 'Is it live or is it Memorex?' The slogan endured for over ten years and covered both their audio cassettes and their video (VHS) products. In the early adverts Ella Fitzgerald broke a wine glass with her voice,[2] and the experiment was repeated by playing back a recording of her on Memorex

[1] With surface noise 'playing' constantly in the background the audience couldn't use its presence to distinguish between the recording and the live performance.

[2] See: www.youtube.com/watch?v=YG8K0yl4_hc [accessed 25 February 2014] for a YouTube posting of one of these adverts. Many examples are also available to view on the internet of singers shattering wine glasses by singing a loud note at the resonant frequency of the glass and in close proximity to it. There seems to be some controversy about whether the original Memorex advert was staged or not, and whether Ella Fitzgerald's 'live' voice was amplified or not. To comply with advertising standards, the advert was probably a stylised recreation of an actual event.

tape. The point of all the adverts was to imply that it was impossible to tell the difference between an actual event and the recording of it on Memorex tape – be it audio or video. The next year the *Deutsches Institut für Normung*[3] established a set of international norms of 'high fidelity' audio recording and playback quality (DIN 45500), laid out in terms of noise and distortion levels and frequency response.

As seen in the previous chapter, this idea of realism, of making the mediating process of recording as transparent as possible is quite problematic. Just what is the acoustic experience that we should be trying to capture? If realism is defined in terms of replicating the experience of being in a specific space where a specific noise happens, that would require recordings seeking realism to be binaural recordings using a dummy head.[4] Aside from recording there is also the question of playback. Ted Fletcher (2005), among others, has pointed out the artificial nature of stereo, especially of a stereo system based on the relative volumes of signals from two spaced speakers (rather than phase differences), and has gone so far as to create a single point monitor system of stereo[5] that uses phase rather than volume to create a spatial image.

We're also very selective about our realism. What about all the low-frequency traffic rumble, the coughing, the rustle of clothing and the squeak of the piano stool that are likely to accompany the musical component of the concert experience? The visual aspects of a concert help us to concentrate on the elements we want to listen to and to ignore these forms of background noise – or at least help us push them into the background. This multi-modal nature of perception is illustrated by the McGurk effect (McGurk and MacDonald 1976). In a video demonstration, the sound 'ba ba ba' (synchronised with the lips) is dubbed onto two faces, one saying 'ba ba ba' and the other saying 'fa fa fa'.[6] The majority of viewers hear the sound that they see: 'ba' when then look at the former mouth and 'fa' when they look at the other. What we hear is strongly influenced by what we see. One obvious result of recording is that it breaks this multi-modal relationship by removing the visual element in performance and thereby disrupts what we would normally interpret as realism. A further twist in this multi-modal

[3] The German national and international organisation for standardisation in measurement.

[4] Dummy head recordings replicate the sound of being in a space by recording using two microphones placed inside the 'ears' of a dummy head. See, for example, Rossing et al. (2001, p. 575).

[5] See: www.tfpro.com/18.html [accessed 8 February 2014].

[6] See a demonstration of the McGurk effect at: www.youtube.com/watch?v=G-lN8vWm3m0 [accessed 20 July 2013].

perception story is that there is evidence (Oohashi et al. 2000) that ultra-high- and ultra-low-frequency sound are not only perceptible (probably through creating sympathetic vibrations on the skin, bones and/or internal organs) but also affect the perceived quality of musical sound. If this is so, the limited frequency bandwidth of commercial-quality digital audio[7] is another restricting factor in recording and reproducing sound realistically. CD-quality audio only reproduces the frequency range of sound picked up by the human ear (i.e. 20Hz to 20,000Hz) so any frequencies above that, which are abundantly present in the sounds before they are digitised, are lost in the digital recording process.[8] And with the further data reduction of MP3 we may have to concede that contemporary recorded music is becoming less realistic rather than more so.

Truth or reality?

The multi-modal nature of hearing is also discernible in the way the visual component helps us to identify and to follow individual elements in a complex musical texture. It is easier to pick out a cello part in an orchestral performance if you can see the gestures of the players. It is easier to understand sung lyrics if you can see the singer's mouth moving. 'Spot' microphones allow a producer or a sound engineer to subtly highlight a particular feature, in the same way that a painter or a photographer can select a particular point of focus in a two-dimensional representation of a scene. They guide us to look in a particular way, and various technological techniques in record production can guide us towards hearing in a particular way. On a general level, lead vocals tend to be mixed 3dB louder than backing tracks[9] to make them stand out, but there are also many other techniques used to make particular features more prominent.[10] It is, in fact, possible to argue that the whole history of record production can be explained as techniques that seek to manipulate the way we listen, to compensate for this reduced listening experience – i.e. listening without seeing.

Despite these complexities in the question of realism, we can nonetheless recognise that both visual and audio representations of a 'scene' can be more or less 'natural'. They can be closer to or further from an actual experience.

7 By commercial-quality digital audio I am referring to CDs, wav, aif and other 44.1kHz file formats. MP3 is of a generally lower quality.
8 Although, of course, higher sampling rates can mitigate this problem.
9 Josh Reiss of Queen Mary, University of London provided this figure in a lecture at the London College of Music in March 2011.
10 See, for example, Owsinski's (1999) interviews with various producers.

In visual art we are very familiar with this dichotomy between realism and artificiality; for example, between photographs and cartoons. As in the case of M.C. Escher and Salvador Dalí, the 'scene' can be a representation of an impossible event or situation, such as a never-ending staircase or a floppy pocket watch. Yet it is still something that is meaningful. We might call it a form of truth rather than a form of reality. What form, then, do cartoon sounds take? Just as visual cartoonists will exaggerate a single feature like Prince Charles' ears, or use a simplified representation of a structure like a line drawing of a three-dimensional structure, so too can a complex acoustic phenomenon be represented with a single parameter. One of the most common examples of this in recorded music is the fadeout. The single parameter of gradually decreasing volume creates the impression of the musical event receding into the distance. If we were seeking to create a realistic representation of this experience, the decreasing volume should be accompanied by a change in the proportions of direct and ambient sound and a reduction of high-frequency content: it should get duller with more rumble and more reverberation or echo as well as getting quieter. With our brain's built-in need to match current interpretation with past experience, we hear a volume-based fadeout as a representation of increasing distance in the same kind of way that we see a 'stick figure' of five lines and a circle in a specific configuration as a representation of the human form. So great is this tendency in human perception that the reduced frequency and dynamic range of Edison's reproduction of Anna Case's recorded voice did little to alter her audience's perception of the realism of the sound.

What is being staged?

If the musical content of a recording arises from one or more performances being perceived over time, the *staging* of the recording refers to aspects of the 'event' that are external to the performances and yet contribute to the meaning we perceive. One key feature of staging is the perceived spatial relationship between the 'performers', and between them and us (the listeners). There are two elements to this perception of spatial relationships: the nature of the environment in which the event is happening and everybody's position in that environment. The level of realism or artificiality in that perception of space allows us to hypothesise a continuum between mimetic and abstract or suggestive forms of spatial staging. For example, the staging on Miles Davis' (1959) *Kind of Blue* album utilises mimetic staging that is strongly suggestive of a band on stage, but that was created using a separate microphone on each instrument and some additional chamber reverb that gives unnatural but perceptually 'useful' clarity. Suede's (1996) *Coming Up*, on the other hand, uses a variety of artificial forms of ambience and close microphone placement that, for example, spreads the drum kit across the whole stereo image and uses different amounts and types of reverberation on the different components of the drum kit.

Staging in the theatre doesn't only involve the choice of theatre and the spatial positioning and movement of actors on the stage. It also involves clothing, make-up, lighting and stage design as markers of atmosphere and character that are external to the actors' performance. The staging of recorded music also includes analogous techniques for altering the sonic characteristics of a performance: the timbral staging. The choice of microphone type and the way they are placed in relation to the performer(s) can affect the timbre in many ways. The gadgetry of the professional recording studio – dynamic compressors, noise gates, limiters, overdrive, distortion, tape saturation, low bit-rate sampling, flanging, phasing, equalisation, pitch alteration – provides a huge range of techniques that can be used to 'dress up' performances in ways that alter the atmosphere and character of the finished recording.[11]

This, however, brings us to the issue of separating out the performance from the staging. This distinction between the creation of the performance and the process of staging it is not always clear cut. For example, is the editing process part of the creation of a performance or part of the staging of it? Editing can often involve the removal of breaths or mouth noises (Savage 2005), which will alter the character of a performance. Once a performance ceases to be the result of a single person's activity it is harder to maintain this distinction, and yet this notion of agency seems to remain central to the way we perceive music. Nevertheless, in the world of film-making it is widely accepted that the editor, designer, computer generated imagery (CGI) technician and others all collaborate with the actor to create the final performance, and that they are all micro-managed by the director. This is just as true for the analogous processes in the creation of recorded music. B.H. Haggin's assertion in the commentaries on Glenn Gould's (1966) *Prospects of Recording* that 'I don't like the idea of Schwarzkopf putting her high C on Flagstad's recording'[12] still rings true in the world of twenty-first-century sound recording. In the world of film, on the other hand, Heath Ledger's

[11] Lacasse (2000 and 2005), in his PhD thesis and a subsequent paper, examined this kind of timbral staging, which will be examined further later in this chapter.

[12] Haggin was one of several musical figures whose comments appeared in boxes annotating Gould's 1966 article in *High Fidelity Magazine*. His refers to a suggestion by Gould that such an edit was a creative possibility that would be 'howled down' by 'indignant purists' (1966, p. 50).

death during the filming of *The Imaginarium of Doctor Parnassus* (Gilliam 2009) sparked a creative twist where the use of editing, other actors and computer simulation not only allowed the film to be completed but became central to the marketing campaign.[13] This reflects society's different notions of the authenticity of mediation in film as opposed to recorded music, but both media nonetheless rely on collaborative creative practice.

The staging cues that we hear in a recording (irrespective of its type) are not exactly those we would hear in the actual situation. Even dummy-head binaural recordings, the method that most accurately captures sound as we hear it, doesn't provide us with a completely accurate picture of an audio scene. We continually move our heads when listening, and the cross-referencing of our knowledge about our head orientation in conjunction with the natural staging information gives a much more vibrant and dynamic picture of an aural scene than any recording can. Most recordings we hear are very unnatural affairs compared with binaural recordings, and recording practice has developed a variety of staging devices to create different sources of interest in recorded sound. However, they are all grounded in the way we perceive sound in the 'real world'.

Did I hear a roar or a lion?

The ecological approach involves the perception of affordances (Clarke 2005, p. 36): not just a sound (for example a roar) or what it signifies (the presence of a lion) but also what it *affords* (danger). And this brings us back to the broader question of demarcation. The term 'staging' implies a neat separation of a core work or performance from the staging process. This is by no means always the case, as we can hear in examples such as Joe Meek's production of the Tornados' 'Telstar' (1962) or Phil Spector's production of Ike and Tina Turner's 'River Deep, Mountain High' (1966), where the character of the sounds seems central to the way they were performed but, at the same time, partially determined by the spatial characteristics they exhibit. And what about edited performances or musical material constructed out of samples? The sound of the space and the timbral shaping of the instrumental performances are an integral part of the 'work' in these instances. The musical meanings – the affordances – that we generate from these recordings flow from the composition, the performances, the electronic processing and the perceived environment as a unified whole. Going back to our lion example, if we hear a roar while on our own in the

[13] See: www.blastr.com/2009/12/how_heath_ledgers_last_fi.php [accessed 8 February 2014].

African savannah the potential affordances would encourage us to run away from it, but the same sound heard in a zoo might encourage us to hurry towards it to get a glimpse of the animal.

On the one hand, our perceptual system has developed in relation to the nature of experience. It is to our evolutionary advantage that we interpret stimuli in terms of agents in an environment, and even if we know that this is not true on a rational level, we cannot help but create an interpretation as if it were true. Thus, although we might know that Stevie Wonder played all the instruments on 'Living for the City' (1973b), we still interpret the music as a multiple-player, co-present musical performance. Although a particular instance of recorded staging may not be 'possible' (i.e. it may be virtual rather than mimetic), we still interpret it as a representation of reality. Thus, although it may not be possible for a single drummer to play a bass drum in a small tiled room at the same time as they play a snare drum in a large concert hall, we create a mental representation of this common form of rock staging that maintains the perception of a single agent – the drummer – and yet also incorporates the conflicting spatial images.

On the other hand, the concept of staging stems from a culturally constructed, ideological definition of the work of art that characterises collaborative forms of creativity such as music and theatre in terms of the output of a single composer or author and its performance by musicians or actors. With this in mind, the word 'staging' becomes an umbrella term for the forms of collaborative creative activity undertaken by any contributor other than the composer, author, musicians or actors. As we have seen, though, when music and theatre are mediated as recorded music and filmed drama these notions of authorship, performance and agency become confused. In music both composition and performance are transformed by the creative possibilities of the mediation process into collaborative activities where the boundaries between creation/performance and staging become blurred. While the radical conceptual shift in the world of music that this involves needs to be explored in more detail, the concept of staging remains a useful analytical tool.

Spatial staging and the sound box

Listening without moving

The production techniques utilised in recorded music are based on a culturally constructed 'ideal' listening position and mental state. In either stereo or surround-sound systems there is a 'sweet spot' where the spatial effects are perceived most effectively, and this positioning of the listener implies that they are going to be both attentive and passive. The majority of listening to recorded music involves neither of these criteria being met. Domestic hi-fi speakers are seldom placed according to listening criteria and are often positioned asymmetrically, on the floor, in a corner or on shelves on the basis of available space, visual aesthetics or the proximity of electrical sockets and cable lengths. A lot of listening occurs with substantial background noise being present, such as in-car stereos or on personal stereos on public transport.[14] In relation to the question of attention, recorded music is frequently used to accompany dancing, as background or mood music in social situations and more broadly as a soundtrack to our modern lives through the ubiquitous use of personal stereos and headphones. It is seldom the subject of our undivided attention.

The culturally constructed 'ideal' listening position and mental state are also based on the normal working environment of a sound engineer. Does it make sense to be mixing dance music while seated (and sober)? Can a sound engineer effectively mix music to be played in a car while sitting in a quiet room? Many record producers have developed strategies to integrate the imperfections of everyday listening experiences into their mixing practice. Bobby Owsinski's (1999) interviews with various producers revealed strategies that included listening to mixes from a corridor outside the studio through an open door, comparing mixes on deliberately low-quality speaker systems as well as studio monitors and listening to mixes with a vacuum cleaner switched on in the studio to simulate the experience of listening with a car engine running in the background.

Does the academic analysis of music involve a different form of listening than 'functional listening'? Can you analyse dance music in a meaningful way if you're not part of the community that dances to it? A fully rounded musicology of record production should surely be including ethnographic studies of 'listeners in the wild' as well as producers in their natural habitat. Clarke has approached this issue using the notion of 'subject-position' taken from film studies to describe the listener's unique perspective on a piece of music resulting from their 'particular circumstances, experience, background and aesthetic attitudes, as well as the specific ... occasion' (Clarke 2005, pp. 92–3). The subject-position steers a course between determinism and a 'potentially infinite plurality' of interpretation. Clarke suggests that the complex nature of the perceptual input provides inherent, complex

[14] For more on this see Bull (2005) and DeNora (2000).

interpretive information. For example, a particular form of audio input might have characteristics associated with a child's voice singing and also possess the acoustic characteristics of sound occurring in a large, reflective enclosed space. We hear what's happening and we hear where it is happening because these are fundamental to the experience of being human and living in the world. Certain members of the human race may also find that this perceptual experience creates cultural meaning relating to the choral traditions of the Christian church as well as to the physical meaning: the voice and the space.

Hearing where you are

The concept of staging as a tool of analysis in record production comes from the work of William Moylan (1992) and Serge Lacasse (2000) but is also related to Trevor Wishart's (1986) thoughts on 'landscaping' in electroacoustic composition and Allan Moore's sound box (A.F. Moore 1992). Lacasse refers specifically to the manipulation of the sound of the human voice, but his ideas are transferable to all recorded sound. The notion of staging refers to the treatment of sound in ways that add meaningful context for the listener to a performance or a perceived musical 'event'. Perhaps the simplest example of this is the addition of artificial ambience to suggest the sound source's placement in physical space – a church as opposed to a bathroom, for instance. As often as not, these types of spatialisation techniques involve the cartoon versions of sound discussed earlier. This is as true of classical recordings that use a combination of 'room' and 'spot' microphones on solo instruments or sections to make them more prominent as it is of pop recordings that use artificial reverberation on a lead vocal: they create the impression of a spatial environment rather than an accurate representation of one.

Edward Hall (1966) coined the term 'proxemics' to describe his theory of the culturally and psychologically (i.e. individually) constructed nature of space. While Hall recognised that wide cultural variations exist in the perception and interpretation of social space, he identified the four categories of intimate, personal, social and public space and, in an interesting parallel with later metaphorical models of embodied cognition, defined them according to criteria arising from bodily sensation and perception. This also relates directly to Johnson's (1990) image schema,[15] and in particular to the centre–periphery schema, where the individual is the core or centre.

[15] Johnson's definition of an image schema is of a mental structure that provides recurrent, structured understanding of different types of experience both physically and metaphorically.

Hall identifies various forms of meaning that can be associated with these proxemic categories, but metaphorical forms of meaning can be identified as well. Based on his own observation and anecdotal evidence, he ascribes a series of national characteristics of proxemic attitudes, describing social constructions of accepted levels and forms of proximity in different cultures. Even if we consider that these assertions were reliable in 1966 rather than being based on relatively crude national stereotypes, they would suggest that approaches to proximity have altered radically in the intervening decades. Their anecdotal nature, however, indicates that more structured and rigorous studies are needed before such specific claims can be reliably made. The same is, of course, true of the types of metaphorical relationships that might be theorised, but they also provide an interesting avenue of analytical and interpretive potential. Intimate space, as defined in Hall's proxemic categories, is associated with physical and emotional warmth but intimacy can also be associated with honesty and sincerity. The use of intimate space in recorded music may then create metaphorical meaning that suggests a personal and direct relationship with the performer. Aside from the musical and artistic meaning that this may generate, this type of relationship may also stimulate 'brand loyalty' towards a star's projected image. See, for example, Doyle's discussion of the way Muddy Waters utilised a sense of intimacy in his recordings for Chess Records in the 1940s (2006, p. 176). On the other hand, the perception of public space in recorded music may suggest the power relationships associated with large-scale concerts and the aspirational relationship that some forms of stardom can generate. I have discussed this in relation to rock music production in 'The Stadium in your Bedroom' (Zagorski-Thomas 2010b).

Hearing the impossible

Further complexity has been added in the last forty years or so of record production through the use of conflicting perceptual messages. If we listen to the recording of Whitney Houston (1992) belting out the final chorus of 'I Will Always Love You' and compare it with Jarvis Cocker's vocal on the first two verses of 'Common People' (Pulp 1995), we notice that the volume of the voice, the high-frequency content, and the level of room ambience are similar. The perceived performance intensities of the two vocal deliveries, on the other hand, are entirely different. Houston's vocal timbre suggests high levels of energy being expended, and Cocker's timbre gives the impression

Thus, the force schema can explain a physical force such as wind, or be used metaphorically such as the idea of love as a physical force (e.g. he was irresistibly drawn to her).

of a throwaway delivery and a world-weary lack of effort. The timbral cue of a quietly 'spoken' voice at a high volume level outranks other conflicting cues to stage Cocker's vocal as intimately close and Houston's as further away. An extra level of complexity is added in Houston's case: although the intensity of the vocal can range from a virtual whisper at the start of the track to a powerful 'roar' at the end, the actual volume remains almost the same, controlled by a combination of compression and mix volume. The false impression we receive of how loud the vocal is at different points in the song, and our sense of how much energy is being expended in Houston's singing, is shaped by the vocal timbre, and this overrides the opposing messages conveyed by the equality of volume throughout.

Conceptual blending

Many authors have discussed the notion of unnatural or impossible auditory scenes in recorded music,[16] but how we interpret them stems from the way they suggest 'real' phenomena rather than the way in which they are 'unreal'. A line drawing of a cube provides a two-dimensional schematic representation of a three-dimensional object, but does so in a way that eschews information such as the colour and texture of the surfaces. Schematic aural depictions of acoustic space similarly provide one or two features of an acoustic phenomenon to suggest a more complex reality. The idea of functional staging that I will expand upon later in this chapter is mostly reliant on cartoon versions of audio phenomena, but I also want to examine the notion of conceptual blending in this context.

Fauconnier and Turner describe conceptual blending as 'an invisible, unconscious activity involved in every aspect of human life', by which an interpretation of a phenomenon is achieved by imaginatively blending two or more different concepts (2003, p. 18). For example, a recording might apply a short, bright ambience of the type found in a small tiled room to the drum kit sounds in the track and a longer, concert-hall style reverb to the vocals in the same recording. Our interpretation of this recording may flag up its artificiality, but we also blend the two concepts to provide a single spatial interpretation of the sounds. We don't hear the impossibility of being in two rooms at the same time. Rather, we hear the extra power and clarity that a short reverb – by increasing the average amplitude of the drums – creates, but take our overall spatial cue from the long reverb on the voice. One acoustic feature is mapped onto a gestural (albeit related to

[16] See, for example, Izhaki (2008, p. 408), Moylan (1992) and Veal (2007).

the environment) feature and a contradictory acoustic feature is mapped onto an entirely different environmental feature in order to allow a single interpretation to be made. There are two conceptual models about how space affects our perception at work here. The first is the idea that the intensity and morphology of ambience is related to our sense of volume and thence to power and performance intensity. The second is that it relates to the perceived size of the space we are in, and therefore to intimacy and the cultural associations of large and small spaces (e.g. a bathroom as opposed to a concert hall). As Fauconnier and Turner might describe it, we create a single interpretation that recognises both models but is restricted to neither.

One of the staple forms of staging in rock music provides an example of this. The low-frequency sounds in a track are recorded and processed with little or no ambience but with equalisation and compression that exaggerates the bass frequencies. The equalisation provides additional low-frequency volume, usually in conjunction with filtering or selective boosting and cutting of low frequencies to avoid muddiness. The compression, by increasing the sustain of these low-frequency sounds, increases the impression of volume by increasing the average but not the peak amplitude. This creates a single feature of the characteristics of large acoustic spaces: more bass in comparison with high frequencies. This is combined with reverberation added to higher-frequency components such as the hi-hat, snare drum, guitars and vocals, which creates the perception of space without the muddiness of reverberation on low-frequency content that 'reality' creates. We get two of the characteristics of a loud performance in a large space – important signifiers of power and energy in rock music – but in a distorted form that doesn't involve the loss of rhythmic and pitch-based clarity that 'nature' would normally insist on.

Timbral staging

The term 'timbral staging' refers to choices and treatments that shape the timbre of the recorded music. These may be analogous to orchestration and arranging, in the sense that they influence the tone or the gestural shape. The idea of orchestration being related to gestural shape may seem odd at first glance but the difference in sound between, say, a trombone and a marimba is not as simple as the relative volumes of the various overtones that determine brightness and other tonal features. There is also a spectromorphology that relates to gesture: the sound of a blown attack as opposed to a struck one and the way in which the trombone can slide between pitches as opposed to the distinct unsustaining notes of the marimba.

What is being staged – again?

If we stage a play, then do we also stage a composition as opposed to a performance? The traditions of Western art music – with a composer creating a score – create the implication that the casting process – the selection of a musician – is itself a form of timbral staging: the 'grain' (Barthes 1977) of the chosen voice adds a character that is external to the composer's voice. This is part and parcel of the complexity that scholars such as Christopher Small (1998) and Nicholas Cook (2000) have identified in the traditional notion of the composed score as a text rather than as a set of instructions for the collaborative creation of a performance. And now, of course, we add a further level of complexity – the editorial control of the producer and engineer over the structure of the patchwork of performances that constitute a recording is yet another cog in this collaborative machine. The choices of musicians to play on a recording – finding voices that blend together or selecting the distinctive character of a particular player's tone – are important creative decisions no matter at which point in the production process they are made.

However, in musical activity – especially outside the Western art music tradition – the performer often carries the status of creative artist: the performance is the 'thing' being staged rather than the composition, or perhaps as well as it. A pop singer's interpretation of someone's song, a jazz group's improvisation around the skeleton of a standard and a folk musician's setting of some communal repertoire are all such instances. In these cases, some or all of the performances are the musical creations being staged and therefore, of course, can't be seen as staging choices.

Dressing up sounds

The musical notion of timbre is often considered to be analogous to colour or texture in the visual domain. This suggests that timbral staging in recorded music may be equivalent to techniques such as set design, make-up, costume and lighting in the cinema. Audio processing techniques such as equalisation, dynamic compression or expansion, phasing, flanging and distortion can enhance and perhaps even change the meaning of a performance. These are things that are normally done by someone other than the 'actor' or 'performer' (but can be done by them), and which may be described as 'external' to them: as post-production in a philosophical – if not strictly temporal[17] – sense. Serge Lacasse has produced a taxonomy of effects and processing (2000, pp. 168–219) based on William Moylan's (1992) work on staging that suggests various forms of meaning associated with these techniques.

Lacasse's work is also paralleled in the field of electroacoustic composition. Denis Smalley (1986) discusses ways of generating meaning in electronic music by creating morphologies that suggest an action and an object; for example, a string vibrating when plucked, a human sobbing, or the smooth mechanical acceleration of a motor. Lacasse extends Moylan's concept of staging to include electronic treatments of sound that impose a timbral shape (or Smalley's spectromorphology) onto recorded sound in ways that suggest the physical manifestation of human emotional activity. This is related very closely to theories of embodied cognition, such as those proposed by Lakoff and Johnson (1999) and Antonio Damasio (2000).

There is of course, though, an ambiguity of meaning inherent in this. I have argued elsewhere (Zagorski-Thomas 2012a) that Clarke's (2005) application of subject-position, Grady's (1997) primary metaphors, Johnson's (1990) image schema, Csikszentmihalyi (1997) and McIntyre's (2012) systems approach to creativity and Bakhtin's (1982) centripetal and centrifugal forces provide tools to create a potential bridge between the producer's intensions and the listeners' interpretations. While I'm not suggesting that there is any absolute meaning, there are certain embodied and culturally constructed potentialities for interpretation.

For example, staging a guitar sound by adding overdrive or distortion creates a spectromorphology for that sound that is similar to the timbre of a shouting voice. By adding a certain pattern of both harmonic and non-harmonic overtones, the staging conveys meaning through relating the guitar sound to the type of emotional human states that we associate with shouting voices. While different individuals and communities may have developed more or less nuanced distinctions and aesthetics, and their interpretations may vary from anger and aggression to good-humoured excitement, they are unlikely – given the bodily metaphor mentioned above – to associate this type of distorted sound with peace and relaxation.

[17] A lot of what is often described as post-production in recorded music (and radio) does not happen 'after' in any meaningful sense. I will return to this idea in Chapters 8 and 9, but for the moment it is enough to mention that editing, the quintessential post-production activity, is occurring throughout the 'production' process of recording performances.

Functional staging

What is it for?

Let's go back to our earlier point that a lot of (if not most) recorded music is created for an audience that is not going to be either seated in a 'sweet spot' or attentive in the traditional concert-hall mode of reception. We use music in a variety of different ways and these ways of listening can affect the way the recorded music is produced. All music has a function (and often more than one), but the function doesn't always have an impact on the approach to phonographic staging.

I'm going to start, therefore, with a short taxonomy of the functions to which recorded music can be put.

1. Focused listening – playback for an individual (or small group) to listen attentively. This happens mostly in the home but can be formalised (e.g. a music society or acousmatic concert) or via headphones in other informal situations. Production will aim for clarity and stylistically appropriate proximity to suggest that the listener is a privileged (best position) witness.
2. Performance atmosphere – playback to simulate or suggest the atmosphere of a 'live' performance. Production will reproduce, simulate or suggest acoustic properties associated with stylistically appropriate communal experience of a performance.
3. Dance – playback in informal (party) or formal (club) situations. Production will ensure musical features important to facilitating the attentional synchronisation of dance gestures to musical gestures are highlighted.
4. Background – playback used for subliminal or peripheral creation of ambience where listeners' attention is focused elsewhere. Production will aim to be smooth and without sudden dynamic or timbral variations.

These functions are not mutually exclusive and different styles of music combine different aspects of these production approaches in different ways.

Focused listening

Music intended for home listening through domestic hi-fi or personal stereo systems tends to involve some balance between the first and second functions in our list. The notion of stylistically appropriate proximity generally relates to the communal activity involved in concert performance of that style. Thus, orchestral music is generally staged to place the listener centrally but several rows back from the stage in a large auditorium. In popular music this form of staging will often employ techniques that suggest intimacy and an individual approach – as if the performance is being whispered in your ear, and is solely for you. Close microphone placement, exaggeration of high-frequency content and the relative high volume of dry signals in comparison to reverberation are all common techniques for suggesting proximity to the performer, and when these are combined with low-energy, intimate performances the effect is even stronger.

In fact, these techniques have become so prevalent that in some styles of music they have become merged and confused with questions of recording quality – the closer they sound, the better the recording. This has also been combined with our continued exposure to unnaturally compressed bass frequencies to create expectations about the sonic characteristics of recorded music that constitute a culturally constructed perception of 'good-quality' recording, which extends well beyond questions of frequency and dynamic range.

Performance atmosphere

The use of production techniques to create the atmosphere of a large-scale communal activity is used extensively in music that is designed for reproduction in a smaller home environment (for example, Queen 1977). Rather than an accurate representation of the listening experience of a large concert hall, though, the muddying influence of reverberating low-frequency sound is usually avoided. Instead, the 'fattening' of the sound that this creates is often suggested through some sort of electronic or tape-based compression of the low end. This gives some aspects of the perception of a large space without the loss of clarity that realistic reverberation would induce: another example of the sound cartoons mentioned earlier.

Many of the conventional techniques of multi-track recording and mixing can be related to this form of virtual staging – of generating psychoacoustic cues that are reminiscent of some features of a particular type of listening experience while avoiding other aspects that may have a negative impact on intelligibility or the musical meaning of a particular sonic feature.

Dance

One factor common to a wide variety of commercial recordings intended for dance is that playback will be through a public address system in a large venue. The playback will thus entail the addition of substantial ambience from the dance venue itself as well as any ambience on the original recording. Reverberant spaces will blur the rhythmic characteristics of a piece of music by making the note onsets less distinct. These note onsets are the perceptual cues that we use to establish pulse and to synchronise dance gestures to musical sound. A characteristic of functional staging in recorded music intended for public dancing would therefore be to reduce the ambience on the recordings of the musical elements that are key to establishing the pulse of the music. In Western popular music at the end of the 1960s and beginning of the 1970s, when clubs dedicated to dancing to recorded music started to become more popular, we see a divergence in drum sounds between dance music and rock music that seems to bear this out. See, for example, Stevie Wonder (1973a) and Led Zeppelin (1973).

At the same time, in dance music musical elements that are more concerned with generating the party atmosphere – most commonly vocals and hand claps – are treated with reverb to suggest large-scale communal activity (for example, K.C. and the Sunshine Band 1975) and contribute to the club 'vibe'.

Background

Productions of music such as Muzak and easy listening are often aiming to be 'wallpaper music': to blend into the background and provide a more or less subliminal accompaniment for some other activity. As our perceptual systems are tuned to attend to change and difference, constancy and uniformity are the tools that can be used to make a recording recede into the background. Mixing and processing that irons out dynamic change and stages the whole musical content in the same acoustic space are therefore common where this is the function required.

Media-based staging

Media-based staging takes the idea of 'location' a step further to include perceptions of time and place that are associative rather than perceptual: where the aural 'footprint' of particular forms of mediation associated with audio reproduction media has been used to generate meaning within the production process. The sound of particular media – specific limitations in frequency range and dynamic range and particular forms of distortion, ambience and noise – will generate associative meaning for audiences with particular forms of cultural experience. These can take two principal forms: chronological associations that relate to historical forms of recording and playback mediation systems. The latter will include sound reproduction systems associated with particular places or activities and mass or personal communication systems. As discussed in the first theoretical interlude, the forms of frequency alteration or distortion that characterise different media constitute an invariant property associated with a specific type of activity or experience. Where these can be mapped onto a specific musical or, indeed, any sonic experience (i.e. where that sonic experience exhibits that invariant property), that form of mediation will be associated with it and some association of the mediation will be attributed to the musical experience. For example, our experience of the way voices are affected by phone lines may be matched with a vocal sound in a recorded song, and we may make the associative connection of communication over a long distance.

This is further complicated by issues of familiarity and expertise that may allow for finer or coarser gradations of differentiation. For example, recognising the sound of early recordings is a broad-based association familiar to most members of post-industrial societies, but hearing the difference between wax cylinder acoustic recording and 1920s electric disc recording, although a relatively easy skill to acquire, is not one that's common in contemporary society. Likewise, recognising the sound of a voice coming down a phone line is a widely acquired social skill, although hearing the difference between a land line and a mobile phone may not be so obvious to most. And getting more esoteric, we may utilise the difference between 16-and 24-bit recording or between good-quality MP3 and a .wav or an .aif file.

When did I hear that?

One reason for media-based staging in record production is to evoke the sound of a particular (or more commonly just a vague) historical period. In the same way that sepia tinting of film and photographs, black and white photography and the particular colour saturation associated with Super8 and other home movie formats are used to denote age, the sound of early recordings is also used. Another crucial aspect of this that should be mentioned is the way particular forms of clarity and audio quality are associated with modernity. This has also become quite tightly entangled with the distinction between expensive- and cheap-sounding record production.

One obvious example of media-based staging is the Beatles' 'Honey Pie' (1968), which has a short fragment of 'old crackly record' at the beginning –

in this instance an obvious reference to the stylistic period of the track. The Buggles' 'Video Killed the Radio Star' (1979) uses a limited frequency range and dynamic compression on the vocals to suggest the sound of early radio broadcasts. This is mixed into a contemporary (to 1979) production sound, and the production itself juxtaposes perceptions of antiquity with those of modernity – the voice and keyboard sounds have the restricted frequency range of antiquity while the female vocals, kick drum and bass have a sound of modernity that was set to become the standard in the 1980s.

Making sounds that resonate

This brings us to a further distinction that can be made about the way media-based staging can create meaning: a way that is related to ideas of familiarity and expertise. Historical references can be grounded in ideas of what might be perceived as cool to a particular target audience – to ideas of authenticity and the perceived authority that stems from speaking with a particular voice. In the early 1990s the 'voice' of late 1960s and early 1970s record production, the sound of analogue tape and valve or tube amplifiers, was used to distance the sound of Oasis (and other Manchester bands of the early to mid-1990s) from the sound of the 1980s. The voice of authority was the perceived golden age of rock, although the way it was used was selective: another form of cartoon.

There are many other examples of particular types of production technology developing an authenticity within a particular musical style – Roland TR808 drum machines and TB303 synthesisers within house and techno in the late 1980s, playing, sampling and pressing to vinyl within the Bristol sound (Roni Size, Portishead) and the anti-synthesiser stance of various rock bands at various points – such as Queen and Rage Against the Machine. In our postmodern age, though, the cache of sonic signatures can go up as well as down, and the 'voice of authority' can be sincere or it can be ironic. Whereas on certain hip hop tracks, for instance, the presence of the sound of vinyl crackle is a signifier of authenticity, of sampling from the original repertoire, in the case of the Mike Flowers Pops' 'Wonderwall' (1995) it is part of the ironic language of retro cheesiness. This highly specialised interpretation/inverted snobbery can be seen in terms of Bourdieu's (1986) ideas of cultural capital – and specifically of Thornton's (1996) idea of subcultural capital: only an audience with the habitus of listening within a particular sonic world will understand the cultural resonances, the subtleties of authority and irony, that allow the 'correct' reading of this audio event.

Rebelling against a sound

Another important way that media-based staging can affect the meaning of recorded music is through a dilettante approach – on the face of it, a superficial, amateurish and partially understood approach to recording. Garage bands from the late 1950s onwards have produced rough and unpolished recordings, and this has led to it being embraced as a production aesthetic in itself. If the dilettante approach is chosen rather than being accidental then it takes on additional meaning. In this instance, professional-quality recording becomes a signifier for the 'establishment' and the rejection of it – the choice to go lo-fi – becomes a political statement: a marker of difference. An example of this can be found in Darkthrone's *Transilvanian Hunger* (1994).

Where did I hear that?

The sound of playback mediation systems can include forms such as Muzak in an elevator or a supermarket, film sound in a movie theatre, AM radio sound or the sound of TV. Mass communication media might include the public address systems in various types of environment: supermarkets, railway stations, sporting events, aeroplanes, etc. This also includes the sound of personal communication media such as different types of telephone calls, walkie talkie radios, police radios, or the sound of astronauts communicating from the moon.

Eminem's 'The Real Slim Shady' (2000) differentiates his voice in the introduction from the main lead vocal by using the sound of a supermarket public address system. Aside from referencing a familiar form of paging – or requesting someone's presence – that relates to the lyrical content, this also is a culturally familiar form of disembodied voice. The role of the narrator, a very common form of disembodied voice in contemporary media, can be summoned in many more conventional ways than this – the sounds of radio announcers or TV voice-overs being two examples. Record production is itself another medium that generates disembodied voices – the paradox that Evan Eisenberg (2005) has described as the performer without an audience and the audience without a performer. Techniques such as this can allow the creation of multiple levels of disembodiment: the staging identifies this version of Eminem's voice as different from the main vocal – a step further away and thus a narrator commenting on or preparing us for the lead vocal.

A further example of this can be found on '10.30 Appointment' by Soweto Kinch (2006). The cultural significance of an interview at a job centre in the

UK – conjured up by the tannoy announcements and the office environment noises – in which the protagonist explains to the employment officer that he wants to be a rapper, is not only very British but is also culturally specific to those claiming state benefits. The ritual humiliation of the ticket and window interview queuing technique is more broadly familiar, however.

On Skee-Lo's (1995) 'I Wish' the introduction to the track is staged as playback with the limited frequency range of a small-speaker AM radio, and this is itself introduced by the sound of a tuning dial being turned. The track is referencing the audio media expected to be one of the primary forms of playback. It also works as an interesting twist on an often-used popular music arranging tool – arranging the introduction as a lighter version of the main theme. Rather than, for example, a solo piano introduction before the band kicks in, this provides a version of the track with high- and low-frequency filtering, which is then removed as the vocal starts.

Hanging on the telephone

The telephone voice utilised by Britney Spears on 'Oops! . . . I Did It Again' (2000) is recognisably treated, and is dropped into the verse narrative of the song a few times – seemingly quite randomly – as an arrangement tool. The familiar staging of telephone communication is used as a tone colour in the vocal arrangement rather than as a cipher for disembodiment or separation – the form of meaning usually associated with telephone references in popular music in the past (e.g. the Electric Light Orchestra's 'Telephone Line' [1976]).

Later in the Britney Spears track a filmic reference to the Titanic movie, in which a diamond necklace is dropped into the ocean by the old lady narrator, is given the sonic characteristics of the reduced sound quality of a movie theatre. The media-based staging in these instances is used to create references to popular pastimes and youthful social life rather than meaning related to the musical and lyrical content.

More cartoons of sound

An important aspect of this, which relates back to issues of familiarity and expertise that were mentioned earlier, is the fact that the signifier – the characteristic that identifies the media in question – is often highly exaggerated. The crackle on the Mike Flowers Pops' record (1995) is so loud that it would have been a signifier of a badly worn record; the vocal track on 'Video

Killed the Radio Star' (The Buggles 1979) has a more restricted frequency range than the actuality of early AM radio; and the slapback delay on the tannoy in 'The Real Slim Shady' (Eminem 2000) has slightly more feedback than the real thing. Gaining the stamp of authenticity, of speaking with the voice of authority, often requires the 'tone of that voice' to be exaggerated.

Theoretical interlude 2

Chapters 6 and 7 will deal with recording technology and the way its design influences the way in which it is used. The constructionist agenda from the sociology of technology is applied to explore how technology develops and becomes disseminated. Both the systems approach to creativity and the constructionist agenda are used to examine how the technology influences the way it is used.

In these two chapters actor-network theory (ANT) is used to explain both the network through which recording technology is produced and disseminated and the network in which it is used to make music. There are two key aspects to its explanatory power: the first arises from describing the participants, their environment and their relationship to each other; the second arises from elucidating the nature of their influence upon each other. The participants (human and non-human) configure each other through their perception of and action upon affordances. This process of configuration can occur through a participant's perception of the physical restrictions and affordances in an environment (including the other participants) and, of course, the capabilities of their own body. This relates to both image schema of embodied cognition and ecological perception. Activities that are physically possible are recognised and reinforced as an image schema.

Another way in which configuration can occur is through the voluntary alteration of our more complex mental representations. Of course, the term voluntary is used in the context of the power structures that have been constructed in the network. If someone is holding a gun to my head and gives me an order, I may voluntarily reconfigure my mental representation of the world to comply with that order rather than choosing to die (or, perhaps more accurately, choosing to see if they carry out their threat). The coupling of the idea of compliance with the reconfiguration of a mental representation may seem an odd one, but those structures involve the scripts of subsequent activity: I reconfigure my mental representation of myself in the script into someone who is going to comply and activate the script. Phil Spector notwithstanding, the use of guns as a tool of persuasion in record production is a rarity. More commonly, I may be persuaded by evidence or argument that I can trust a particular person to lead an activity and tell me what to do. Much of my script-based activity in the studio may have been determined by previous learning, but there will always be some element of configuration – asking, showing, persuading, telling, etc.

Two ideas drawn from the social construction of technology (SCOT) are also important in the next two chapters. The first of these is to examine how the technological frame – the agenda that determines the types of questions that are asked in the design and development process – is set. We can see the technological frame as a kind of sociological mental representation of the mindset of the participants: although they don't have to agree on how and why something should be done, they do agree on the context for framing the question. The second idea is to compare the action script inherent in design and the interpretive flexibility seen by participants in a technological frame. These are both, when seen from the perspective of ecological perception/embodied cognition, reliant on the perception of affordances. The idea in SCOT that different types of user will have different relationships with the supposedly inherent action script – the designer's intentions – relates to the fact that users' different existing knowledge structures will cause them to perceive different affordances in the same object. Similarly, interpretive inflexibility within a technological frame relates to the fact that a participant's existing knowledge structures are equivalent to the technological frame and they will, likewise, afford interpretation – flexible or otherwise.

The way the systems model of creativity is brought into the discussion in these two chapters relates primarily to defining the cultural domain and the social field. Csikszentmihalyi (1988) discusses the generality of society rather than the specifics of psychology. The cultural domain is the set of rules, conventions and knowledge involved in the relevant form of creative practice that is available globally, not just those available to the particular individual under discussion. McIntyre (2011) examines how the domain's structure, accessibility, flexibility and so on are related to Bourdieu's theory of cultural production (Bourdieu 1993). However, there's no distinction between the knowledge, rules and similar that the individual has internalised and those that they don't know but that are 'out there', which may or may not be potentially accessible to them. This is one of the reasons why I think that the systems approach is better suited to a broader approach than to the detail of a specific case.

6 | The development of audio technology

A history of what?

The history of recording technology

Jacek Mastykarz worked in Polish television sound in the 1970s, but became a record producer/engineer at the recording studio in Theatr Stu in Krakow in the 1980s and later moved into live sound for large festivals. During the 1980s he engineered and produced for Polish bands such as Maanam, Skaldowie, Lady Pank and others. He recalls:

> In 1980/81 I was responsible for bringing the first 24-track Studer and many other bits of up-to-date equipment to the studio in Theatr Stu. At that time most studios and radio stations, including Polskie Nagrania (the biggest record production studio in the country) operated a 16-track. As I recall, in the 1970s *Korowód* [an album] by Marek Grechuta was recorded on an eight-track. The 16-track was standing in the corridor awaiting a compatible console.[1]

In the last two chapters we've been examining the way we perceive and interpret recorded music although, of course, that has important ramifications for the way it may be produced. We've also discussed the ecological approach to perception. One of the defining characteristics of this approach, so much so that it is enshrined in the terminology, is the centrality of the physical environment with which we interact in the process of perception. The things around us, including those that we design and make ourselves, help to define how we think and perceive. We conceptualise our perceptions in terms of the 'things' that may have caused them and build conceptual models of these 'things' in terms of the outcomes they might afford. This gives us a theoretical basis for how we might study technology, along with a theoretical bridge between the psychology of embodied cognition and ecological perception and what Wiebe Bijker terms the 'constructionist program' (1995, p. 6) within the history and sociology of technology, taking

[1] Personal email communication with Jacek Mastykarz in September 2012. Translation by Natalia Zagorska-Thomas.

in systems theory, actor-network theory (ANT) and the social construction of technology (SCOT).

But what does this tell us about Jacek Mastykarz and his description of the way recording technology spread in Poland during the 1970s and 1980s? Well, the very choice of the example sets an agenda about innovation. He is discussing the innovations that occurred within the context of the recording industry as it existed under the Polish communist regime of this period. This isn't about the dates at which these forms of multi-track recording technology were invented, but if it were, what could we say about them? The development of optical multi-track sound systems for film started in the 1930s[2] and commercial multi-track magnetic tape systems appeared in various forms in the 1950s. However, there are several strands of the timeline that we could follow here. We could start by looking at when the discoveries that made these technologies possible occurred. We could then move on to look at when the first working prototypes were made and then when the first commercially available products were released. But the Mastykarz example points us towards yet another aspect of the history of technology: the story of when and how these technologies came to be distributed around the world and of their usage.[3]

In order to provide an explanation as well as a description of these events, we need not only to gather these kinds of evidence together but also to place them into a theoretical framework: to provide an interpretation. Mastykarz was working in a musical culture where, partly due to the restricted access to the latest developments in recording technology, performers remained in an older model of performing/recording practice for longer. The sound of Polish rock music from this period is different from that of Western countries not simply because the musicians lacked the technology to copy that sound. While that may have been a partial aspiration, they also remained more firmly entrenched in a model of creative authenticity based on live performance. The lack of opportunity to establish a working method (and a sonic signature) that was based on complex studio manipulation and multi-tracked performances encouraged them to develop different creative practices based around co-present performance in the studio. The aim of this chapter is to examine how this combination of the psychology of embodied

[2] Although its origins go back to Charles Hoxie's pallophotophone in 1922.

[3] I explored some of the issues about recording technology in Poland under communism in a 2012 paper at the Society for the History of Technology conference in Copenhagen called 'The Influence of Recording Technology and Practice on Musical Performance in the Recording Studio in Poland between 1960 and 1989'. I'm hoping to find the time to expand this into a journal article in the future.

cognition and ecological perception and the sociology of ANT, SCOT and the systems approach to creativity can provide such a theoretical framework for understanding the development of audio technology. The first step in that journey is a discussion of the nature of the evidence we can draw upon.

A history of things

The choices we make about research and data gathering are ideological. They are based on our pre-existing beliefs about what is important or significant. The literature on the history of recording is permeated with the history of the technology. The literature on the history of musical performance, on the other hand, is more concerned with the history of techniques than instrument technology. That organology is such a marginal topic in musicology and, indeed, that the study of Western art music focuses not just more on composition than performance but also more on harmony and form than on instrumentation and timbre, all speak volumes about this inherent ideology. I would argue that this ideology stems from the Cartesian dualism of mind and body. Western culture for the past three centuries has revolved around the valorisation of the intellectual over the physical. Despite evidence to the contrary, Western art music has developed the mythology of composition as an internal, cerebral act, divorced from the physicality and gesture of instrumental performance.[4] Recorded music, perhaps ironically as it severs the direct connection between the performer and audience, allowed performers to create for posterity and thus created a mechanism by which this inequality between performance and composition could start to rebalance. Also, the last quarter of the twentieth century saw a strong intellectual shift away from Cartesian dualism and towards embodied cognition: the notion that our intellect and our bodily experience are inextricably entwined. As this shift becomes more firmly embedded in our intellectual culture as the twenty-first century progresses, I think we will continue to see fundamental changes in the ideological substrate of all academic disciplines. One such change can be seen in the trend to examine what material culture can contribute to the history of ideas and society.[5]

With this in mind, the study of material culture in relation to recorded music has centred on the development and dissemination of recording and production technology. In the mid-1920s we hear the change from

[4] See Cook (2000, pp. 63–8) for a discussion of this form of mythology.

[5] MacGregor's *History of the World in 100 Objects* (2010) is a highly popular example of this trend in the UK.

acoustic to electric disc recording, and after the Second World War we witness the widespread introduction of tape-based recording, which was developed in Germany during the 1930s. Although Alan Blumlein patented a stereo recording system in 1931 and multiple tracks were used in film recording earlier than in the music industry, it was not until 1958 that the first commercial stereo records were released. During the 1960s and early 1970s tape track numbers expanded to three, four, eight, sixteen, then twenty-four. Simultaneously, there was a change from valve to solid-state electronics, followed by the introduction of digital recording around 1980 and the move from tape formats to hard-disc recording in the late 1990s. During all these periods there were developments in product design that had a profound impact on recorded sound, such as improvements in microphones, mixing consoles or speaker design, or the development of noise gates, the digital delay and tape noise-reduction systems. Variations on this type of narrative can be found in resources such as the Audio Engineering Society's 'Audio Timeline'[6] and in books such as those by Morton (2000) and Chanan (1995), which also provide a more interpretive commentary.

To assist musicology in the understanding of record production, we need to focus on the availability and usability of these technologies. I'll address the latter in the next chapter, but I want to start by examining various aspects of the former. What are the factors that determine this availability? And what kinds of narrative should we develop to describe them?

A geography of things

First, though, there is a further question to be addressed here about how evenly technology has been distributed around the world throughout the history of recording, and how variations in distribution have affected the approaches to, and the sound of, record production in different places at different times. While in the first half of the twentieth century many of the major record companies disseminated their technology around the globe fairly evenly,[7] their studios were exclusive places where only relatively few musicians got to record. And notice that I referred to 'their' technology. The development of recording technology at this time was still very much an in-house process undertaken by record companies and broadcasters, and

[6] See: www.aes.org/aeshc/docs/audio.history.timeline.html [accessed 8 February 2014].

[7] EMI, for example, started studios in India, Australia, Africa and South America in the early 1930s at around the same time it established Abbey Road in London, and generally kept them all up to the same technical standard.

the differences in patent ownership and technical preferences between these organisations meant that the equipment involved varied quite substantially. In the post-war period, as the recording industry grew in both size and profitability, the manufacturing industry producing recording technology also grew, and many more businesses that were independent of the record companies and studios developed. The USA and Western Europe, particularly the UK and Germany, dominated the supply side of this industry for most of the century, but Japan also became a major player in the last two decades. Having said that, there were thriving audio technology sectors in many other countries. Many of these were confined to their local markets but some expanded into exports.

Particular developments in local production facilities around the world have led to the establishment of unique recording practices that can have a major impact on recorded music. Thus, the importing into the Congo of a mono tape recorder by a Belgian musician, Bill Alexandre, in the 1950s had a notable effect on the spread of Congolese rumba (Stewart 2003, pp. 41–4); the establishment of the Shifty portable eight-track facility in South Africa under the apartheid regime helped to develop black music recorded for a black audience (Sheppard 2003, p. 669); and British suppliers' offloading (at a reduced price) of portastudio technology that failed to sell in the European market to Nigeria had an impact on access to the modes of production in the West African music industry in the 1980s and 1990s.

A history of tools

Affordances

A key feature that differentiates between things and technology is the notion of affordances, a term that is found in both ecological perception and ANT. As an abstract noun we use the term technology to refer to the application of scientific knowledge for practical purposes, but when we refer to things as technology we refer to machines or devices that apply this scientific knowledge for a practical purpose: in other words, tools.

In *The Ecological Approach to Visual Perception*, Gibson says:

> The theory of affordances is a radical departure from existing theories of value and meaning. It begins with a new definition of what value and meaning *are*. The perceiving of an affordance is not the process of perceiving a value-free object to which meaning is somehow added in a way that no-one has been able to agree upon; it is a process of perceiving a value-rich ecological object. Any subject, any surface, any layout has some affordance for benefit or injury to someone. (1979, p. 140)

In other words, an object is perceived in terms of the use (or otherwise) that it affords. There's a circularity here that I think serves to clarify this connection between embodied cognition and ecological perception. Our perceptions of light, sound, smell, taste or touch are constructed in terms of what might have caused light to reflect from something's surface, sound or smell to emanate from something and taste or touch to result from our bodily contact with something. We can then actively attempt to reconceptualise something in other terms, as in the disassociation of sound and source that we may attempt in acousmatic listening, but that is not the basic way in which we perceive. When I say our perceptions are constructed in these terms I mean that we interpret them in terms of the conceptual models we have constructed for entities and events in the world. One aspect of the circularity occurs because these conceptual models are themselves constructed from prior experience. For example, I may have learned through multiple, reinforcing experiences that the perception of a particular form of sonic morphology is associated with air resonating in a tube. That learning process involves the establishment of progressively stronger associations between acoustic, visual and tactile stimuli that form a multi-modal,[8] schematic, conceptual model. These conceptual models form an interactive network that ranges from basic image schemata[9] that are the building blocks of conceptual categorisation to complex conceptual models that reference a whole range of other schemata and models. To continue with our example, my experience of flutes may have created a conceptual model that calls upon a long, thin object schema and a blown pipe sonic schema but that also allows variations such as 'finger holes or keys' and 'wooden or metal' that will, in turn, relate to particular characteristics of tone or articulation. Some of these features – particularly the basic image schema – will relate to universal features of human experience (such as blowing/whistling or the long thin structure of a finger or arm) and others are culturally and experientially specific (such as the types of flute and flute music I may have experienced). Either way, though, these conceptual models are constructed from experience and our experiences are then interpreted according to how they fit with these conceptual models.

Another aspect of circularity brings us back to the notion of affordances. Whenever our perception fits with a conceptual model there may be features of the model that have been experienced in the past that are not being experienced now. With our example, if I see someone holding a flute but

[8] By multi-modal I mean utilising experience from all of the senses.

[9] See, for example, Lakoff's discussion of the trajectory schema and the long, thin object schema in relation to the Japanese classifier *hon* (1990, pp. 100–13).

not playing it, I will perceive the affordance of a particular type of musical sound. There's a further aspect of affordance in that the interconnected nature of these conceptual models provides a mechanism for Fauconnier and Turner's (2003) conceptual blending. Thus, if I see a cardboard tube, by virtue of the fact that its long, thin, hollow nature is also referenced in my conceptual model for a flute (and other blown instruments), I may also perceive that it affords the making of sound. A third type of circularity relates to the neurological connection between perception and action. In Chapters 1 and 4 I discussed the shared neural activity between perceiving an action carried out by another and carrying it out ourselves. This type of understanding of affordance is framed in terms of action – of what to do. An architect friend of mine once explained this type of visceral surrogate experience very clearly by saying: 'Look around this room. No matter which object you choose, you can imagine, to the point of almost tasting it, what it would be like to experience putting any of these objects in your mouth.' Perhaps because it is a method of exploring our environment that we use continually as a child and very little as an adult, this brings home so strongly to me the connection between our perception of what an object is and the physical activity of exploring similar objects in the past. My sensation of an affordance is couched in the experiential terms of what I might do or what might be done and how it might affect me.

ANT

ANT also includes the notion of affordance. Indeed, Latour explicitly references Gibson in *Reassembling the Social: an Introduction to Actor-Network-Theory* when explaining the need for including 'non-human' actors in the theoretical framework (2005, p. 72). In ANT the social only exists in as much as it is performed by the human agents involved in a network. It is therefore reliant on the psychology of interaction and communication to express how these social activities and relationships are formed and maintained. I shall return to the question of usage in more detail in the next chapter, but for now I want to explore how the existence and positioning of non-human actors or agents might be incorporated into the theory. Latour says:

> Thus the questions to ask about any agent are simply the following: Does it make a difference in the course of some other agent's action or not? Is there some trial that allows someone to detect this difference? . . . These implements, according to our definition, are actors, or more precisely, *participants*, in the course of action waiting to be given a figuration.

This, of course, does not mean that these participants 'determine' the action, that baskets 'cause' the fetching of provisions or that hammers 'impose' the hitting of the nail . . . Rather it means that there might exist many metaphysical shades between full causality and sheer inexistence. In addition to 'determining' and serving as a 'backdrop for human action', things might authorize, allow, afford, encourage, permit, suggest, influence, block, render possible, forbid and so on. (2005, pp. 71–2)

In terms of the development of audio technology, the tools of record production, we've seen that we want to establish why, where, how and by whom these tools were brought into existence and also who is given access to them and under what circumstances. The why is perhaps most easily explained in terms of affordances. There are two mechanisms. First, which existing knowledge and technology afforded the creation of any given new tool? Second, which potential benefit of an as yet non-existent piece of technology (i.e. which potential affordance) was identified as a reason for creating this new tool? To use the technology that afforded overdub recording on a multi-track tape format as an example, the following quotation comes from the article that describes how Ross Snyder developed the technology that allowed recording on one head and playback on others simultaneously, which led to the creation of the eight-track tape machine sold to Les Paul for $10,000 in 1957:

Ampex has special ability to construct precise, stacked, vertically aligned, multichannel magnetic heads . . . By 1956 the technology could produce such heads with rejection of track-to-track cross talk sufficient to deliver performances clearly separated. Also, new erase heads could efface tracks individually. These accomplishments made the Sel-Sync scheme newly workable; it would not be possible without them. Its time had come, as it had not, earlier.

The Sel-Sync invention was mine. Nothing like it had been discussed earlier, but the technology now encouraged its creation. Certainly I invented the scheme intending to improve the recording process for those doing overdubs for any reason, and Mr. [Les] Paul was on my mind. I had high hope he would find it a useful contribution to his art. (Snyder 2003, p. 210)

Ross Snyder's slightly awkward English notwithstanding, this quotation illustrates the why perfectly and the rest of the article covers a lot of the where, how and by whom. All the technical preconditions that afforded this next step were in place. Indeed, Ampex considered it a reconfiguration of existing technology and, as such, no new patent was filed. Les Paul had been working with 'sound on sound' recordings for some time by bouncing recordings between two tape machines (and disc cutting machines in earlier years) and adding a new layer of performance with each bounce. The drawback was that each new bounce degraded the quality of the existing recording. The potential affordance of this new technology was to allow the same musical process to occur without the loss of audio quality. This article and other documentation allow us to construct quite a neat actor-network model to represent the process by which one of the groundbreaking developments in audio technology took place.

The question of access, though, is probably of much greater importance in terms of how this development affected the sound of recorded music during the subsequent years. Despite Les Paul and Mary Ford using the Ampex eight-track recorder to make records from 1957 onwards, there was no demand for it as a commercial product. Aside from its expense, it introduced a certain amount of hum into the recording process and there were very few artists who wanted to work with large numbers of overdubs as Les Paul did. For the vast majority of technicians and musicians it provided an affordance that was surplus to their requirements. What it did encourage Ampex to do, however, was to introduce the technology into their three- and four-track tape recorders that were released in the early 1960s. The problems with noise came from packing the eight tape heads into a very small space; this was less of an issue with three or four tape heads. Three-track technology did provide an affordance that was desirable at the time. Although musicians preferred, and indeed had little option but, to work together in the same space at the same time, contemporary popular music styles required an often quiet singer to compete with a band or a small orchestra. For the most part this was achieved by screening the singer from the band and giving them a separate close microphone to sing into, but more recently – in the late 1950s and early 1960s – a single iteration of the 'sound on sound' bounce described above was sometimes used. A three-track tape machine with Sel-Sync heads afforded a stereo recording of the ensemble on two of the tracks followed by a separate vocal take with no loss of quality. These three- and four-track machines paved the way for the eight-track technology in two ways. The profitability of the three- and four-tracks ensured further research and development money that solved the issues of noise. In addition, the intervening decade after 1957 brought about a change in culture among musicians, some of whom started to see the musical affordances of the creative recording techniques that more tape tracks would allow.

Places as tools

More broadly, there are other aspects of the application of technology that have different implications for recorded sound. In particular, studio design, room size and acoustic treatment have a significant impact in this respect and have certainly been affected by the application of scientific knowledge. Susan Schmidt-Horning (2012) has looked at studio acoustic design in the 1940s and 1950s, and this can also seem to be driven by the twin horses of supply- and demand-based affordances. On the 'supply' side, new knowledge about how to control the frequency content of reverberation through acoustic treatment afforded the design of rooms with adjustable acoustics. On the 'demand' side, improvements in recording and reproduction quality were making the shortcomings in studio design more apparent in the recorded product.

I have observed elsewhere that the difference in sound between American and British record productions in the late 1960s and early 1970s was due in some part to the larger size of 'live' rooms in the UK (Zagorski-Thomas 2012b). The demand side of affordances in this issue is made more complicated by the rapid changes in instrument design (particularly guitar amplifiers and effects) and musical styles that made a clear understanding of what was desirable more difficult. The development of the acoustically dead Westlake style of studio design in the early 1970s was a big influence on studio design and made a highly significant difference to the sound of recordings. Later designs such as stone-, slate- or timber-lined drum rooms exerted a similarly powerful if very different influence. The desirability of the affordances that these developments offered must be seen in the context of the marketing that went on to stimulate that demand and the large income streams that music production was generating at the time. The huge cost of this kind of acoustic treatment raises the question of economics in general. The costs of setting up a studio to match the shifting capabilities of professional practice rose steadily throughout most of the twentieth century, but recent developments have taken us back almost to the point of Fred Gaisberg in 1910, in the sense that a relatively inexpensive and portable recording set-up that doesn't require years of special training to operate can produce recordings whose sonic characteristics meet professional norms.

Innovation and mythology

The way we tell it

Back in Chapter 3, I discussed the idea that a theoretical model was not descriptive. There is no actual network, just a messy reality, but if our model is a good one the messy reality will behave *as if* it were an actor network or the actor network will predict or explain behaviour *as if* it were the messy reality. In another pleasing form of circularity, the theoretical model provides a schematic representation of the messy reality of the way our minds work, in the same way that the theory itself describes our conceptual models as schematic representations of the messy reality of experience. And there is a third schematic level that resides somewhere between these two.

My use of evidence that purports to represent the reality of a situation to support my schematic explanation of it is, of course, problematic. Going back to the example of Ross Snyder, the validity of my schematic representation rests on the veracity of his statement. Of course, there are supporting statements from other Ampex employees who were involved, and he does cite certain documents that further support his case but, as we shall see in the next section, there are also statements to the contrary. There is no unequivocal evidence that the truth doesn't lie somewhere in between these two conflicting stories. I am using the evidence I have to create a narrative that will stand instead of messy reality because, of course, I have no access to the reality of a historical event. That 'he said, she said' narrative then becomes the evidence base for my theoretical explanation. This is by no means a problem limited to the humanities and social sciences: the scientific method labours under the same problems. The trick in all these instances is to try to recognise where there might be holes or distortions in the data or a flaw in the extrapolatory logic and to tell the right story. Because, when it comes down to it, the narrative structure that we create from historical evidence is exactly that: a story.

Ideology and story telling

Historical narrative is always ideological. Just by choosing to tell one story rather than another we are making an ideological statement: that's the basis of canon formation. If we talk more about the Beatles than about Motown, we're making an implicit statement about what we think is more important. Of course, though, we can't talk about everything, and in any case not everything is equally important. The problem is that an unspoken and unchallenged ideology may become embedded in the formal structures of research and teaching and make it difficult for us to see the wood for the trees. Even if the question about the Beatles and Motown is asked, it is likely to elicit a response that complains that it is not comparing like with like: the Beatles was a group; Motown was a company. And yet that demonstrates yet another unchallenged ideological position that underpins musicology in general: what is an acceptable 'unit' of creativity in the field of music? In Western art music it is the lone composer. Although with opera he (another unspoken ideological restriction – gender) is allowed to work with a librettist. In jazz and popular music the question is more problematic. For certain styles of music the composition is less important than the performance – generally styles from the African-American tradition like jazz and gospel. Others, like rap and reggae, often value original lyric writing while 'allowing' the backing track to involve stock 'riddims' or sampled fragments of other tracks. And in rock music the composition of original material backed by an honesty or integrity of performance is valued. But despite this variety, when it comes to the forms of creativity there is still a tendency to look for an individual when it comes to the creative force. Even with the Beatles where the Lennon/McCartney partnership was one of the few examples of collaborative creativity where there wasn't an acknowledged, or publicly perceived, leader or figurehead, both fans and scholars have spent more time trying to pick out which pieces of which songs were written by which Beatle than assessing the creative impact of the team on any individual's writing style. All music-making – and record production is no exception – is a collaborative activity, even in terms of the legacy of influence that previous musicians and teachers have on subsequent generations. We shall examine this in more detail in Chapters 7 and 8 but the point for the moment is that the shadow of the nineteenth- and twentieth-century cult of the romantic or modernist artist, a lone genius, is one of the key ideological positions that has formulated the narratives of musicology. That's not to say that we shouldn't elevate any one character above any others, but we should, as has been slowly happening in the past two decades or so, examine how that exceptional character fitted into and was produced by the creative network or system that surrounded them. That may range from the way Mozart tailored his vocal writing to suit the style and technique of Adriana Ferrarese, Louise Villeneuve, Francesco Benucci and the other singers of the first performance of *Così fan tutte* to the way Hank Shocklee, Chuck D and the rest of the Bomb Squad utilised a creative network that included themselves plus a range of electronic technology and the sampled creative practice of others to produce Public Enemy's *Fear of a Black Planet* (1990). Surely the richness of these kinds of narratives of collaboration and interaction should enhance our appreciation of creative activity – but that's another ideological position. The real issue leads on to our next point: while you can't avoid holding an ideological position, you can interrogate what you (and others) are doing more thoroughly to try and identify and flag up the effect of these kinds of position.

The idea of conceptual models that are formed and reinforced by further experience that fits with these existing models is attractive to me, partly because it feels like the kind of system that may have formed through evolution. There's an efficiency in processing power usage that flows from schematic representations. We don't need to keep reinventing the wheel or, more accurately, we don't need to keep re-perceiving the wheel. We can use a few key features to suggest that conceptual model and then we can just ignore (or rather pay less attention to) that area of perception until something changes to draw our attention back to it. The fact that our attention wanders from the repetitive and is drawn to difference and change is, on the one hand, to state the obvious, and yet is also at the heart of perception and musical creativity. There is, however, a downside to this efficiency. We are forever, both consciously and subconsciously, seeking to match our experience to a conceptual model. In fact, this type of pattern matching is a very basic human motivation and it means that we are drawn towards the simple explanation. The very fact that something offers itself as an explanation means that we've found a match between some experience and some schematic features.

This takes us back to Thomas Kuhn's paradigms in *The Structure of Scientific Revolutions* (1962). We tend to hang on to existing ideas and explanations for longer than we should, and it takes us longer to be convinced of something's newness than to be convinced that it fits with some existing knowledge. In short, we're prone to stereotypes and clichés such as 'the Beatles invented everything', 'African-American musicians weren't technical innovators' and 'an increase in clarity makes a recording more natural'. And this brings us back to the story of Ross Snyder and the Ampex 'Octopus' eight-track. Les Paul was a clever and creative man who customised one of Ampex's first tape machines in the late 1940s to allow himself to overdub 'sound on sound'. He was also the first to purchase an eight-track; indeed, as we've seen, Snyder suggests he had Les Paul in mind when he came up with the idea of Sel-Sync. So it seems quite obvious that, if we're looking for a single inventor of multi-track recording, conflating everything into Les Paul makes for the neatest package. Indeed, a trawl through a few websites provides quotes such as 'He invented multi-track recording and overdubbing, using those techniques for the first time in 1947',[10] which is sufficiently ambiguous to allow several versions of the narrative to be true. There are, however, some more specific and contradictory accounts:

> In 1953, Les Paul conceived the idea which would revolutionize the recording industry forever: the multi-track tape recorder, a device which would enable a musician to lay down multiple parts in synchronization with each other, thus

[10] See: www.encyclopedia.com/topic/Les_Paul.aspx [accessed 8 February 2014].

allowing one musician to become a 'one man band'. It was economically significant because it allowed retakes without erasing previously recorded tracks. First presented to Westrex (who turned it down), the eight-track recorder became a reality after a long, expensive, arduous collaboration with Ampex (the original prototype was a disaster). (Doris 2013)

Les Paul was a very innovative man. Not only did he invent the solid body electric guitar as we know it today, he also made overdubbing and multi-track recording possible. Paul had the idea to combine the record head and the playback head into one unit, allowing artists to overdub in real time with no delay... Based on Paul's discovery, the company Ampex released a four-track recorder with Sel-Sync (Selective Synchronization) in 1955. (Schonbrun 2013)

And on Les Paul's website we find:

Les' re-invention of the Ampex 200 inspired Ampex to develop two-track and three-track recorders, which allowed him to record as many tracks on one tape without erasing previous takes... In 1954, Les continued to develop this technology by commissioning Ampex to build the first eight-track tape recorder at his expense. The machine took three years to get working properly, and Les said that by the time it was functional, his music was out of favour, so he never had a hit record using it. His design became known as 'Sel-Sync' (Selective Synchronization), in which specially modified electronics could either record or play back from the record head, which was not optimized for playback but was acceptable for the purposes of recording an 'overdub' (OD) in sync with the original recording. This is the core technology behind multi-track recording. (Les Paul Foundation 2013)

So where does the 'truth' lie? Certainly nowhere clear cut and probably in some confused and confusing middle ground involving miscommunication, misunderstanding, faulty memory and simplification. If we let go for a moment of the idea that there has to be a single person who had a single idea that counts as the invention of multi-track recording, then the problem becomes less intractable: there was messy reality which behaved *as if* there was a network of actors in which Les Paul was a key player and Ross Snyder was also important.

Peter Doyle's podcast of a talk that he gave at both the Art of Record Production conference in Cardiff and at Monash University (Doyle 2009) deals quite explicitly with this problem of 'well-worn' or archetypal narratives in history. I shall return to the specifics of his argument in Chapter 10 because it deals with the creative impact of various businessmen (and the examples from the mid-twentieth century are all men) on the production process. Doyle uses these examples to illustrate the pervasive stereotypes that:

characterise the relationship between the creative artist and his/her first point of contact with 'the business' – be it producer, engineer, manager, agent etc. Descriptions of the artist–producer relationship, I will argue, typically invoke a set of deep and enduring narrative tropes – mythic, archetypal, folkloric, literary and pulp – and these almost unfailingly operate to the detriment of the producer. One near constant has been the valorisation of the artist as romantic, often tragic, indeed, as 'sacrificial' figure, and with it a concomitant tendency to typify the producer/mentor/facilitator/'suit' figure as venal, mendacious exploiter, and as unrepentant corrupter of artistic purity.[11]

While Doyle doesn't accuse academics of this – his examples focus on journalism, biography and the media – he does point to the absence of work in these areas and claims that it demonstrates a tacit ideology in the academic accounts of record production that valorises the artists above the 'button pushers' and the 'button pushers' above the 'bean counters'. The current trend towards more complex and nuanced accounts of these creative systems/networks starts to redress this balance.

Several authors cover various aspects of the technical developments,[12] but less frequently considered is the way in which the sound of recordings changed as a result of technological innovations. Although this has been charted to a certain extent in technical papers for the Audio Engineering Society, the data is often in the form of numerical specifications and measurements. There have been some interesting discussions on the internet about why we find certain types of distortion attractive in recording.[13] It seems that recording engineers make equipment choices that represent a practice-based manifestation of this phenomenon in all genres of music and from all musical cultures. Examples of this can be found in Wallach (2005, pp. 141–2) and Moehn (2005, p. 61), who both describe preferences for older analogue tape technology over the sound of newer digital formats in Indonesian *dangdut* and Brazilian *samba enredo* respectively.

The dissemination of technology

Earlier in this chapter we looked at how we can use the lens of history or of geography to examine this development of audio technology: the physical parameters of space and time. Of course, the way these technologies and

[11] This quotation comes from Doyle's written abstract for the podcast, which can be found at: www.digitalpodcast.com/items/7696234 [accessed 10 May 2013].

[12] See, for example, Mee and Daniel (1990) and Cunningham (1999).

[13] For example, see Boss (1998). This example was discussed in Chapter 2.

their uses came to be distributed through space and time is determined by a whole range of factors. The development of the knowledge necessary for their creation is one of these but, as we're starting to see, so are the economics, politics (including gender, race, age and sexuality), logistics and other forms of knowledge such as those that allow the maintenance or customisation of invented technologies.

Economics and dissemination

There is a lot to be said about the way the cost of technology affects its distribution. On a basic level it is true to say that the relative cost of new technologies at various points in history has either encouraged or inhibited the spread of those technologies. The introduction of the relatively cheap tape machine technology (in comparison to disc cutters) at the time of the post-Second World War boom, particularly in the USA, led to a large-scale dissemination of that technology and a growth in new small studios and record companies. This spread wasn't uniform, however, and the dissemination into Africa, Asia, the Middle East and South America was on a smaller scale and over a longer time period than that in the USA, Canada, Europe and Australia, for example. The more expensive multi-track tape technology of the 1960s, 1970s and 1980s was a very different process, with by far the greatest concentration of investment in studios happening in the USA, the UK and – to a lesser but still very significant extent – in France, Germany, Canada and Australia. Elsewhere in the world the major record labels or state organisations[14] invested in these sorts of facilities but, in the case of state-owned companies, they were often combined with radio or television facilities and performed dual roles.

From the 1980s onwards, with the advent of both portastudios[15] and Music Instrument Digital Interface (MIDI), hobbyist and semi-professional equipment once again started to be able to rival expensive systems for quality – enough for many records, particularly in the dance music market, to be made on this kind of 'project studio' equipment. Aside from usually

[14] For example, in communist countries the main record companies and their recording studios were state-owned.

[15] Portastudios were cheaper cassette tape formats for multi-track recording that appeared in 1979 and grew in popularity during the 1980s. Of varying quality, they were all of a lower standard than the semi-professional open reel tape machines, which were similarly of a lower standard than the very expensive large format analogue and digital tape systems. In the 1990s digital cassette tape systems – notably the Alesis A-Dat and the Tascam DA88 – provided cheaper systems that grew in popularity until the development of computer-based Digital Audio Workstations.

being of lower audio quality, the other way this equipment was made more cheaply was by reducing the range of features and parameters, which also had the effect of making it easier to use. This twin process of cheaper and easier access to record production encouraged the sort of explosion of demand for recorded music-making in the 1980s and 1990s that cheaper guitars, drums and amplifiers had done for rock band performance in the late 1960s and 1970s. Once again, though, the limited availability of PCs like the Atari ST[16] in areas like Africa and South America meant that the spread of this cheaper technology was less extensive and slower.

Bijker has defined the 'technological frame' of any given question as the way problems were identified and problem-solving strategies were determined (1995, p. 272). This is one of the key definitions in the SCOT model of the constructionist approach. He also suggests that to understand a particular phenomenon we need to define the way in which the environment we're examining is configured: whether there are no dominant technological frames, one or several. For example, looking at how the initial stages of multi-track recording developed, we can identify two technological frames that developed roughly simultaneously. Thus, Les Paul was at the centre of one such frame, identifying the problem in terms of the multiple overdubs he wanted to be able to use in his recording. Ross Snyder and Ampex were quite strongly influenced by this frame, not least because of the $10,000 Les Paul was prepared to pay for a machine that solved the problem as he framed it. If we add to this the fact that Les Paul was a well-known pop star who arranged stunts to pretend to 'demonstrate' his multi-tracking method on television at the time, we can see that Ampex might easily be persuaded that his ideas were the way forward.

What might be considered the most widespread technological frame at the time might be considered to be invisible (to Ampex) because it existed in the continuing common professional practice of the time: the issue of getting a single vocal (or instrumental) track overdubbed on top of an existing mono or stereo recording. There was, however, an existing and commonly used practical technique to get over this problem: bouncing from one tape machine to another while recording the new vocal and mixing it onto the new tape with the existing backing track. There was a slight loss of quality, but there didn't seem to be a clamour to solve the Sel-Sync issue from this

[16] Atari ensured their success in the home music market in 1985 when they incorporated MIDI in and out sockets in their ST computers, which then became an industry standard machine for several years.

part of Ampex's market. The financial impetus from Les Paul (both direct in the form of the cash and indirect in the form of what proved to be a non-existent prospective market) prompted a solution in the form of a product that virtually no-one other than he was interested in. Nonetheless, the development of that unwieldy eight-track technology then led to the solution of the problem in the other technological frame: three- and four-track tape machines utilising Sel-Sync. This is, in some respects, an example of the phenomenon that Bijker terms 'problem redefinition'.

Another slightly later example illustrates another term used by Bijker: 'inclusion'. By the second half of the 1970s, the technological frame of professional recording practice had developed an 'interpretive inflexibility': the participants had developed a fixed idea of the problems and solutions involved in recording. These involved expensive, acoustically treated recording spaces with large format multi-track tape machines, mixing consoles to match and a wide-ranging set of microphones and outboard equipment that was constantly in need of updating to stay at forefront of the market. This meant that the socio-economic units involved in this activity required large amounts of capital both to enter the market and to remain there (although there was extensive use of equipment leasing arrangements as well). In Bijker's model, therefore, their level of inclusion in this technological frame was deep, and this immersion restricted their ability to see beyond the restrictions of that frame. This can be seen in the way that, after the advent of MIDI and the development of good-quality semi-professional multi-track tape machines, it was the more nimble new entrants to the market rather than the older studio companies that led the trend for small programming rooms for the emerging hip hop and dance music markets. Once the business model for this smaller type of studio space had developed out of the semi-professional technological frame, the larger studios followed suit and started to install smaller programming suites alongside their larger studios.

However, we shouldn't restrict ourselves to this supply side of the economics of the dissemination of technology. The traditional notion of demand in economics is based on consumer knowledge: knowledge of price and availability, knowledge of the available range of products and services and knowledge of their desires or the relative utility or satisfaction that spending their money on A rather than B would afford them. Obviously our knowledge is never complete or perfect, and the questions of availability and the utility (or otherwise) of waiting will also be addressed in the section on logistics and distribution that follows. However, the relative utility we garner from the consumption of different goods is in a constant state of flux – our tastes change, we're influenced by advertisers, even the very act of buying something can alter the amount of satisfaction we receive from it.

All these complexities exist in the world of consumer products, but who is the consumer in the world of record production? For the most part, it is a business in the middle of the supply chain: a company that buys both products and skills from other suppliers to allow it to work as a service industry in part of the process that creates a product – the master recording – that its customers (record companies or musicians) then turn into a subsequent product (LP, CD, MP3, etc). These two sets of consumers, record companies and musicians, can have conflicting demands about the nature of the product – something we'll examine in more detail in Chapter 11. Bijker's notion of inclusion does, however, extend to include the way potential customers are 'enrolled' in the adoption of a particular technological frame. Although record companies often owned the studios they used, they were also often arranged in separate divisions with their own financial targets, and the artist and repertoire (A&R) departments didn't always remain as deeply included in a particular technological frame as their colleagues in the recording studios. Thus, dance music labels within major labels – such as Fourth and Broadway within Island Records in the late 1980s and early 1990s – broke out of the technological frame of the large studio format of recording much more quickly than Island's recording studios. However, both musicians and record company executives also frequently became and remained enrolled in that kind of technological frame because of the glamour and prestige it afforded, as much as for the needs of the recording project at hand.

Politics and dissemination

There are a great many aspects to the politics of technological dissemination and I'm going to start at what we might call the macro level: the influence of government policy, and in particular trade agreements, on the spread of recording technology. The General Agreement on Tariffs and Trade was a process that started in 1947 and continued up to 1994, under which countries of the United Nations gradually negotiated reductions and removals of trade restrictions and tariffs. The rounds of negotiations in 1963–7 and 1973–9 in particular reduced the expense of imports and exports of various types of electronic goods, one result of which was the large growth of Japanese imports in the 1980s. During the late 1990s and early 2000s the US restrictions on the export of high-performance computers under their

International Traffic in Arms Regulations impeded the spread of the cutting edge of hardware for digital audio workstation (DAW) systems.[17]

I've also already mentioned the way some countries financed state-owned recording facilities, usually sharing space and technology with radio and television broadcasters. This was an ideological choice that reflected these governments' feeling that recorded and broadcast music was an essential part of their nation's cultural output and, therefore, that it needed to be supported. This was usually accompanied by preferences or even restrictions on the types of music it was appropriate for the state recording and broadcast organisations to be seen to be supporting. This type of ideological slant wasn't restricted to governments either. During much of the twentieth century the major record labels subsidised their classical music arms, partly because of the preferences and prejudices of their management and partly because it was seen to add prestige to the company.

In a musicology that aims to encompass the whole gamut of music around the world, the term 'minority' to cover the notion of anything non-Anglo-American, male and heterosexual becomes ridiculous. There are fewer men than women in the USA and the UK (CIA 2013), the population of the rest of the world far outnumbers the Anglo-American population and, although the figures about homosexuality are not reliable, it is entirely possible that the gay population of the world is larger than the population of the USA and UK combined. However, when it comes to the economics of recorded music and the distribution of the related technology, the history of both the money and the ownership of the technology makes that term meaningful again. Indeed, it also makes sense to see the UK situation as another marginalised community in relation to the USA. If that is our agenda – to examine how the politics in countries and communities outside the mainstream of commercial US music affected their access to and subsequent engagement with recording technology – how is that to be done? There are studies (such as Porcello and Greene 2004 and Zagorski-Thomas 2012b) that look at the specific ways countries have developed their usage of recording technologies, and there are books (such as Meintjes 2003, Stewart 2003 and Veal 2007) that look at scenes or musical styles in a particular country in depth. These can look at questions relating to the ideology of aesthetics, such as why particular music styles such as Indonesian *dangdat* (Wallach 2005) or Brazillian *samba enredo* (Moehn 2005) both continued to favour analogue rather than digital

[17] At that time the export of the kind of computing hardware required to process multiple channels of audio files was considered to be a threat to US national security interests; restrictions were placed on the sale of such hardware abroad.

recording. They can relate to more conventionally political questions, such as how particular colonial and post-colonial networks of Greek and Belgian traders affected the development of Congolese rumba (Stewart 2003). They can also relate to issues of national, racial and/or cultural identity, such as Veal's (2007) and Sean Williams' (2012) examinations of how the culture of Jamaican reggae engaged with technology to produce dub.

And, of course, this discussion needs to engage with those who have worked on the margins in other senses. In much of the history of recorded music women have been absent (except perhaps as performers) from this discussion. Richard Burgess has summarised some work he did with Katia Isakoff on these issues (2013, pp. 194–213). Not only have women been absent in the histories but their absence has also been largely ignored or played down. As Oudshoorn and Pinch have said: 'Historians did not consider it relevant in situations where women were absent, thus reinforcing the view that men have no gender' (2003, p. 4). We will return to this when we discuss the use of technology in the next chapter, but for the moment I want to remain focused on the issue of distribution and access. Despite the many exceptions that Burgess and Isakoff have noted, women have been largely excluded from the mainstream of studio work as engineers and producers. On the other hand, Wolfe (2012) examines how the availability of cheaper technology and the resulting increased potential for self-production has provided more favourable conditions for women to get involved in the nuts and bolts of production.

This is an area where I think there is a great deal of scope for existing work in popular music studies to be framed in terms of the technologies and processes of record production. For example, Tim Lawrence's description of how the gay scene in New York's Sanctuary club in 1970 was instrumental in encouraging DJ programming and performance techniques that helped shape the future of DJ practice and the development of dance music is a case in point (2003, pp. 33–53). Lawrence provides a close reading of how DJ practice and the sociology of the club's clientele worked together to encourage the development of a more 'full-on' approach to song programming, blending and mixing techniques. Although he doesn't engage with the theoretical models or literature of SCOT, this provides a great example of how a marginal community's access to and relationship with technology and its environment has had a huge impact on the wider musical world. In relation to a more class-based distinction that was nonetheless also heavily informed by questions of race, Richard Peterson describes the uneasy relationship between the mainstream of popular music and the variously labelled folk, hillbilly, rustic, cowboy and country market (1997, pp. 185–201). In the book as a whole, Peterson tracks the many esoteric and idiosyncratic ways that country musicians negotiated a path between their personal roots and popular culture, and how the industry struggled to balance prejudice about class, notions of authenticity and the economics of the mass market. Thomas Porcello (2005) has undertaken a related analysis that discusses how the trope of 'liveness' in recorded country music from Austin, Texas, is represented in the recorded sound and is also used to differentiate the music of Austin from what is perceived as the more commercial and polished sound of Nashville.

David Edgerton has examined the politics of 'techno-nationalism' and race in relation to the distribution and use of technology and, although he doesn't deal explicitly with recording, discusses the highly contradictory nature of some national narratives of inventiveness and technical aptitude (2006, pp. 103–37). He also points out that the racial politics in both colonial powers and countries like the USA with significant ethnically defined immigrant communities has often limited access to technology and education about its production and usage. Anne Danielsen discusses the representation of black culture as primitivist in relation to her analysis of the funk grooves of James Brown and Parliament, and although she discusses their music in terms of composition and performance practice, provides a useful model for analysing music and musical performance within a socio-cultural contextual frame (2006, pp. 20–39). Andrew Blake (2012) looks at how the Indian Suvi Raj Grubb worked within the world of British classical music production between 1960 and 1985, and how the complexities of class and post-colonialism created a confusion of both aesthetic conservatism and political radicalism. All the above examples can also be discussed and examined in terms of how these political factors determined the affordances available within a network or helped to establish or inhibit a particular technological frame, the level of inclusion of the various participants or the forms of interpretive inflexibility involved.

Logistics and dissemination

This aspect of SCOT ties in very closely with the notions of ecological perception and embodied cognition. Understanding logistics is quite a practical affair, and professional experience or practice as research is an important element in this kind of research. Many of the problems and advantages encountered in the logistics of technological dissemination only come to light in the process of actual enactment. For example, reading through some of the managerial memoranda in the EMI archive in Hayes revealed that there were unanticipated problems to do with humidity when the EMI technicians exported their disc recording systems to the Dum Dum studio EMI established in Calcutta in the 1930s. Producer/engineer Ian Little also explained in an interview about working with Duran Duran (Buskin 2004) that one of the problems of working in George Martin's AIR Montserrat studios[18] was that when they had a severe problem with the tape machine that the in-house maintenance engineer couldn't fix, they had to fly a repairman in from Miami – presumably at the studio's expense, but an expense that was reflected in the daily rate.

These types of logistical issue are obviously tightly entwined with economics: many problems with the environment, local infrastructure and transportation can be solved if there is enough money to deal with it, as there was at Montserrat in the 1980s. At the same time, the internal logic of a particular physical and economic environment is always part of the creative system (Csikszentmihalyi 1988) or field (Bourdieu 1993) in which the participants work. Chris Kirkley describes the ways in which the logistics of music distribution and self-production have come together in West Africa to create a new music 'scene', in which peer-to-peer transmission by both fans and musicians becomes a much more intimate process than it is on the internet:

> In much of West Africa, cell phones are used as all purpose multimedia devices. In lieu of personal computers and high speed internet, the knockoff cell phones house portable music collections, playback songs on tinny built in speakers, and swap files in a very literal peer to peer Bluetooth wireless transfer.
>
> The songs chosen for the compilation were some of the highlights – music that is immensely popular on the unofficial mp3/cellphone network from Abidjan to Bamako to Algiers, but have limited or no commercial release. They're also songs that tend towards this new world of self-production – Fruity Loops, home studios, synthesizers and Auto-Tune. (Kirkley 2011)

Knowledge and dissemination

The last of these issues around the question of dissemination of technology is that of knowledge: how to use and maintain the relevant technology. There is a history of amateur electronics and mechanical engineering that,

[18] George Martin and John Burgess's Associated Independent Recording (AIR) is a production company that was established in 1965 and has opened three recording facilities over the years. AIR Montserrat was a residential studio set up on the Caribbean island of Montserrat in the 1970s. It was closed down after damage caused by Hurricane Hugo in 1989.

in particular, grew out of employment in the military, telecommunications, radio and broadcast media and a few other areas that provided basic training in electronics, mechanical engineering and electrical repairs. In tandem with this, the appearance of commercial hobby kits and literature in the 1950s and 1960s contributed to the dissemination of these forms of knowledge too. These hobbyists range from people such as Joe Meek (Cleveland 2001), who seems to have had a relatively limited knowledge that he employed very creatively, to Thomas Boddie in Cleveland, Ohio, who designed and built his own recording and pressing facility in the 1950s and 1960s,[19] to Geoff Frost in London, who started working for the BBC before becoming a sound engineer in the 1960s and moved on to designing and building Sound Techniques mixing consoles, as well as running the studio of the same name.[20]

Edgerton describes the ways in which maintenance of complex electronic technology like that used in recording has become much more specialised, leading in some cases to the cost of repair being higher than the cost of replacement (2006, pp. 75–102). This is made more complicated by the software-based nature of contemporary production. The generic components such as the computer in a production set-up might fall into that category, but the more specialised components such as the audio interface are more complex: the choice is between the relative low quality of the cheap yet replaceable and the high quality of the expensive, which might require expensive maintenance or repair. Another factor in this process is that with the consumerisation of recording technology more legacy equipment is available. I shall return to the notion of the 'vintage' as opposed to the obsolete in the recording world later, but this older equipment is often very cheap, and the difference from high-end equipment is not always as clearly demarcated as it used to be. That said, though, this vintage technology is expensive to maintain because the requisite knowledge can command a premium price in a niche market, and spare parts are often hard and/or expensive to get hold of. The judgements between these types of technological frame, extremes that we might distinguish as 'buying with built-in obsolescence' and 'make do and mend', depend on access to different types of knowledge, and the determinants of the existence and maintenance of these types of knowledge base are ideological as well as economic.

The software element of contemporary production and, to a lesser extent, the generic computer hardware provide parallels with electronics hobbyists

19 See: http://ech.case.edu/cgi/article.pl?id=BRC2 [accessed 24 July 2013].

20 See: www.soundtechniques.co.uk/about.html [accessed 8 February 2014].

in earlier periods: communities or working relationships often grow around a particular expert hobbyist to whom the others can turn for advice and help. This often results in informal hierarchies of expertise, many of which now exist as forums on the internet. This is, not surprisingly, more software- than hardware-based.[21] The software and creative knowledge-sharing community that has grown around Cycling 74's Max/MSP programming language is a case in point. This modular system allows beginners and experts to share common ground in a very similar way that hobbyist clubs did.

Homogeneity and globalisation

Edgerton balances his notion of techno-nationalism with the term 'techno-globalism' to discuss the homogenisation in technological availability and usage that has spread around the globe in the latter half of the twentieth century and the start of the twenty-first (2006, pp. 103–37). I've already mentioned that the reduction in trade restrictions was a key issue. Aside from the question of access, the more important issue of price competition was a great equaliser. When there were tariffs charged on the import of goods from the USA to Europe, and vice versa, it obviously made the imported goods disproportionately more expensive and the majority of buyers would only be prepared to pay the difference if there was a marked difference in quality. So, while the quality of German Neumann microphones did ensure they sold in the USA as well, British mixing desk manufacturers such as Trident in the 1960s found they couldn't penetrate the US market.

Once the economic barriers to trade were lowered and eventually removed, manufacturers also set about creating homogeneous products that were all compatible. While this process has been chequered with various successful and failed attempts by individual manufacturers to generate sufficient demand and sales quantities of particular formats to create a de facto process of standardisation, there has also been a steady process of discussion and negotiation. For example, the MIDI protocol was developed by various industry professionals, companies and the Audio Engineering Society in 1983; and the International Electrotechnical Commission (IEC) formed in 1906 and the International Organization for Standardization (ISO) established in 1947 started to collaborate in 1987 to develop standards for information and communications technology.

[21] Although several of my students build their own 'vintage' effects pedals.

The change from hardware to software products that has characterised the last decade and a half in particular, although not without clashes of compatibility by any means, has seen a further move towards globalisation. While the manufacturers of the DAW platforms have maintained the exclusivity of their session file architecture,[22] there has been a homogenisation of audio files and plug-in formats that has allowed and encouraged a particular structure of support industry. There are a few market leaders in the field who benefit from the prestige and stability of a large established organisation, but the industry also supports a lot of small-scale companies and freelance programmers. In many ways, this is a more extreme version of the economic structures of the 1970s and 1980s, when larger microphone, mixing console and tape machine companies provided a technical, physical and economic context for a large number of smaller effects (and to a lesser extent microphone) manufacturers. The software revolution exacerbated this position, principally by lowering the financial and technical barriers to entry for new companies. There is also the fact that the need for a physical product has also receded. Although software was initially sold on disc, the download culture has lowered the cost of product distribution for software companies to virtually nothing and, of course, it costs the same to deliver to the house next door as it does to the other side of the world. I'm not aware of any writing on the structure of the DAW and plug-in industry that examines any explicit connections between the economic structures and the sound of contemporary production, but Eliot Bates has examined contemporary studios as:

> acoustic environments, as meeting places, as container technologies, as a system of constraints on vision, sound and mobility, and as typologies that facilitate particular interactions between humans and nonhuman objects while structuring and maintaining power relations. (2012)

As we shall also see in Chapter 11, this kind of structuring process is quite a common emergent property of industrial management systems. As particular sectors of an industry get larger and more inflexible, the solution (as viewed from within) can only be envisaged in terms of subcontracting, as the alternative – replacing the larger institution with smaller ones – is unthinkable from within the managers' technological frame. They are not going to be the turkeys voting for Christmas. The DAW manufacturers'

[22] And, in fact, the number of DAW software platforms with a significant market share seems to be shrinking and subject to the same fairly aggressive take-overs and trade wars that have been seen with record companies.

solution to different types of technology being appropriate for different types of music-making was not to abandon the market share of their existing product and create a broader range of different DAW style products,[23] it was to encourage a diversity in plug-ins through a subcontractors system. There may also be an ergonomic logic to the creation of a technological frame of this sort, but that doesn't mean that the level of inclusion of the management of those larger companies in that particular technological frame wasn't also an important factor.

Product differentiation

Of course, this process of homogenisation raises the question of how these commodities then differentiate themselves from each other. Indeed, the DAW companies have a similar problem and one of the ways in which they attempt this is through the range of plug-ins that they provide as part of their package. The other is through the notion that the design of their human–computer interface is targeted at a particular market sector: put crudely, one could say that Avid's ProTools is aimed at professional studios and those interested in recording acoustic audio, Apple's Logic is aimed at those wanting to combine recording and composing and Abelton's Live is aimed at DJs who also produce their own tracks.

One crucial way in which recording technology has been marketed to create clearer product differentiation is through the use of iconic producers, vintage equipment and recording studios. One of the early examples of this was Ted Fletcher's JoeMeek range of audio equipment, which he launched in 1993 to the professional market but which in 2001 was taken over by a US company that developed products aimed at the semi-professional and hobbyist markets. More recent examples can be found in the range of plug-ins by Waves,[24] which produces a series of products in association with Abbey Road Studios that emulates a lot of the 1960s technology used on the Beatles' recordings. These include the RS56 'Universal Tone Control . . . originally introduced in the 1950s and used in Abbey Road Studios to prepare recordings for the record-lathe', the King's Microphone emulator with buttons for George V, George VI and Queen Elizabeth, and the REDD equaliser:

[23] Although that kind of diversification has happened (e.g. Abelton Live, Reason, Melodyne, Fruity Loops and Max/MSP are examples of the smaller, less generic DAW platforms competing with Logic, Cubase and ProTools, etc.).

[24] See: www.waves.com/plugins [accessed 24 July 2013]. Waves also creates plug-in emulations of Automated Processes Inc (API) and Solid State Logic (SSL) mixing desks, and collections with celebrity producer endorsements like the Eddie Kramer collection.

London's Abbey Road Studios were at the epicenter of a seismic shift that rocked the world of music during the 1960s, and changed the course of popular culture forever. The Beatles, the Hollies, Pink Floyd and countless other luminaries made musical history at Abbey Road Studios, trailblazing a revolution that resonates to this day.

And at the heart of it all: The REDD consoles, custom-designed, built by and named for Abbey Road Studios' in-house Record Engineering Development Department. Renowned for their silky smooth EQ[25] curves, extraordinary warmth and lush stereo imagery, there's something magical about the REDDs that sound like no other consoles.[26]

The intriguing case of these analogue emulation plug-ins returns us to the notion of schematic representations. Some of the characteristics of the original technologies are emulated – the visual layout and some aspects of the sonic 'footprint', for example – while others, such as noise, the physical interface and (un)reliability, are not. Although these can be highly sophisticated and useful production tools, they are what they are – digital audio plug-ins – and they provide particular forms of desirable distortion and sonic colouration rather than any real link with the past. The selective schematic nature of the marketing descriptions reminds me of the joke: he was sleeping like a baby – woke up every four hours screaming.

How technology sounds

How does it sound now?

One important aspect of the discussion about how technology sounds can be summed up in the following quotation:

Chet Atkins was playing his guitar when a woman approached him. She said, 'That guitar sounds beautiful'. Chet immediately quit playing. Staring her in the eyes he asked, 'How does it sound now?' (Gottlieb 2009, p. xi)

And the two alternative sides of the argument about how well this applies to production technology as well as to instrument technology can perhaps be summed up by Brian Eno's (2004) characterisation of the studio as a musical instrument and Michael Jarrett's (2012) description of the ideal nature of

25 EQ is a common industry abbreviation for equalisation, the adjustment of frequency content in an audio signal. An ubiquitous form of this are the treble and bass controls on audio playback devices.

26 See: www.waves.com/plugins/red [accessed 24 July 2013].

the producer for many of the people he interviewed: that of transparency. Of course, though, the nature of the guitar does have an impact on the nature of the sound and on the way the guitarist plays it. It has physical properties that not only affect how the strings resonate but also partially configure what the guitarist can do and, perhaps more importantly, is encouraged or discouraged from doing by those properties.

Thus far I have skimmed over the idea of distortion and quality and, although I will return to this in Chapter 10 in relation to audience aesthetics, the notion of 'good' and 'bad' sound also needs to be addressed in relation to the sonic imprint of technological mediation. First, though, we have to deal with the question raised in the last chapter, that there is some 'original' sound that has to be captured in the studio, or anywhere else for that matter. I would hope that my position is clear on this by now: there is no more a process of 'capture' in recording than there is in photography or film. The technology that has been developed produces a mechanical or electronic schematic representation of an event by exploiting a particular feature of the way that activity in the world makes air behave. This may seem unnecessarily circuitous but I think it is a crucial point. Recordings flatten aural sensation in the same way that photographs flatten visual sensation – not only is some detail necessarily lost in the transfer process, but the fixing of the 'image' negates the fundamentally interactive nature of perception of an activity or scene. By creating a schematic representation, either aural or visual, we are creating something that is fundamentally different from the thing itself. Therefore, although the audio representation cannot be realistic in any absolute sense, it can not only be more or less convincing as a representation of a performance but can also have any of the other types of characteristics that we might associate with representational art. Thus, we might think of the aural colouration that analogue tape gives to sound as equivalent to the characteristic colouration of Super 8 film or other forms of pigmentation that stem from the chemistry of film. I don't want to make any further comparisons between sound and vision but I do want to discuss the nature of distortion and the construction of more or less abstract or representational audioscapes through the production process.

The complication that I've already observed is that the term 'distortion' implies an original or un-distorted entity that can be acted upon. That would be a hypothetical entity, the kind of mental representation of our interpretation of our senses that we would also make in the presence of the original activity or performance. There is no objective 'original' in either case – just our interpretation of what might be happening. In the 'objective' world there are only atoms (or whatever particles there actually are). There is no you or I that have finite boundaries and defined entities. The borders between the atoms of my skin and the atoms of the air are always in a state of flux. I am always being permeated by air, water, light, gamma rays and so forth, and the atoms that (roughly) constitute me today are always changing. The objects that I see in the world are a mental interpretation of light, sound, touch, etc. and, while we share enough aspects of representations of those objects for the purposes of communication and communality, my interpretations are different from your interpretations.

So, after that mildly existential diversion, the notion of the 'original' is subjective, interpretive and constructed, but in the majority of cases in a recording of a piece of music I have a mental representation of what might be happening in what sort of space to make that sort of sound.[27] In Lakoff's idealised cognitive models there is the notion of the prototype, which is based on a representation of what is interpreted as happening rather than on the specific aural characteristics of the sound. If I can also hear characteristics in the sound that don't match that mental representation – tape compression or noise, the subtle overdrive of a microphone pre-amp, the frequency and transient alteration of a microphone and so forth – these are what I'm labelling as distortion. And just as photographers and others who take the time to acquire the relevant skills are better at noticing the vagaries of depth of field or the chemistry of film colour, there are people whose aural skills are more developed than others, who can not only notice but also identify the causes of these types of distortion.

As I mentioned earlier, though, there's another aspect to this issue: the construction of representational audioscapes. Whether we're talking about the acoustic period of recording at the start of the twentieth century when musicians were positioned in relation to the recording horn, the multiple microphone set-ups of the 1940s and 1950s where recording and mixing were generally a single combined operation (whether to disc or tape) or a hundred or more tracks of overdubbed audio in a ProTools session being mathematically processed and summed by a computer, these are all constructed representational audioscapes. The least distorted type of construction is a binaural stereo recording, where a dummy head has microphones instead of ears and the sonic characteristics of having a denser concentration of atoms between our ears (i.e. a bony head) is replicated with acoustically treated materials. However, as realistic as a dummy-head binaural recording

[27] And in the examples where I have no literal form of interpretation, such as electronic music, I construct an interpretation based on my experience of things that bear schematic resemblances to this abstract sound – using conceptual blending and metaphor more than empathy.

might be (until you move), the history of recorded music seems to suggest that we mean something else when we talk about quality and clarity.

I've already mentioned in earlier chapters the multi-modal nature of perception and the fact that recorded music, by removing the visual mode, makes it harder for us to focus our attention on a single musical component, something that we normally achieve in a concert situation by looking at that 'component'. Many of the developments in audio technology are designed to allow the 'shaping' of sounds, various types of frequency and dynamic distortion, which permit the construction of a representational audioscape that uses schematic manipulations to make certain features more or less prominent. In the mid-1940s Decca developed Full Frequency Range Recording, which meant that there were no longer any audible frequencies that were not reproducible in the recording process. The dynamic range of the human ear – the range from the quietest to the loudest possible heard sounds – is about 140dB, although music doesn't usually extend that far (a symphony orchestra's range is about 80dB in a concert hall). In the 1950s the best possible dynamic range on a tape recorder was about 68dB, and by the 1970s – with the help of Dolby noise-reduction systems – this went as high as 100dB, although vinyl records and cassette tapes never got above 70dB. The 16-bit digital dynamic range of compact discs is around 90dB, and this goes up to 144dB with 24-bit high definition recordings.

The upshot of all this is that for domestic high fidelity the quality of recordings in the 1950s was about as good as it was going to get until digital recording came along in the 1970s. In the 1960s one of the key developments was Dolby noise reduction, which increased the dynamic range of low- and high-frequency sounds by 10dB and 15dB respectively. As the low and high extremes were seen as the markers of audio quality – these are the areas that older and cheaper forms of recording failed to reproduce – the exaggerated presence of these frequencies became associated with the notion of quality and the increased headroom that Dolby allowed in these areas, allowed mixing and mastering engineers to fill up that space. To put it bluntly, distorting the low and high frequencies of a recording was seen as a marker of audio quality and that super-reality of the implausibly bright and the implausibly deep have maintained that status ever since. In a perhaps less loaded statement of the phenomenon, a schematic exaggeration of a particular feature produces the exaggerated corollary of the normally perceived meaning of that feature: audio quality.

Returning to the idea of greater clarity flowing from the exaggeration of one or more components in an audioscape, tools such as equalisation, noise gates, dynamic compression and stereo panning – in conjunction with greater separation at the recording stage through microphone selection and placement and multi-track recording techniques – allowed exactly that. Whether it was the relatively subtle enhanced clarity of Walter Legge's classical recordings for EMI, the delicate but artificially created space of Teo Macero's *Kind of Blue* production (Davis 1959), or the blatantly artificial sparse staging of Prince's *Sign 'O' the Times* (1987), the common denominator is the use of some or all of these techniques to draw our attention to some features at some moments and to other features at other moments. To put it bluntly: creating a distortion of an actual or constructed performance for the sake of perceptual clarity. And to once again attempt a less loaded statement of the phenomenon, a constructed schematic representation of an actual or constructed performance, highlighting some features and inhibiting others, produces the impression of greater clarity in an audio scene by facilitating and suggesting an unambiguous interpretation. Thus, while the narrative of the technological frame of recorded music was always described in terms of quality, clarity and fidelity, the unspoken part of that narrative relates to the notion of schematic clarity. The design agenda for audio technology manufacturers was then framed in terms of separation, removing the extraneous and exaggerating or enhancing particular features, rather than representing the activity as it happened in the room where it was recorded.

Designing the sound

As I have indicated, the next chapter is going to deal with the notion of the user and how the design of a product may configure the way they use it. Before that, I want to examine how the impetus for product innovation in the audio industry has worked and how this musicology of record production can examine it in more detail. As Paul Théberge has noted in relation to synthesiser technology, during the 1980s there was a gradual change in emphasis in the marketing of synthesisers from (to simplify) 'lots of control' to 'lots of presets', as the industry reconfigured itself from being a supplier to mainly professional musicians to being a supplier to a mainly hobbyist market (1997, pp. 75–83). This same trend can be seen within the DAW market, particularly with plug-in interfaces and their design.

Changes in design and innovation in audio technology can have an impact on the character of recorded sound in a number of ways. For instance, a series of incremental changes in a particular type of product may generate a wider palette of sonic options, one example being the development of microphone technology or dynamic compressors over many years. There have also been modifications that cause a sudden improvement (or a sudden change) in an existing technology, such as the replacement of the tape delay by the digital delay. While not changing the nature of the effect, this altered not only the quality of the delay sound but also the level and nature of the control that could be exercised over it. There are examples too of the introduction of a new technique or procedure that changes the recording process in some way. Thus, the advent of noise gates in the early 1970s had a significant impact on the amount of space in the sound of popular music, and hard-disc recording around the turn of the millennium made cut-and-paste editing so easy that it changed conventional working practices and hence the shape and feel of recorded performance. What's important to grasp is that the nature of the sonic change the technology produces is only part of the story. At least as important, and probably much more so, is the fact that new technologies involve new interfaces and, very often, the change in the way of physically performing a particular task (like linear editing, for instance) makes more of a difference to the sound of the musical output than the sound of the new technology.

To return to the notion of vintage audio (see also Bennett 2012) as evoking a kind of nostalgia, the audio equivalent of sepia tinting, this last point about the nature of the interface is particularly relevant. The difference between a software emulation controlled by a mouse or a touch screen – albeit with a graphic representation of the original physical object – and the knobs, buttons and tactile surface of the actual hardware are bound to induce very different working practices, even if the sonic imprint of the processing technologies are the same. However, software designers know what people want (or they soon find out when they don't) and the ergonomics of computer control is now firmly embedded in their market, if only because of the cheapness, ease of use and portability that it offers. Another point Paul Théberge makes, though, is that it is possible that the information which initially sparked this change of tack on the part of manufacturers – the lack of user-programmed sounds in keyboards returned for servicing – may well have been the result of musicians seeking to protect their own sounds from being 'bootlegged' rather than a lack of interest in user-programmable features. He goes on to say:

> Which interpretation is correct is perhaps less important than the changing perception of the user that began to take hold within the industry from this point onward. As far as the manufacturers were concerned . . . ease of use and ready access to 'libraries' of exciting, prefabricated sounds would increasingly become the basis on which new instruments were marketed and sold. (Théberge 1997, p. 76)

The key thing that needs to be incorporated into any model of SCOT is not just that the designers' job is to accommodate the demands of the users but that their notion of that demand is just as liable to be distorted as any other schematic representation of the world built on incomplete and subjective interpretations.

7 | Using technology

Ergonomics of recording technology

A history of usage

In his article 'All Buttons In' in the *Journal on the Art of Record Production*, Austin Moore (A. Moore 2012) performs some comparative tests on the Urei/Universal Audio 1176 dynamic compressor, and one of the settings he uses when compressing a mono ambient drum recording is the 'all buttons in' mode. The design of the 1176 provides quite a small number of parameter controls: input and output levels, attack and release rotary controls, four preset compression ratio buttons (which also change the threshold control) and four buttons to select what the meters shows. By using a Field Effect Transistor, Bill Putnam (who first designed the unit in 1966) created a compressor capable of very fast response times. For the non-technical reader, a compressor is an automatic volume control that monitors the signal being sent to it. When it rises above a certain level (the threshold) the compressor reduces the volume of the output signal by a certain amount (the compression ratio). The attack and release settings control how quickly the reduction takes effect and how quickly it returns the volume to its original level once the signal goes back beneath the threshold. As David Felton describes in an *Attack Magazine* article:

> In addition to the four standard ratios selected via push buttons on the front panel, engineers soon discovered a secret (and unintended) trick up the 1176's sleeve. By pushing in all four buttons simultaneously, the unit can be forced to behave in a completely different manner to the way in which Putnam intended, with seriously assertive results. The high ratio, often distorted results of this 'all buttons in' (or 'Brit') mode can be explosive on drums and aggressive on bass. (Felton 2012)

Moore's article (A. Moore 2012), forty-five years after the original launch of this product, demonstrates that this mode has become standard practice: he points out that not only do the producers and engineers he cites discuss this mode in interview but it is also referenced in the manual that Universal Audio produces for the unit. Furthermore, the company has also produced a software emulation plug-in version of the 1176 and the promotional text on the website says:

> The four Ratio buttons determine the degree of compression; lower ratios for compression, higher ratios for limiting. Disengaging all the Ratio buttons (Shift+Click the currently selected ratio) disables compression altogether, but signal continues to pass through the 1176 circuitry. This is commonly used to add the 'color' of the 1176LN without any gain reduction. At the request of users, the wide range of 'Multi-Button' combinations possible with the hardware is now possible – including the famous 'All Button' sound.[1]

This example demonstrates several of the issues about the usage of technology that started to emerge from our discussion about the technology itself in the previous chapter. The limited options on the original design place restrictions on what the user can and can't control. Other, particularly later, compressor designs provided separate threshold and ratio controls, for example, that made the machine more difficult to use but more flexible. The users' discovery of the 'secret trick' demonstrates a process that has only recently been integrated into scholarship on technology: that users don't always obey the rules, and that when they don't it can often have positive and creative results. And yet, despite or because of the relatively limited options available on the 1176, it remains such a popular item that Universal Audio can still sell both hardware and software versions forty-five years later, albeit with certain updates (although all updates happened before 1974).

The systems approach to creativity

I have mentioned Csikszentmihalyi's (1997) systems approach to creativity several times, along with Phillip McIntyre's (2012) application of this model to record production and other forms of musical creativity, and I want to examine the strengths and weaknesses of this approach now in a little more detail. One of the key strengths of the systems approach is to recognise that creativity is not a solo activity. In the model, an individual is seen to be working within a cultural domain of rules and conventions and within a social field that evaluates and judges their creative output. The individual, while working within a cultural domain, can choose to obey the rules and conform to the conventions or to break some of them and react against certain parts of the domain. I've chosen to utilise Bakhtin's (1982)

[1] See: www.uaudio.com/store/compressors-limiters/1176-collection.html [accessed 25 July 2013].

notion of heteroglossia in relation to this type of activity as I believe it gives a more nuanced approach towards the domain. Instead of the notion of an unproblematic domain of rules and conventions, the notion of heteroglossia provides a range of potentially contradictory pressures that the individual can engage with in different ways. In some instances they will align themselves with the centripetal forces of conformity over a particular issue and in others they will align themselves with the centrifugal forces of rebellion.

Of course, within this cultural domain the notions of conformity and rebellion are subjective and negotiated and vary between the varied communities that operate within that domain. Thus, for example, if I was a record producer operating in the early 1970s, I might take a centripetal approach to using the Urei 1176 when it comes to compressing vocals and use the approach suggested in the manual, but a centrifugal approach when it comes to compressing drums and use the 'all buttons in' technique. Of course, that centrifugal approach might become centripetal to a smaller subset of producers who all swear by that technique. What is rebellion in the mainstream becomes conformity among the 'rebels', and quite often in social structures over time the rebels become the mainstream. And while I might be conventional among my peers in my cultural domain when it comes to my approach to compression, I may be entirely unconventional when it comes to EQ or microphone selection.

In terms of the social field, I approach that in the same way. The social field doesn't aggregate out to a uniform set of opinions about the value of the individual's creative activity. The various gatekeepers and audiences that constitute the social field will have different priorities about which aspects of an output are important, as well as different opinions about its value. Another area where I have imported external ideas into the systems approach is through Pierre Bourdieu's ideas about the different forms of capital (1986). Economic, cultural, social and symbolic capital are all utilised by the members of the social field to attempt to gain dominance for their judgements. On the economic level, the spending power of an audience and its ability to buy the output and thereby confer value on it is one basic use of capital. Cultural capital relates to tacit and explicit knowledge that confers power on an individual; social capital relates to power that stems from a person's position within some social grouping and symbolic power relates to ideas such as prestige and honour.

There is a certain amount of overlap here: I might be considered to have prestige because of the advantage my knowledge confers upon me, which might also flow from a social position such as a newspaper editor – a position my knowledge helped me achieve – and my economic capital may have helped me achieve all three of these other things. They can be seen as functionally distinct, however, as the specific advantages that flow from wealth, knowledge, social position and prestige are all different. The way I see these forms of capital relating to the social field is that different individuals and communities will value them in different ways and to different extents, and these evaluations will help to determine the effect of these judgements on the creative individual, the other members of the social field and the way these judgements will affect the various forces at work in the cultural domain.

For example, if Chris Lord-Alge, the producer, is receiving critical praise from the music press and the trade press and commercial sales are doing well, that can be analysed in terms of the forms of capital that are putting weight behind these various assertions of his expertise and success. Lord-Alge may have a low opinion of the music press and take their praise with a pinch of salt, but might value the more peer-based and technically informed praise of the trade press because of the different forms of capital it employs – i.e. the creative field affects the creative individual. At the same time, the journalist in the trade press may be very impressed by popularity in the mainstream music press and may be reinforcing their opinion of Lord-Alge's work, based on the very opinions he dismisses – i.e. part of the social field affects another part of the social field. (This is all hypothetical, by the way. I have no special knowledge of Chris Lord-Alge's opinions or of anyone who may have written about him!) And finally, Lord-Alge may have praised the use of the 1176 on vocals in an interview with the trade press and provided information on the types of settings he prefers. This, in turn, may have affected the norms of practice of a group of engineers and producers who admire the work of Lord-Alge – i.e. the individual's work, mediated by the social field, affects a part of the cultural domain.

One of the key problems for me with the systems model of creativity lies in triangulating the individual with the cultural domain and social field. The very problem that this model is meant to address is the fact that an individual's creativity needs to be examined in relation to others – those that preceded them and influenced them at the very least. Indeed, most creative practice is in some way collective. How does the systems model represent and explain collective practice? Should each individual in the collective whole be represented separately with their own domain and field or should, as Phillip McIntyre recently suggested to me,[2] we substitute a 'black box' of a creative team into a single creative system? If the former, then how do we represent the interaction between the members, and does this suggest

2 This was in a question and answer session at the end of his paper with Paul Thompson at the eighth Art of Record Production conference at Université Laval, Québec City.

that they each have their own, albeit overlapping, domains and fields? If the latter, then how do we represent the interactions that take place within the 'black box'?

The social construction of technology (SCOT)

An alternative approach that we've also already mentioned is SCOT, developed by scholars such as Wiebe Bijker (1995), Trevor Pinch (Pinch et al. 2012), Nellie Oudshoorn (Oudshoorn and Pinch 2003) and others. This is a large and developing body of work but there are several key ideas that I am drawing on. First is the notion that there is some kind of action script implicit or explicit in the design of any piece of technology – it affords being used in some ways and not in others. This ties in nicely with affordances in ecological approaches to perception, and the action script seems analogous to an action schema in embodied cognition. Second, this implicit script in design shouldn't be focused on without proper recourse to the users. Feminist approaches in SCOT have turned towards the participants who have tended to be ignored within the history of technology: the users of the technology. Obviously this was a key issue in our Universal Audio 1176 example. A third important aspect is the notion that technologies move from interpretive flexibility towards stability. This idea can be applied to both the design/manufacture side and the user side.

Thus, in the period around 1966, Bill Putnam lived in a world where there was still a good deal of interpretive flexibility about the kinds of technology that might be used to build a dynamic audio compressor, and that made it more 'natural' to look around and discover the possibility of using a field effect transistor (FET) rather than a transistor-based voltage controlled amplifier (VCA) or one of the other possible technologies. By the end of the 1960s and until the advent of digital audio, the technologies of dynamic compression types had reached stability: tube-based, diode bridge, optical, VCA and FET compressors. For the purposes of this chapter, my focus is on users and, in a summary of recent research, Nellie Oudshoorn and Trevor Pinch identify three classes of user:

1. end users: those who have some skilled knowledge of and are affected by product innovation;
2. lay end users: those who are in a similar position but who are not privy to whatever expert discourse surrounds the product's development;
3. implicated actors: those who are silent or not present but who are nonetheless affected by the technology.

(2003, pp. 1–28)

Configuring the user

Several scholars have approached the question of how the ergonomics of new recording technology developments have shaped changing professional and creative practice. Zak has described the way in which multi-track recording techniques have changed the creative process for many musicians (2001, pp. 130–41). Paul Simon's *Graceland* album (1986) was partly written by recording extended 'loops' of basic sketches played by African musicians and then using the 'feel' to suggest structural editing and rewriting. It has also become common practice for writers to use sounds as the basis of an idea. Peter Gabriel's creative process involves recording any experimentation that occurs in the studio and utilising it as a springboard for the development of ideas, or storing it away for future use. These techniques evolved from changes in the technology rather than the technology being developed because there was a desire to make changes to the compositional process.

This brings us back to another related theoretical model, actor-network theory (ANT). Woolgar (1991) asserts that those who develop and produce technology are configuring the user through the design process rather than social negotiation, but it is still a process of configuration. Furthermore, the notion of the user as they exist within the network of the design process is imagined or constructed by the designers rather than being a representation of the actual individuals or groups, until, that is, we get into the world of focus groups and beta testing. Indeed, the designers themselves are configured in their process of design both by that imagined or constructed user and by the structure and ideology of the organisation in which they work. This configuration of the design process is further mediated by journalists, public sector agencies, spokespersons, role models, etc. In short, the implicit or explicit action script or scenario that is inherent in any design can be extensively shaped by other figures in the network and, as this is ANT where non-humans can be participants in a network, that can include the design technology that they use and other factors in their working environment.

We must also explain these action scripts or scenarios in terms of the affordances that the technology offers. It may be possible to complete a task in several ways: the different types of edit screen for Music Instrument Digital Interface (MIDI) information in various sequencer software packages springs to mind. So we should not consider 'configuration' to be a necessarily straitjacketing term. However, the affordances offered by a new product and the action scripts that they imply can also be seen to create new, or reinforce old, geographies of responsibility (Massey 2004). 'Who does what' is a fundamental categorising principle of workflow, and the history of sound engineering and pretty much every skilled activity is littered with contests and arguments over demarcation. Indeed, this is one of the key points that Steve Albini argues about the use of digital audio workstations (DAWs) instead of tape, and about his assertion that he's not a producer, he's an engineer or a recordist.[3] On the former, he asserts that the design of tape machines is centred on the 'capture' of a performance, whereas the design of a DAW centres on the notion of manipulating that recording once it has been 'captured', and that isn't his job. On the latter, he asserts that his job is to facilitate the recording according to the wishes of the musicians he's working with, and that the term 'producer' suggests that he should take some kind of creative control. Both instances clearly relate to Albini having an ideological stance on his job demarcation: on the participants' geographies of responsibility. This rejection by Albini of the work scenario suggested by the design principles of DAWs relates back to 'all buttons in' on the 1176. Both of these activities involve an alternative script to the one 'handed down' in the design of the technology, and this type of activity has been labelled the antiprogram by Akrich and Latour (1992, p. 261). I shall return to this idea shortly.

Seeing sound

This brings us to another way in which the ergonomics of music production technology have influenced creative practice. Contemporary non-linear recording software has added the visual dimension to editing sound in a way that simply wasn't present in tape-based formats. Even during that period it was not unknown for engineers and producers to cover the VU meters on the mixing console with tape because they felt that they should make their judgements of sound quality purely from an aural perspective, without any visual influences. Recordists now have a graphic representation of every recorded sound wave available to them on screen, as well as a visual representation of the arrangement in the form of a block diagram showing which instruments have been recorded (or copied) at which points in the song. This would seem to encourage the user to think of sound as an object rather than a stream (which is arguably the way tape machines encourage users to conceptualise sound). There is a potential rich vein of research in the

[3] Albini has argued different aspects of his case in many places; one example is an interview he gave at the sixth Art of Record Production conference at Leeds Metropolitan University in 2010: www.youtube.com/watch?v=yRAc3hx5pok [accessed 8 February 2014].

study of how this (relatively) new visual aspect to the recording process has affected creative practice in the production process. This continuing process of atomising the act of composition and record production and exposing every aspect of performance to closer and closer scrutiny has resulted in a clinical quest for technical perfection that often comes at the expense of aesthetic considerations. As soon as the technology to fix blemishes exists – through the use of compression to even out dynamics or of Auto-Tune to correct pitch inaccuracies, for instance – the pressure to utilise it is brought to bear. The inherent script or program (in Akrich and Latour's terminology) or the way the technology configures the user (in Woolgar's) creates the pressure to conform. This pressure can also be applied if something looks 'wrong' on screen, even if the 'flaw' hasn't actually been heard.

The choice of visuals, of what is represented, when and how, is a very powerful influence on the user. The representation of music as a visual pattern that can be measured against a time grid is a fundamental shift in the technological frame that is having a profound effect on the way recorded music sounds and, thus, how performers try to play live. Unlike staff notation, this is a post facto representation of what is there, rather than a set of instructions for how to create or interpret a performance. While this kind of representation isn't taking over in folk, classical, jazz and other musical forms that don't get recorded to a click track, the technology of tempo extraction, of analysing a piece of audio and creating a conceptual time grid that works, is improving all the time. Indeed, this kind of tempo extraction is increasingly being used in classical and jazz musical analysis,[4] if not yet in commercial production and editing. The idea that when we listen to music we create some kind of internal abstract interpretive pulse through a combination of embodied entrainment to what we perceive to be happening and a prediction of what we expect to happen next is entirely in accordance with my ideas on the psychology of music. The idea that this is the same for everyone, that there is a 'correct' pulse that can be extracted from music by a computer algorithm and that it can be represented by a grid with lines on a screen (rather than, say, a gestural shape) is not.

As we've said, the nature of the visual representation strongly affects the way we think about music and, since the advent of MIDI, the representation of rhythm in sequencing and DAW software has been much more nuanced than the representation of pitch. With MIDI sequencing I can quite easily move a note slightly ahead or slightly behind the beat of the grid and the software reflects this by offering groove and quantise templates that specify

[4] Using software such as Sonic Visualiser (www.sonicvisualiser.org/ [accessed 26 July 2013]).

grids that can be as asymmetrical as I like. Not only that, but when something is played I can specify which notes I want corrected and which notes left 'human', and I can specify a percentage amount of correction; for example, correct anything near a quarter note 100% but only correct the eighth notes in between them by 70%. And once the technology of time-stretching audio files was developed[5] these same techniques could be applied to audio.

This sophistication of rhythmic editing wasn't matched in what you could do with pitch. Despite the fact that the technical possibility was afforded by MIDI to bend the pitch of notes, software designers didn't engage with this in the same way. I spent a large amount of time laboriously drawing pitch bend curves into various different software sequencers during the 1980s and 1990s, and it seems in retrospect that some template algorithms for slides, vibrato and tremolo should have been just as easy to implement as the highly sophisticated rhythm manipulation. Just where the causality lies is unclear: were the software designers more interested in rhythm than pitch? Or was there no demand from the users? In some ways, the problem was embedded in the structure of the MIDI protocol: portamento, tremolo and vibrato were treated by manufacturers as being inherent in the sound itself, something you programmed in the synthesiser (the instrument) rather than in the sequencer (the player). Once that interpretive flexibility had been removed by the universal adoption of the MIDI protocol, we can see that Bijker's (1995) notion of inclusion is once again relevant here. Such was the widespread acceptance of MIDI as the technological frame, the stability of interpretation as to what form it took and the deep level of inclusion that all participants felt (users, software designers, product manufacturers, etc.), there was little or no discussion about such fundamental principles of visual representation as whether gradations of less than a semitone should be represented on something like the 'piano roll' editing page of a sequencer.[6] At the moment, the visual representation of pitch in audio files is non-existent in most commercial DAW software, Melodyne[7] being the notable exception, and plug-ins like Auto-Tune that alter pitch focus their visual representation of activity on what the technology is doing rather than the pitch of the audio.

And what do these visual representations do for the way we think about timbre? The arrange page in MIDI sequencers that first emerged in Cubase

[5] Altering the playback speed of a section of digital audio without altering its pitch or vice versa.

[6] The piano roll edit page represents pitch vertically with a grid of semitones and time horizontally. Notes are represented as blocks, rather like the holes in a piano roll for a player piano.

[7] See: www.celemony.com/cms/ [accessed 26 July 2013].

has become the standard for DAWs such as Logic and ProTools as well. This too puts time along the horizontal axis and the vertical axis is divided into tracks. In the original MIDI version these were assigned to different MIDI channels, and thus each track represented a different sound: this in turn had been based on the late 1970s/early 1980s model of multi-track recording in popular music – a separate microphone and therefore tape track for every instrument. However, the construction of arrangements by representing separate instrumental parts as coloured blocks on the grey background of the arrange window grid meant that you were creating a kind of colour chart of the orchestration. Unlike tape, it was possible to see where the musical activity was on the different tracks, like a score. In a recording where all the musicians are in the same room and play the arrangement in real time, there are simply a series of blocks (the number of microphones/tracks being recorded) that start at the beginning and stop at the end. The amplitude of the sound file does show the level of activity on each of the microphones, and that is usually visible on the screen, but ambient microphones for the whole ensemble rather than close microphones for specific players will confine the information to overall amplitude rather than giving a visual representation of the arrangement.

And that only relates to timbre in terms of instrumentation rather than the timbre of the individual musical components. These can be represented visually with spectrographs but their use is, so far, confined to musical analysis rather than to production. All of this suggests that the representation of timbre is as or less nuanced than that of pitch. As far as I can tell, the main thrust of research in this area is aimed at the design of interfaces,[8] which is certainly throwing some light on the topic but is not primarily concerned with the way in which visual representation affects the way we think about sound and recording.

Production technology as a consumer product

If these issues of scripts and configuration can be boiled down to a pressure to do whatever can be done rather than whatever should be done, it is built into the system of creative practice by the commercialisation of the process. By offering a large amount of consumer choice in products that do particular things and none in others (for example, in areas for which only time, perseverance and ingenuity are necessary rather than a form

[8] See, for example, the work of Josh Reiss at Queen Mary, University of London (e.g. Reiss 2011).

of product) – and by making sure that the consumer products are advertised/discussed and the others are ignored – the domain/field structure is manipulated in a particular direction. The problem, though, with explanations like this is that they can very easily make capitalism sound like a conspiracy. The domain/field structure is manipulated not by a single force or some kind of sinister cartel but as an emergent property of the many conflicting affordances, goals, prejudices and unintended consequences of the disparate participants in the system. How then should we be explaining the ways in which consumerism is affecting users' relationships with recording technology? Are users being configured to create music in ways that utilise particular forms of technology for purely commercial reasons? How much of the domain relates to 'ease of use' or creative potential and how much to maintaining the plug-in (consumer-driven) methodology? What are the forces behind the technological frame?

Paul Théberge and SCOT/ANT/creative systems

Paul Théberge (1997), as mentioned in the previous chapter, has examined this question in relation to the changes that occurred in the musical instrument industry. He charts the way in which keyboard manufacturers in the 1980s and 1990s helped to alter the way musicians viewed their instruments. The continued changes in the technology, and other factors to do with marketing, fostered the view that a keyboard was a consumable object that should be regularly upgraded. This can be identified as part of a more general trend whose effect is creeping into recording practice too. The market for plug-in effects and processors for the desktop sound-recording market has seen a similar move towards offering a large number of preset options (such as 'rock hi-hat EQ', 'techno hi-hat EQ' and so forth) rather than simply providing a variety of adjustable parameters.[9] This is encouraging changes in working practice: rather than continually monitoring and tweaking the parameters of an effect or processor to fit the changing sound of a mix, an option is selected and maintained until it grates enough to be replaced by another. In particular, the pressure from a market built on gadgets is to alter the technological frame – the problem-solving paradigm – from one based on finding the right process to one based on finding the right 'thing'. This seems slightly ironic in a world where musicology seems to

[9] Although, as opposed to the hardware version of this phenomenon that Théberge describes in relation to synthesisers, presets in plug-ins tend to be either an addition to programmable features (rather than a replacement) or a feature of designs that are emulating vintage hardware units.

be slowly altering its ontological frame from one where music is construed as a thing to one where it is seen as a process.

As we saw in the example from Théberge's work in the previous chapter, the manufacturers don't get it all their own way: users are neither as easily understood nor as easily configured as they perhaps might like. Alice Tomaz de Carvalho (2012) discusses the continued influence of the older professional studio model of recording in the discourse on home recording in the internet forum and 'hobbyist' magazine literature. Added to this is the further complication that recording technology manufacturers are continually trying to expand their market to include performing musicians as well as those from a programming/production background. To return to the systems model, there is a clear need to understand how the various participants in the marketised aspects of musical creativity fit into the system. On the one hand, the monetised portions of the internet and the extensive market for self help literature (the hints and tips from experts with various forms and levels of cultural capital), not to mention the many universities and private colleges selling courses in the subject area, amount to selling access to parts of the cultural domain of rules and expertise. On the other hand, there is the social field with an equally extensive network of equipment and plug-in reviewers reinforcing the notion that all you need to do is find the right 'thing' to solve your sonic problems. This, however, is interestingly matched not only by the discourse that Tomaz de Carvalho identifies of internet knowledge brokers – perhaps unsurprisingly – suggesting that knowledge is more important than technology but also by a parallel competition, or at least a tension, in education between theoretical understanding and professional experience.[10]

Within the constructionist approach in the history of technology, feminist approaches have been instrumental in bringing the user into the frame – not just the female user. By examining the areas in which women have been particularly active in the history of technology, as users rather than inventors or manufacturers[11] (see, for example, Trescott 1979), scholars developing this feminist approach have opened up the subject of users as active participants in the definition, development and potential repurposing of technology. This is particularly relevant in the field of record production. The categories of use mentioned earlier in the chapter (end user, lay end user and implicated actor) take on further implications when discussed

[10] In the UK, the Music Producers Guild is part of a course accreditation organisation (Joint Audio Media Education Support) for university courses in recording and production.

[11] Obviously, this isn't to suggest that women have been absent from invention or manufacture in audio technology, but they have been marginalised and vastly outnumbered.

in relation to a highly commercialised example such as early twenty-first-century recording technology. With something like a tennis racket or a vacuum cleaner there is little scope for the kinds of nuanced selling that occurs in the recording market. While I can aim to persuade the user to buy a better/more expensive model, these are not technologies that have a rich and complex market for enhancements or accessories. Furthermore, these are not markets where the nuances of improved performance can be tracked so explicitly against these enhancements and accessories, or in which demand may be so closely (and in some instances inversely) related to the type of user you are. For example, a lay user with limited expertise may be more likely to buy simple-to-use products with more presets, and a more expert end user might aim to buy fewer more powerful (and correspondingly more complex and expensive) products: products that lend themselves more readily to a user's antiprogram as well as the designer's program.

Creative abuse

As we've seen, Akrich and Latour describe the antiprogram in terms of resistance to the 'program' that is inherent in the design of the technology. They use the terms 'subscription' and 'de-inscription' (Akrich and Latour 1992, p. 261) to explain this choice between subscribing to the program and using the technology in the manner it was designed, or de-inscribing oneself from the technology: rejecting or renegotiating the program. As others have pointed out, in particular feminist writers in the SCOT school of thought, this is seldom an act of outright rejection, and the renegotiation is often better described as a creative interpretation. Hirsch and Silverstone discuss the domestication of technology as a process by which it is not just brought into the household but is absorbed into creative practice and working life in four stages:

1. appropriation – the act of acquiring it;
2. objectification – creating a pattern of usage and display;
3. incorporation – the way it turns out to be used – something that may or may not be the intended way and can be seen as an articulation of creativity;
4. conversion – the process through which the user and the technology engage with the outside world.

(2004, pp. 9–17)

The notion of conversion was discussed by Hirsch and Silverstone in relation to domestic media technology, and this related to the way the users engaged with the external media that the technology afforded them access to. By applying this model to both professional and home recording studio environments I am generalising some of the terms, but I would certainly contend that it is relevant to both.

There are ways in which all four of these stages of domestication can become subject to renegotiation or creative interpretation. Second-hand markets and software piracy are the two main ways in which the stage of appropriation can be renegotiated. By using a cheaper (or free) method of acquisition there is often a cost to be borne in terms of functionality or aesthetics. There may be specific features that are faulty or absent, or there may be cosmetic wear or damage that might influence the user's or others' perception of it (the processes of objectification and conversion): either the patina of age conferring some kind of authenticity or the appearance of damage giving an impression that it is less efficient or professional. Objectification, of course, relates more to hardware than software and, again, has a slightly different meaning in a studio situation (even a home studio) than the kinds of domestic consumer technology that Hirsch and Silverstone are discussing. The objectification of recording technology usually involves the inclusion of the technology within a more complex technological system of production. This could be as simple as a computer with headphones or speakers, or as complex as a full studio set-up in several rooms with a complicated network of hardware. Situating the technology within this set-up involves considerations of how the user expects the system to work (an interaction with the incorporation stage) and, potentially, repositioning the item or restructuring the system in the light of further interaction with the incorporation stage. Once again, the issue of how the system looks as well as how it performs will have an impact on both the user's and others' perception of the environment as professional, efficient, modern, etc.

These tropes can be seen in relation to our notion of the program and the antiprogram in the broader sense of the norms of the cultural domain as well as the specifics of any given item. Incorporation is, perhaps, the most obvious site for creative interpretation. As we've said, the objectification process is highly related to this. In the case of a hardware patchbay, for example, the wiring process is so long-winded and disruptive that substantial changes in order to facilitate different working practices are much less likely than, for example, exchanging one effects rack unit for another. Having said that, every working studio is in some way an expression of the thoughts and working practices of the people who designed and use it. Using other people's studio set-ups not only gives you unforeseen insights about ergonomics and your own creative practice in general but is also a window into their character. The conversion stage, in some ways, relates to exactly that point. In most instances, a studio will involve some kind of collaborative activity, whether we're talking about a professional facility that might host projects with different engineers and producers as well as different musicians, or a small home set-up where there will often be some other performer in addition to the owner/user.

One of the great triggers for creative reinterpretation of studio technology is for a technician or producer to be set a problem by someone, usually a musician, outside the technological frame or cultural domain – i.e. someone with no clear idea about what is or isn't possible with the technology, who is thinking backwards from the 'what I want it to sound like or feel like' perspective. Thus, for example, John Lennon stating that he wanted his voice on 'Tomorrow Never Knows' (The Beatles 1966) to sound like the Dalai Lama singing from a mountain top prompted Geoff Emerick to take their repurposing of a Leslie rotating speaker a step further than before and record John's voice through it.[12] On the same album, for 'Paperback Writer' and 'Rain' (The Beatles 1966), in response to Paul McCartney's complaints about his bass sound, Emerick also rewired a large speaker to work as a microphone (Ryan and Kehew 2006, pp. 420–1), one of the few examples I can think of that constitutes such a literal antiprogram. In fact, the technical engineer from Abbey Road at the time, Dave Harries, recalls: 'We were reprimanded for improper use of equipment. They told us we couldn't use it because it wasn't a real microphone' (Ryan and Kehew 2006, p. 421). In a term that I think captures the essence of this type of reinterpretive activity better than the antiprogram, Andy Keep (2005) coined the phrase 'creative abuse'.

If the notion of the antiprogram is better seen as a reinterpretation of that program (or the way a specific piece of technology might configure a user) rather than as a rejection of it, Sam Bennett's notion of anti-production as a rejection of the mainstream aesthetic of recording practice might be viewed in terms of rival interpretations of what should constitute such an aesthetic. In her conference paper (2010) and her forthcoming book, an expansion of her PhD thesis (2014), Bennett examines both the deliberate use of nominally outmoded technologies and unorthodox techniques or processes as creative practice through a series of case studies. In fact, the iconic nature

[12] They had previously recorded some guitar through the rotating speaker for an earlier, discarded version of the track. The Leslie speaker was designed for use with the Hammond electric organ and created a 'swirling effect by rotating a baffle and "horn" around the bass and treble drivers inside the speaker cabinet' (Ryan and Kehew 2006, pp. 423–4).

of some of the producers who engage in these kinds of practices – Steve Albini, Mark Ronson and Jacquire King, for example – have served to suggest that in certain sectors of the record production domain they should be seen as centripetal rather than centrifugal forms of activity.

Practical knowledge and heteroglossia

With practice as research being a very 'hot' topic in musicology at the moment – specifically, how to differentiate between creative practice and practice as research – the idea of experimenting with technology to develop new techniques in the context of professional practice seems highly pertinent. I would contend that judgements of this sort are usually a question of value rather than definition. Discovering something new seems like an everyday occurrence: it is discovering something useful that is the tricky bit. Not only that, but in questions of research, as I discussed briefly in the first two chapters, the decisions about which subjects are appropriate to study at university level and how they should be approached is a question of ideology. I imagine that I am more likely to be able to persuade a research council that discovering a new way to repurpose a new piece of music software through practical exploration constitutes valid practice as research than I am to persuade them that my new way of using a wah-wah pedal does. While this may be a facile example, I hope it makes the point that being old, being technically simple and being commercial are not attributes that fit with mainstream ideas about using technology in practice as research.

This is a point where the ideas of cultural and symbolic capital intersect with heteroglossia. Certain types of centrifugal and centripetal activity happen in sectors of the cultural domain with different levels and types of capital, and this once again marks a problem of demarcation in the systems model. Among the communities that lionise the work of Steve Albini, for example, his work is interpreted in terms of the way it represents centrifugal activity to a constructed notion of the 'mainstream', and yet an aspirational individual working within that world is likely to define themselves in terms of centripetal activity to this notion of the 'other', in which Steve Albini may sit somewhere central. In short, there is a very real question about whether we should be exploring the internal mental representations of the communities that make up a cultural domain on the individual level of psychology, or trying to schematise a generic one at sociological level. Put crudely, are we trying to explain what the participants *think* they're doing or what they're *actually* doing?

To return to the SCOT model for a moment: actors with high or low inclusion in a particular situation are either invested or not in a particular technological frame. It determines the likelihood of centrifugal or centripetal activity – the development of the antiprogram. They are less likely to draw on the standard problem-solving strategies in that frame and more likely to identify 'presumptive anomalies' (Constant 1980, p. 15). To return to the Albini example, his immersion in the 1980s Chicago punk scene gave him a low inclusion in the traditional sound engineering world and a high inclusion in both the punk rock performing world and a kind of guerrilla, lo-fi recording world that made a virtue out of recording in rehearsal halls and small gig venues.

On a more general level, Timothy Taylor (2001) espouses a practice-based theory of technology. The design of the technology creates a structure that limits the influence of the recordist's agency and will mostly determine the primary form of usage. However, the agents are also involved in 'consuming' or utilising the technology. They 'undermine, add to and modify those uses in a never-ending process' (Taylor 2001, p. 38). Authors like Bobby Owsinski (1999) offer privileged access to the 'hints and tips' of respected professionals: hints and tips that are generally about unorthodox and centrifugal activity rather than mundane technical orthodoxy such as signal path and gain structure. Indeed, this type of 'creative abuse', in my experience, carries more professional or cultural capital than the technical knowledge that was previously more valued. Thus, engineers would seem to set more store by the innovative use of technology (e.g. misusing noise-reduction technology to get a 'warmer' string sound, or using a speaker as large diaphragm transducer [microphone] to get a 'fatter' bass response) than by detailed technical knowledge (e.g. an understanding of the history and physics of different stereo microphone placement techniques, or a knowledge of room acoustics). The engineers, perhaps unsurprisingly, will be assigning value to practice that favours agency on behalf of them as users rather than determinism on behalf of practical orthodoxy or the technology itself.

In many ways, then, with this narrative of rebellion and mavericks being established as a kind of studio version of trashing the hotel room, how romanticised is the notion of non-conformity and wildness in the popular music recording studio? Stories of giant bags of cocaine, orgiastic behaviour and unconscious rock stars having to be carried to their limousines at the end of a hard day in the studio may well have been true in the 1980s, but my experience was of hard – if not always productive – work. Going back to our Bobby Owsinski examples, however, it does also make sense to bear in mind that the notion of the creative artist (as opposed to the commercial craftsman) in popular music is built solidly around the romantic ideal: a frequently tortured or self-destructive character, whose solitary inspiration comes through flashes rather than through hard work for long hours. For a producer in that tradition, who identifies themself as a creative force rather than a production manager, their internal representation of what creativity is will be more likely to send them in the direction of lateral thinking than conventional problem-solving techniques.

More about affordances

In this last section on creative abuse I want return to the idea of affordances and how the specifics of a situation can suggest ways to innovate and solve problems. Bob Olhsson has said:

> Sgt. Pepper's is not a recording, Sgt. Pepper's was the solution to the various problems they came up with in the process of producing the record. You put something on and then you have to figure out something to put with it that'll make it work, and you couldn't go back whereas now, you've got this huge palette and you can do anything, but you wind up with it all being so conceptual that it is lame. There's no magic, no opportunity for the recording to come out any better than your concepts. (Stevenson 2002)

In June 1957 Buddy Holly and the Crickets were recording in Norman Petty's studio in Clovis, New Mexico:

> 'Peggy Sue' started life as a Buddy Holly composition called 'Cindy Lou' . . . In its original incarnation, as featured in live performances, the song was slower, and had a Latin beat. But while the band were warming up in the Clovis studio, J.I. thrashed out a rolling rhythm known as a paradiddle, often used as an exercise by drummers . . . Buddy liked the effect so much that he immediately suggested using it on 'Cindy Lou' . . . the drumming was so loud that Norman Petty had to get J.I. to set up his drums in the reception area outside the studio . . . As J.I. [played], Norman Petty made his most significant contribution to any Holly recording, flipping the control switch of the echo chamber on and off so that the drumming became a rolling beat, coming and going like waves on a beach. (Gribbin 2009, pp. 83–5)

So, while the solution to the problem of the loudness of the drum pattern was to place J.I., the drummer, outside the studio, this afforded two ideas for innovation that contributed to the unique sound of the record. The first, as partially described in Gribbin's account, was that there was little or no spillage onto the drum microphone from the sounds in the studio because they were in a separate room. This allowed Petty to send the drums to the echo chamber (Petty's attic with a speaker at one end and a microphone at the other) without sending any of the other sounds and this afforded the creative possibility of alternating between the microphone immediately above the drums and the sound of them returning from the echo chamber. As they were recording the track straight to mono, Petty had to do the mix, alternating between the two faders, live as the performance happened. The precise details of the second innovative aspect of this recording aren't so clear. What I suspect happened is that, with the drums having no hi-hat or ride part because J.I. was playing the two-handed paradiddle on the drum and the echo chamber sound made the detail in that even less clear, someone decided that the plectrum striking the strings of Holly's guitar created a shaker- or scraper-like sound that suited the track. By putting a microphone in front of his strumming hand as well as in front of the guitar amplifier, we hear the guitar part as two distinct sounds: the rather dull (in frequency terms) guitar chords providing a harmonic wash from the amplifier sound and the crisp scrape of the plectrum on the guitar strings providing a bright rhythmic impetus. Again, without the removal of the drums from the studio this additional feature would not have been possible either, as the drums would have spilled onto the plectrum microphone, drowning the very quiet sound of that rhythmic scrape.

Through this example we can see affordances as a form of configuration – the creation of the right conditions for that idea to emerge. This 'softer' notion of configuration is about the way all participants configure their mental representations in response to stimuli and interpretation. Any given possibility may or may not emerge, but it has to be afforded by the situation. Another aspect of this is that affordances should be seen as something that requires the active engagement of users (in SCOT) or perceivers/interpreters (in ecological perception) and involves creativity in the forms of interpretation and reaction to the potential.

Technology and the conceptualisation of music

How tools make us think

That return to the notion of affordances also brings us back to the notion of tools and to the idea of being configured in a wider sense. By that I mean not just being configured about how to do a specific job by the affordances offered by a specific tool but also about how tools make us think. In his book *Making*, Tim Ingold (2013) discusses the fact that practical skills like drawing aren't a matter of transferring a mental image onto the page via the medium of the pencil tool. Instead, he proposes that the physical activity of muscle movement and haptic feedback are an embodied part of the mental process of creation. There's a continual feedback loop of thinking and doing, and the combined flow of consciousness, gesture and the affordances of the materials creates the final outcome (Ingold 2013, pp. 20–1). Although Ingold doesn't cite Csikszentmihalyi (1997) on flow, there does seem to be some common ground here, and Nakamura and Csikszentmihalyi list factors such as the merging of action and awareness and the loss of self-consciousness as necessary conditions for flow (2009, pp. 195–206). This ability to perform complex tasks without normal conscious attention suggests to me some kind of direct access of a relevant action script, although without a coherent theory of conscious attention it is impossible to suggest what kind of mechanism that might be.

In terms of embodied cognition, in order to conceptualise something we have to be able to construct an empathic or metaphorical link between it and some aspect of our physical experience that has been stored as a schematic representation. We mentally redo an activity in order to interpret the experience of a new one. In the simple case of seeing a person raise their arm, the mental activity has an obvious empathic relation. In a more complex case, such as watching a bascule bridge[13] rise, the mental activity may involve that same arm-raising activity in a conceptual blend with some schematic representation of a steel structure involving sensations of hardness, weight and size that creates a metaphorical relationship between my past experience and this current perception. Other characteristics of the various mental schemata involved in this conceptual blend will suggest potential affordances, such that the combination of size and weight with the knowledge that arms that go up can also come down might suggest the affordance of it crashing back down again. A new activity – particularly a new engagement with a 'tool' – allows, or perhaps forces, us to think in a new way: to create new connections between this activity and other activities for which we already have experience (and schematic representations).

The move from linear, tape-based recording practice to non-linear, hard-disc systems has also had a powerful effect not just on recording practice but also on the way artists and producers conceptualise a piece and envisage the creative process. Many of the historical developments that Zak mentions in *The Poetics of Rock* (2001) can be seen as creating music through what might be described as 'organic development' (in terms of progressive

[13] One that is raised and lowered like a drawbridge.

growth), whereas the 'cut-and-paste' methods of desktop systems have encouraged composers to work in a modular fashion. It is becoming less common for any musician to play their part from beginning to end during the recording process. Non-linear practice often involves the producer or engineer aiming to record a 'good chorus' and a 'good verse', which are then copied and pasted to create the arrangement structure. This change in working practice has led to many composer–producers conceptualising session musicians in the same way as they might envisage a sampler: as a sound source that generates modular units to be assembled and manipulated in the creative process. Sampling has to some extent altered the idea of composing to include collage and assemblage in ways that were previously perceived to be the domain of the DJ (the editor, the selector and the impresario), driving changes in the way non-linear recording is used. Indeed, the most successful software packages in this field have evolved out of MIDI sequencing software, thus further reinforcing the idea that non-linear recordings should be manipulated in the same way as MIDI sequences. This, in turn, encourages constant timing and playing with a click track to facilitate the editing process. Without going into the nuts and bolts detail that these examples would entail, I think it is easy to see how these changes in tool technology have altered the kinds of empathic and metaphorical links that might exist between the participants and their perceptions of what they are doing.

One further example that links this to the discussion on vintage technologies in the previous chapter is the plug-in emulation of vintage hardware. As I mentioned, by buying the software version as opposed to the hardware (assuming that the emulation is actually good!) the sonic imprint of various aspects of the circuitry may be faithfully reproduced, but the ergonomics of the controls are different: mouse- or touch screen-controlled instead of by knobs, sliders and buttons. My physical engagement with the controls, then, will not only make me act differently but I will be conceptualising the process and the tool in a different way, and am thus surely more likely to get different kinds of results.

How thinking makes us use tools

Finally in this chapter we reverse the previous question and look at how our conceptual models may affect the way we use tools. In some ways that has been what the rest of this chapter was about in any case: the way we engage with domains and fields, the notions of action scripts and configuration. In this section, though, I want to look at the broader process of social interaction through technology. We can see this bigger picture as a discourse that is played out through the design, promotion, distribution and use of technology.

For example, to return to Les Paul and Ross Snyder, in this instance an idiosyncratic 'super-user' set a design agenda that the rest of the network/social field wasn't particularly interested in until more or less a decade later. However, a limited version (the three- and four-track machines) was marketed and taken up by many (principally to overdub lead vocals). That's not to say that this development wouldn't have happened without him: Ross Snyder informs us that the technology was all pretty much in place anyway. But without that specific design agenda being set by Les Paul, who is to say how the specifics of multi-tracking might have progressed?

In some ways we might see Melodyne as a similar type of technology. In this instance, a technology that requires the fragmentation of audio into component parts seems to flow from a desire to turn audio back into notation. There are great technical problems with achieving this, but Melodyne is beginning to surmount them. It seems to me, though, that it is a conceptual model based on mechanical forms of articulation and notation (discrete scalar divisions) that stem from a particular dominant form of music in the West.

This suggests that the broader cultural currents of musical ontology play a key role in setting the agenda for technological development. There is a circular motion in specific domains and cross-fertilisation between different domains that occurs as new product design suggests new rules of creative practice and, potentially, new ways of thinking about music, performance and recording practice. Individuals may use some, break some and disseminate these new versions of the 'rules', and these changes may also suggest some rewriting of the broader conceptualisation of music, performance or recording practice that seeps out into the professional and public consciousness. This, in turn, encourages further creative practice in the domain of new product design, and the cycle continues.

Theoretical interlude 3

As we've seen, these schematic representations or simplifications are at once useful and problematic. They can aid our understanding but they are also a reflection of our underlying ideology. The key lies in the nature of usefulness. They are useful because they help us to achieve our goals, but what are the goals of analyses like these? Are we aiming to characterise similarities and commonality through the identification of unifying themes? Or are we concerned with pointing out differences between times, places, musical styles, technologies or individuals, in which case the relevant schematic features are variables? Obviously, this is closely tied to the age-old and basic activity of ensuring you have clearly defined research questions before you engage in a study, but identifying research goals also goes to the heart of the nature of knowledge. What kinds of thing can we know about social and creative activity, and of what kind of use can they be? At the 2009 Art of Record Production conference I was on a panel with Nicholas Cook and Allan Moore about the academic study of record production and we were asked by record producer and sound engineer Haydn Bendall what we thought was the point of all this research. I can't remember the precise details of who said what, and unfortunately it wasn't recorded, but the gist of the response was that there were two potential reasons: one was the pragmatic approach of doing research that somehow helped in the 'doing' of production; the other was the more general and perhaps less immediately useful goal of understanding human musicality and the way we engage with and interpret music. In short, they are the distinctions we made in Chapter 2. In any particular research project, the goals will lead to the identification of the research questions and that will help to determine the methodology. However, the other determinant of the methodology is the research context: the pre-existing knowledge and understanding about the subject. My argument in this book has been that there is a good deal of pre-existing knowledge and understanding about the nature of human psychology and social and creative activity that is slowly being absorbed into musicology, but that there should be a more systematic approach.

Our understanding of the way groups of people engage with technology – whether that is musicians and their instruments, recordists and their studios or anyone else – needs to be consistent with both our understanding of human psychology and with a clearer understanding of the process they're engaged in. Clarity about the nature of music-making, both live and recorded, is as important as clarity about the way the participants think and behave. In Chapters 4 and 5 I looked at how ideas from the ecological approach to perception and embodied cognition can help us to understand the ways we interpret music and the kinds of schematic mental representations we construct in relation to music and music-making. In Chapters 6 and 7 I looked at how constructionist approaches to the history and sociology of technology can provide a richer understanding of the recording process. In the next two chapters I look at how these two approaches can be integrated to provide a consistent theoretical framework for investigating the complex social and intellectual processes through which recorded music is produced. In fact, I'd go further and suggest that the same framework should be applied across musicology in general.

While, as I've said, the specific methodology for any particular project will depend on the specific goals and research questions, the overall research context suggested by this theoretical framework requires an engagement with four questions.

1. Who and what are the participants involved in the study? By conflating the human and the non-human, this question takes Latour's stance that the socially constructed nature of technological objects means that they should be treated in a similar way to human participants. The human activity inherent in their design and construction means that they embody affordances that are the result of a deliberate process of configuration. For the human participants this may be a simple matter of identifying some specific individuals, or it may involve a more schematic categorisation, such as a social grouping based on roles, gender, class, etc., engagement with a particular musical style or using a particular analytical frame such as Moore's persona (A.F. Moore 2012b).
2. What can be said about the types of knowledge and understanding involved in the study? This may be done at the relatively low level of describing the conceptual models that would be involved, or it may involve a more schematic description such as Csikszentmihalyi's domains and fields (1997) or Bourdieu's notions of cultural and social capital (1986).
3. What can be said about the types of activity involved in the study? Although this may seem to be aimed at production- rather than reception-focused studies, the activities may be cognitive as well as

physical. They may involve the way the participants reconfigure their own conceptual representations as a result of their perception, or they may be about a more active performance of social relationships. And again, they may be discussed in more schematic terms such as Bakhtin's heteroglossia (1982) or Clark's joint action theory (1996).
4. What can be said about the ecology or the environment in which this process is occurring? What types of place and physical conditions are involved, and what types of affordances do they offer?

These are basic questions, but framing them within this theoretical approach provides a clearer set of ways in which they can be tackled. Before I move on there are a few further issues that I want to address.

In relation to actor-network theory (ANT), the question of whether an environment such as a recording studio should actually be considered a designed 'thing' arises. As particular aspects – such as isolation rooms and acoustic treatment – produce affordances, the answer is that they should. Indeed, once we base ANT on ecological perception there is no practical difference between the psychological responses to the environment, things or people. They are all processed according to invariant properties and affordances. Another issue that arises now that we are dealing with collective activity in ANT is notions like power, roles, persuasion and trust. Power structures and roles are determined not only by who wants to configure whom (and in which ways) but also by who is willing to be configured, in which ways and to what extent. All forms of configuration, and therefore power relationships, are negotiated. Persuasion, the creation of trust and any other social activity that involves the exercise of power or concerted activity can be seen as a process of aligning two sets of goals through reconfiguration. There's an explanation of the mechanisms through which that can happen in Chapter 8.

Three additions to the theoretical model are described in the next two chapters and I want to briefly outline how they fit in. The first is Gell's (1998) idea of retentions and protentions as a way to describe the collaborative transfer of knowledge over time. These terms relate to knowledge that is passed down from a previous time period and knowledge that is passed forward to another. These forms of knowledge only exist to the extent that they exert an influence by configuring the mental representations of the current or future users/participants. However, the mechanisms and chronology of transfer and therefore potentially dead and unborn actors may have to be included in the network.

The second is Clark's (1996) joint action theory, which was developed as a way of understanding language as a shared activity. This form of analysis involves searching for phases and dimensions of congruency and discrepancy between participants in an activity. Thus, the various phases, goals, co-ordination devices and roles that are involved in script-based activity are analysed in terms of how the participants align themselves with each other through this kind of shared activity. In short, it can be seen as a way of representing the confluence and disparities between the actors' mental representations of a group activity.

The third of these additions is Goffman's (1956) use of ideas from dramaturgy to examine roles in the social activity of everyday life. Both the adoption and recognition of stereotypical roles is, of course, related strongly both to script-based activity and to the schematic nature of the roles that they involve. Participants can trigger very strong and complex associative meaning by suggesting the activation of a script-based process. These scripts can place us in different roles that change how we feel about ourselves because the highly complex self schema is inflected by cross-domain mapping to whatever we are doing. There is no separate self as such but, by the same token, we are never being exclusively defined by a single role in a single script.

8 | Training, communication and practice

Collaborative activity

Performing social relationships

In 1970 UK rock band the Troggs were recorded arguing in a recording studio. The resulting tape was circulated among recording professionals and musicians and has since even been released on CD, as well as being widely available on the internet. The recording is credited with being the inspiration for a scene in the rock documentary parody *This is Spinal Tap* (Reiner 1984), and this extract from a transcription gives a flavour of the form of communication found throughout the tape (as well as mimicking/mocking the UK West Country accents of the band members):

REG PRESLEY (VOCALS): 'Well, just fuckin' think, then.'

RONNIE BOND (DRUMS): 'Don't just keep saying they're not loud enough. Oi know they're fuckin' right. Oi can hear it ain't right. Weeell, fuck me.'

REG: 'You can hear it is fuckin' not right, too.'

RONNIE: 'Oi fuckin' can, and Oi'm the one that's playing it so Oi don't want to hear ... fuck ... fuck ... in me fuckin' head, that's what Oi gotta fuckin' do, then Oi'll do it. Yer big pranny.'

(Tum-tum-tum-ti-tum, goes the bass guitar. Tum-tum-tum-ti-tum, tum-tum-tum-ti-tum ...)

REG (QUIETLY): 'Fuckin' drummer. Oi shit 'em. Duh duh derh duh duh derh, duh duh derh duh duh derh.'

(Enter the guitar)

REG: 'One, two, a one, two, three, four ... Yer doing it fuckin' wrong!'

RONNIE: 'Oi know Oi am.'

REG: 'Dubba dubba dubba chah, dubba dubba dubba chah, dubba dubba dubba chah, dubba dubba ... You din i' in the beginning. Bloody hell, Oi can't play to tha'.'

RONNIE: 'Nor can fuckin' Oi.'

REG: 'Well, you're fuckin' doin' it!'

RONNIE: 'Well, Oi can't fuckin' play to it either.'

REG: 'Hahahaha. Why don't you just do what you fuckin' started out doing – dubba dubba dubba chah. On your top one, dubba dubba dubba chah. Dubba dubba dubba chah.'

(Snow 2013)

In a 1991 article about the tape we hear from Presley two decades later:

'I wonder', muses Reg Presley, now 47, 'how people take this, because in actual fact it was humorous to us at the time. I wonder whether people think it is serious or what ... We'd been badgered by the record company to go in and record, and at that particular time I had just vague ideas of songs. Normally we'd go into the house of one of the boys, or even use the village hall, and rough them over. That was the procedure. The thing is, that time, we weren't ready to go into the studio. Normally in the Troggs, as they were then, there was miles and miles of arguments until we got what we wanted, but because we hadn't gone through that preliminary stage, the arguments that would probably have happened in the village hall or somebody's room, happened in the studio. It was quite amusing because we were getting nothing down, and I told them before we went in here that it was very doubtful that it would ever happen that way.' (Snow 2013)

Whether or not Presley is rewriting history, the example highlights many of the issues involved in collaborative activity in the studio – what roles the participants were taking on, what kinds of knowledge they had (or needed) and how they communicated and interacted.

Bruno Latour suggests that the social only exists in as much as it is performed (2005, pp. 1–17), in much the same way that Christopher Small (1998) talks of musicking rather than music, and Herbert Clark (1996) describes language as a joint action rather than a thing. All three are concerned with the reification of a process and the problems that thinking of 'the social', 'music' and 'language' as things bring. Similarly, record production is a process rather than a thing, and a process that involves the performance of social relationships, music and language, as well as the process of using technology. The specifics of musical performance in the studio will be addressed in the next chapter but before that I want to look at how record producers and sound engineers work with the technology and each other, and how they learn these skills.

Distributed creativity

In the past few chapters I've described a variety of approaches that academics have developed to analyse creative practice and our engagement with technology. Surely it is now time to nail my colours to the mast and make a stand on which approach I favour. My problem is, though, that I think making such a decision is like asking a carpenter to choose between a saw and a hammer: they are both useful tools but neither is sufficient on its own. More than that, I don't think these analytical tools are incompatible and, in fact, what I'm trying to do in this book is to demonstrate that a particular model of the human mind, based on the ecological theory of perception and embodied cognition, affords an understanding of human social behaviour that can be represented through a variety of different models. I have also said that these models aren't descriptive: they provide schematic representations of the 'messy reality' that allow us to express an ideological position about the importance of certain features in relation to others. Just like any ideological position this is based on evidence, and in this instance the evidence relates to this model of the human mind.

Thus, the systems approach to creativity (Csikszentmihalyi 1997; McIntyre 2012) seeks to represent the way expert activity is performed in terms of the individual working within a cultural domain of procedural and theoretical knowledge and conventions, and a social field that evaluates their creative output in a variety of ways. As a way of developing a broad overview I think this can be a useful model. However, when we're talking about distributed creativity and a group of individuals the model gets more problematic. Each of these individuals will have their own internalised cultural domain built on their experience and knowledge, which in some areas will overlap with those that others have internalised, and in some areas may be unique. And the same goes for the social field. However, the systems model was designed for an overarching view of the cultural domain and the social field, and this kind of fragmentation introduces a whole range of problems, not least being that if the domain and field become representations of the individual's experience of knowledge and judgement, why should we represent them as separate parts of the system?

When we get down to this level of detail about the individuals working together in a system I feel that actor-network theory (ANT) and the social construction of technology (SCOT) provide a better depiction of this type of interaction. We can try to represent the way these participants try to perform the social activity of distributed creativity. However, for me, all these theoretical models need to be understood through the lens of the ecological theory of perception and embodied cognition. Making sense of either the domain and field in a creative system or the ways in which actors perform their social relationships and configure and are configured by the other actors in a network relies on this model of the human mind. The knowledge and judgements in the systems model are determined by the event and person/object schemata of the participants: their conceptual models of scripts, roles, affordances and goals. The social relationships and configuring activities in ANT and SCOT are determined by how their interactions cause the participants to alter or reinforce these conceptual models.

Of course these approaches don't cover all the bases either, but this does provide me with a system for interpreting and evaluating other approaches that ensures an overall theoretical coherence. For example, the idea of retentions and protentions that Georgina Born (2005) borrows from Alfred Gell (1998) provides a useful way of explaining the transmission and creation of a body of processual knowledge within a culture. Gell also characterises collective artistic activity as the 'extended mind', and applies this both to individuals over time and to groups of individuals. In this model, retentions and protentions combine tradition and innovation in various ways to create schools of art, styles, an *oeuvre*, etc. He describes both French conceptual artist, Marcel Duchamp's *oeuvre* and the Maori tradition of meeting house design as examples of the extended mind developing through retention and protention. The metaphor of an extended mind – like those of the triangular system of creativity[1] and the network of actors – provides a useful schematic way of understanding this complex jumble of individual minds and bodies changing over time, which is entirely consistent with the model of perception and cognition.

While Linda T. Kaastra's (2008) application of Clark's (1996) joint action theory to musical performance might seem more relevant to the next chapter, she and others (Arias-Hernandez et al. 2011) have applied it to aircraft maintenance analysis as well, illustrating its potential use in the study of recording practice. In many ways Clark's theory, which was originally developed as a way to understand language as an activity, serves as a bridge between our conceptual model and ANT. He undertakes a detailed analysis of language as a social activity involving shared and individual macro- and micro-level goals; phases of activity and single actions with negotiated entrances and exits; and identified common ground and co-ordination devices between participants. This joint activity occurs along several 'dimensions of variation': scriptedness, formality, verbalness, co-operativeness and governance (Clark 1996, p. 31).

Thus, we could look at the Troggs' tape in terms of both the global goal of turning the germ of an idea into a finished, recorded song and

[1] Csikszentmihalyi represented the systems model graphically with a triangle, in which the individual, their cultural domain and the social field each constituted a corner (1988, p. 329).

the local goal shared by Presley and Bond of getting the drum pattern right. We could look at this as a phase of activity in the creative process that is happening in an inappropriate space for them: the recording studio instead of a rehearsal/pre-production space. And we could examine how co-ordinating devices such as singing or playing parts to each other – normally devices through which musicians like this can develop ideas – seem to be hindered by the talkback process.[2] Dennis Berger, the producer, is present but not participating in this stage of the discussion, despite there having been a discussion a few minutes before about the importance of leadership from a producer. In relation to the dimensions of variation, from the perspective of most producers (and musicians) this process is not following a standard script for studio work, and yet Presley's later commentary suggests that this argumentative process is a standard script for the Troggs, just not in this environment. At the same time as this is apparently a very informal process (judging from the language of the participants), the formality of the setting – an expensive recording studio rather than one of their homes or a village hall – presumably adds a level of stress to the process that is not usually present. With the dimension of verbalness, much of the activity that seeks to achieve the goal is vocal but not verbal: Presley repeatedly sings examples of what he wants the drummer to play. As to the co-operative nature of this activity, while it appears confrontational and antagonistic, Presley does assert that this is their established working method, albeit in a different environment. And finally, the governance: this session occurred after an acrimonious split from their previous producer, Larry Page, who was autocratic but successful. The producer they're working with on this session is unwilling or unable to take control and has ceded the creative leadership to Presley, but Presley seems unable to command sufficient respect from the other band members, despite their seeming acknowledgement of his leadership of the band. Clark's framework provides an intermediate schematic level of representation between the individuals' mental schemata (or Lakoff's idealised cognitive models [1990, pp. 68–76]) and the higher-level descriptions of ANT and SCOT.

Roles in the recording process

Erving Goffman's (1956) application of the notion of dramaturgy to the social activity of everyday life is another such schematic approach that can

2 Presley is in the control room of the studio and Bond is in the live room. Presley is speaking through a talkback microphone, which is fed to Bond's headphones.

be seen to be congruent with this conceptual model. Despite the sexist and xenophobic stereotypes from the 1950s that he often uses as examples, the notion of role-playing and adopting and recognising different characters for different social and professional situations is a useful one. In fact, the notion permeates many of the studies of creative practice found in both record production and performance studies.[3] Performing a particular role also relates back to the notion of heteroglossia: just as individuals have many ways of speaking that relate to different situations, they also have many different roles or characters that they take on in different circumstances.

One of the earliest texts to deal with this issue in relation to recording was Edward Kealy's (1979) article 'From Craft to Art: the Case of Sound Mixers and Popular Music', which is concerned with the development of the role of the sound engineer through the period from the 1950s to the 1970s. Kealy identified three modes of professional practice:

1. The craft/union mode, in which sound recording was considered to be a craft, and training and organization were formulated and controlled by trade union bodies which functioned within the large corporations that owned the majority of recording studios.
2. The entrepreneurial mode, which saw the development of more adventurous techniques and less formal, though still 'on the job', training procedures. This mode was associated with the establishment of small, 'independent' studios in which the engineers were often the owners and were also, at least to some extent, self-taught and/or more prepared to experiment.
3. The art mode, developed out of the work of a few exceptional producers, such as Phil Spector and Joe Meek, who inspired both artists and engineers/producers to consider the application of technology as a creative act.

(1979, pp. 3–29)

Kealy provides a good basic model, especially for the USA and the UK, but there are significant differences between even these two countries. The entrepreneurial mode was much less significant in the UK until after the establishment of the art mode. There may also be good reason for arguing that large record companies awash with money from pop record sales in the late 1960s and early 1970s contributed to the development of art mode techniques through the amount of freedom they gave musicians in the studio. As far as other parts of the world are concerned, many countries bypassed these models almost entirely and remained with the craft/union mode until the introduction of cheap digital technology enabled them to move beyond Kealy's model.

[3] See, for example, Davidson and Good (2002), Bayley (2011) and Burgess (2013).

The main problem with Kealy's model, though, is that he doesn't distinguish between the sound engineer and the record producer. Much of what he describes as the entrepreneurial mode and the art mode are in fact developments in the job of the record producer rather than the 'sound mixer'. In fact, it is hard to justify the idea of clearly defined roles that characterise either job across the board in any given historical period. At the same time as the highly unionised practices were developing in the major record labels' studios, there was also a range of smaller entrepreneurial studios that included both product designers who moved into sound engineering and musicians who came to the job from the opposite direction. In Chapter 6 I described how the maintenance and repair of electronic equipment has become increasingly specialised, and this is a trend that can be seen in the skill set of sound engineers as well. The requirement for sound engineers to be able to maintain, repair and customise the studio's equipment reduced steadily in the latter part of the twentieth century, and this change in the skill set that characterises their role in the studio has led to a similar change in the forms of practice and innovation they engage in. Whereas in the 1960s we see sound engineers thinking about problems in terms of their electrical engineering skills – such as Geoff Emerick rewiring a speaker as a microphone to record a deeper bass sound on the Beatles' 'Paperback Writer' (1966) – in the 1970s and 1980s the innovation focuses more on the use of existing technology, such as the example of 'all buttons in' mode on the Urei 1176 discussed at the start of Chapter 7. Twenty-first-century sound engineers have certainly continued to fix their role more as creative users of technology than as creative manipulators or customisers, and we will return to that shortly. Richard Burgess' typology of producer roles assigns these sorts of attributes as 'subsets of functionality', but they also relate to the technological frame in which a producer develops their skills (2013, pp. 7–26).

The role of the record producer initially developed in isolation from the technology[4] and out of the managerial roles of the record company. The managers of the artist and repertoire (A&R) departments would oversee marketing and distribution of the product as well as the production process: selecting (or delegating the selection of) the music and the musicians, managing the logistics and finances of the recording sessions and being responsible for the overall technical and aesthetic quality of the finished product. As the business of production began to entail larger unit sales of a

[4] Although one could argue that Fred Gaisberg combined the roles of sound engineer and record producer right from the beginning of the acoustic period of recording at the start of the twentieth century.

smaller number of musical products (and subsequently larger unit sales of a larger number of musical products) the process of production tended to become more fragmented and involved more specialised roles – especially in the larger record labels. This led to a wide range of different approaches, not just because of these historical changes but also related to different stylistic developments and the differing needs of different types of artist. In cases where the artist was not the composer, the producer often continued to have a critical role in the selection of repertoire, and more generally in the commercial decisions about who and what were going to be recorded and released.

Thus, in the classical world and with pop artists such as Frank Sinatra and Elvis Presley, the producers continued to perform an editorial and managerial role in the A&R departments of larger labels. With pop artists who wrote their own material producers often doubled as talent scouts, but as the star system developed throughout the twentieth century so too did the range of approaches to record production. For example, the model of the producer as a creative hub who selects artists as vehicles for the producer's own creative projects[5] began with producers such as Mitch Miller in the 1950s and progressed through others such as Joe Meek, Phil Spector, Mickey Most, Trevor Horn and Pete Waterman to Dr. Dre and Fat Boy Slim. This model is also closely related to that of the self-producing artists such as Stevie Wonder, Prince and Mike Oldfield, and the solo dance music producer/artists like Juan Atkins, Derrick May and Ronnie Size. At what might be considered the opposite end of the spectrum are producers such as Phil Ramone, Steve Albini, Walter Legge, Hugh Padgham and Nigel Godrich, who work more as creative enablers, creating the right environment for the artists they produce. Then there are also producers such as John Culshaw, Brian Eno, George Martin, Teo Macero, Tony Visconti and Rick Rubin, who work as creative partners with artists – providing some musical or editorial input of their own and yet not taking over control from the artist.

But these differentiations on the grand scale don't do justice to the complex range of approaches that become apparent on closer inspection. There are myriad forms of collaborative activity that take place in the studio, and the roles producers adopt reflect their personalities and abilities, the personalities and abilities of their collaborators, the goals that have been set and the environment in which the process has to take place. As Goffman points out, members in a team activity need to negotiate the roles they perform not simply in terms of what one member chooses to do but also in respect to

[5] What Virgil Moorefield has described as the 'producer as composer' (2005).

how the other members may choose to 'play along' with that performance and the circumstances of the social situation they find themselves in (1956, pp. 47–65). A producer who wants to take an authoritative leadership position can act in that manner, but it will only work if the other participants are prepared to engage in some form of submission: are prepared to trust in their leadership or have been persuaded to submit to that leadership by some other means.

And, of course, leadership can manifest itself in a variety of forms: aggressive (or just active) authority; a benign or friendly assumption of superiority; the authority of greater experience, expertise or knowledge; various forms of inclusive persuasion; leading by example; and, of course, leading by dint of an externally imposed authority, which in the case of record production is often the financial power of a record company. Certainly, in the more formalised environments of large record companies and/or sessions involving large numbers of participants such as orchestral or big band recordings, a producer needs to accommodate that formality in the role they choose to play. The logistics of large numbers of people in large spaces require the presentation of a different kind of public persona than the intimacy of working with a solo artist. All these forms and levels of formality in leadership are built upon the mutual process of configuration, of aligning goals, scripts and any other relevant mental representations. However, these forms of alignment are only approximate and need only be partial. Just because a producer persuades a backing vocalist to sing a particular line on a recording, it doesn't mean that they have to like it or share any of the producer's other goals for the project.

The process of mixing provides another example of the kinds of social and collaborative practice that require a constant process of configuration and realignment. Just as with the editing process that we'll discuss in the next chapter, there can be a variety of levels of immersion on the part of the different participants. Very often the producer or mix engineer will mix the music without the musicians being present, but when they then play the mix to the artists this can often involve a sudden shift in mental representation from the sound they'd become used to or had been expecting and the actual sound of the final mix. Or, if the musicians present their own mental representations of how the music should sound, it can often result in some version of the Ian Gillan quotation: 'Could we have everything louder than everything else?' (Deep Purple 1972).[6] In any event, the process

[6] Gillan is recorded talking to Deep Purple's live sound man on the *Made in Japan* live album and appears to be jokingly repeating what the sound man has just said to him.

usually involves extensive negotiations between the participants (including the record company executives), during which there is a gradual progress towards some compromise. The mutual configuration process involves a combination of the process of habituation – getting used to it through repeated listening – and an ongoing process of schematic assessment. This will sometimes relate to specific components (e.g. the guitar's not cutting through) and sometimes to more general features (e.g. the low end is too muddy), and the mix engineer's job is to develop a strategy for fixing that problem without creating another one.

Consuming and utilising technology

Over the past century or more, but particularly in the last fifty years, technologies used in the production side of all industries have undergone a process of increasing commercialisation. Whether in the large-scale marketing of barbed wire to farmers in the USA in the last quarter of the nineteenth century or the use of scantily clad women to market power tools to building workers from the 1970s onwards, the trend has been towards converting the process of buyer-led commissioning of customised production machinery into seller-led marketing of standard products: what might be called a trade-off of price for uniformity (or at least a reduction of choice).

As we've seen in Chapter 6, there has been a similar shift in music production technology, from record companies and studios building and maintaining their own equipment to the almost complete commercialisation of these types of production technology. Of course there were always companies supplying technology to others, but not only were there more record companies and studios making their own 'tools', the level of marketing, advertising and other promotional activity to those that didn't was much lower. One pressure that resulted from this shift, as we've already mentioned, was to change sound engineers from manipulators and customisers of technology into selectors of products or presets. At the same time, this same process of consumerisation might also be seen to be freeing up engineers in terms of choice of venue: contemporary technologies are much more portable and modular, and don't necessarily tie recording sessions to traditional studio spaces in the ways that the technology did between around 1930 and 1990. But the problem with making any generalisations like these is that there are always counter examples: life is always messier and more complicated than a series of linear trends. Identifying trends is another form of schematic representation, another indicator of the way our minds work – choosing specific features as more important than others and looking for patterns that help us achieve our goals by providing a useful simplification of the world.

People and technology

Another aspect of schematic representation is the notion of categorisation. This will also be discussed in Chapter 10, but the notion of belonging and identity that is discussed extensively in popular music studies also relates to the feeling of belonging to a skilled or valued profession. I'll discuss later how language can be used to identify and communicate these forms of identity, but the basic principle involves the recognition of some form of cognitive alignment with another individual. We can identify this in terms of a shared technological frame or common aspects of a cultural domain, but the underlying psychological process is one of identifying someone as having similar mental representations of your surroundings – i.e. the same way that humans establish any sense of belonging or identity.

When new students join our courses at the London College of Music it is possible to identify a whole range of features that they use for self-categorisation, which often form the basis for the relationships they start to develop. These can range from nationality, race, gender and class to musical tastes and drinking habits. As the music technology courses unfold it is interesting to see how students often categorise themselves and form groupings on the basis of how they use the equipment – on the technological frame. This can, of course, be strongly aligned to musical taste as well, but it is noticeable that even where that isn't the case students will tend to create easier relationships with people who use and understand the technology in a similar way to them. We are engaged in an incessant process of perceptual learning and categorisation that informs all aspects of our existence. Tribalism seems inherent in the categorical and schematic nature of human thought processes.

Training and learning

Modes of learning

Two modes of learning have remained fairly consistent throughout the history of recording: that of getting access to some equipment and learning through trial and error; and that of observing someone who knows what they are doing, getting them to explain and subsequently copying them.

Indeed, if we allow for those explanations to be both practical and theoretical and to be in either verbal or written form, these two modes cover all forms of training and education on the subject throughout the history of recording. However, the forms of access to the technology and the types of expert knowledge (and the forms of access to that knowledge) are the crucial variables. For the majority of the history of recording, the apprentice system – in various levels of formality – was the principal route of entry and method of knowledge transfer. Disc cutters, tape operators and assistant engineers were trained on the job by existing professionals, sometimes in very formalised settings such as the large studios owned by the major labels. This relates to Kealy's (1979) craft/union mode, but the same process also occurred in more informal one-to-one relationships such as those found in Kealy's entrepreneurial mode. However, at the same time there was also a thriving tradition of the self-taught, and throughout the twentieth century many people – both in the entrepreneurial mode and in a hobbyist setting – transferred skills from experience in the armed forces, the broadcast and telecommunications industries and elsewhere, as well as engaging in formal and informal programmes of learning. This kind of self-taught entry into the industry was often incremental, as in the case of Rudy Van Gelder's gradual move from professional optometrist and hobbyist sound engineer to full-time recordist and mastering engineer between the 1940s and the 1960s (Skea 2001).

The lowering of barriers to entry through cheaper equipment that was simpler to use accelerated during the 1980s, and this created another new mode of learning: the practical use of PC-based systems in conjunction with a plethora of semi-professional and amateur books, magazines and, more recently, websites and internet discussion groups. These changes in the cost of entry have manifested themselves globally, albeit not equally, in different geographical and stylistic markets. Thomas Porcello and Paul Greene's edited collection *Wired for Sound* (2004), concerning the use of music technology around the world, shows that this PC-based change has affected working methods, accessibility and stylistic development across a whole range of musical cultures. My colleague at the London College of Music, Andy East, has observed that Africa was often used as a 'dumping ground' for music technology products that weren't selling in the developed markets in the 1980s.[7] Four-track portastudio tape recorder models that failed to sell in the UK ended up in Nigeria. It would make an interesting ethnographic study to investigate whether specific items of technology

[7] Personal communication, 2004.

influenced the sound of records produced in local markets at particular times, and how this related to this kind of product distribution.

One distinctive difference in the development of record production outside popular music in North America and Europe (particularly the UK) is the relative absence of an art mode until the spread of PC-based systems and the dance music-led cult of the producer. This seems to be true even of South Africa in the 1970s and 1980s, when there was a small, powerful group of producers in the black music sector. Their power was not related to a particular 'sound' or to their artistic manipulation of recording technology, but was based on their ability as talent scouts and promoters.

Thomas Porcello has identified a significant change that began in the 1980s – namely, the shift from apprentice and practice-based learning to formalised post-secondary education (2004, pp. 735–7). Although he is referring to the USA and Canada, the same trend can be seen in the UK and elsewhere in the proliferation of institutions such as the School of Audio Engineering around the world (some forty schools in over twenty countries) and the development of distance-learning schemes such as those offered by the Audio Institute of America. The Audio Engineering Society website[8] also lists courses in thirty countries outside North America and Europe, and the number of degree-level courses with titles such as 'Sound Engineering', 'Music Technology', and 'Sonic Arts' has expanded exponentially since the mid-1990s. This, of course, amounts to a fundamental shift in the nature of the cultural domain and social field, as it alters not only where and how people learn but also what they learn.

What is taught?

Once again, we come face to face with a question of ideology in education and research. Should recording arts/music technology courses in universities be based on the art school/conservatory model or on a more academic and theoretical model? If the former, they are competing with the commercial trade school model of organisations like the School of Audio Engineering. And this trade school model is in danger of training students for a sector of the industry that is relatively small, especially in comparison to the increased numbers of students studying in this area. The improved quality of 'semi-pro' equipment has prompted universities and other organisations offering recording courses to attempt to make a clear demarcation between what they teach and 'bedroom' recording, despite the fact that a significant

[8] See: www.aes.org/education [accessed 8 October 2007].

proportion of commercial product is produced in cheap, PC-based project studios – the 'bedrooms' in question.

If the course is based on the academic/theoretical model then a further question lies in determining the balance between theory and practice. This book is obviously making an ideological statement about the value of theory, but not necessarily about the balance with practice. For me, the problem this book is addressing – as I stated in Chapter 1 – is not that I believe that recording arts and music technology courses in universities should necessarily shift their balance towards theory, but that the theoretical basis currently available is patchy and incoherent. In order to satisfy university requirements for academic rigour, courses often include tangential material as their theoretical content. By theorising a musicology of recording and recorded music I aim to fuel a discourse that has been emerging for several years about how to improve the academic rigour of our discipline. Additionally, the aim is to improve communication between music and music technology/recording by spotlighting the extensive common ground: common ground that is already being mapped by scholars from both sides.

One of the dangers of theorising the content of a practice-based creative activity is exactly the kind of outcome that might be desirable in non-creative forms of practice – homogeneity. This is a frequently cited issue in music performance pedagogy: that by formalising the rules of how one should learn to play the system starts to churn out performers who all think in the same way about performance, and therefore play in the same way. For example, Collier (1994) makes this point about jazz education in the USA. The increased efficiency that a formal system based on solid theory provides means that the overall level of skill goes up, but the greater homogeneity in approach – jazz players learning the same rules about chord/scale relationships, for example – means that the overall level of innovation goes down. The educational system creates an overall increase in centripetal behaviour because the cultural domain is so formalised or, in ANT/SCOT terms, the participants' level of immersion is very deep and thus their propensity for identifying presumptive anomalies is reduced.

Configuring ourselves

By laying the emphasis on teaching rather than learning in the previous section, I am acknowledging (although not acquiescing to) the reversal of Humboldt's[9] philosophy of how a university should be organised:

[9] Wilhelm von Humboldt (1767–1835) was a Prussian philosopher and minister for education, who helped to shape the German and other subsequent university systems.

students learning through research, with lecturers providing supervision. The emphasis on the activity of learning rather than the passivity of being taught is my point. To quote Latour and Woolgar:

> The result of the *construction* of a fact is that it appears unconstructed by anyone; the result of rhetorical *persuasion* in the agnostic field is that participants are convinced that they have not been convinced; the result of *materialisation* is that people can swear that material considerations are only minor components of the 'thought process'; the result of the investments of credibility, is that participants can claim that the economics and beliefs are in no way related to the solidity of science; as to the *circumstances* they simply vanish from accounts, being better left to political analysis than to an appreciation of the hard and solid world of facts! Although it is unclear whether this type of inversion is peculiar to science, it is so important that we have devoted much of our argument to specifying and describing the moment at which inversion occurs. (1986, p. 284)

One of the criticisms levelled at ANT by those in the SCOT camp is that the notion of configuration places the agency all on one side: the person whose activity is curtailed or whose mind is changed is a passive recipient. As I will lay out more fully in the last section in this chapter, I see configuration as a two-way street. In order to believe a fact, we have to actively engage with it and not simply be told it. In Latour and Woolgar's example above, the reason that participants may be 'convinced that they have not been convinced' is that for the process of configuration to take place, they have to actively adopt the idea. In order for configuration to work we have to be offered the affordance of it and then configure ourselves by choice.

Relationships and power structures

For me, one of the problems with the writing on power relationships that I have encountered is that it tends towards one of two ideological positions. Either human nature is such that everyone is involved in a struggle for power or we are essentially collaborative and power structures are somehow a distortion of nature. I don't think that psychology (or evolution) is as simplistic as that. There may well be some basic urges that affect and, in some instances, determine our thoughts and behaviour, but domination and submission – the building blocks of power – are far too complex to be the subject of basic urges. My position relates back to the idea of immersion and the identification of presumptive anomalies, but applies this at the psychological rather than sociological level. At any point where I recognise a discontinuity between my goals or interpretation of some aspect of the world and someone else's, there is the potential for conflict. This may involve my wanting them to do one thing and their wanting to do another, their believing one thing and my believing another, etc. Depending on my level of immersion in this discontinuity, I may decide that I have no option but to attempt to configure their mental representation of the situation to conform to mine, or I may identify a presumptive anomaly: an alternative interpretation of the world on my part that no longer requires them to share my opinion. That alternative interpretation may be as simple as: I don't care enough about their opinion to try and change it, or may be something like: I don't think I can configure their opinion/goal with the resources currently at my disposal so I will develop an alternative strategy. In practical terms, I can choose to try to configure them, to allow them to configure me or to try to avoid the discontinuity somehow.

Configuring each other

I'm going to talk about the specific methods we can use to configure others in the last section in this chapter on communication and language, but for the moment I'm going to talk about the general mechanism. One key feature of that general mechanism is the theoretical model I'm using of the cognitive structures for representing knowledge. On the very basic level, as we have already discussed, interpretation works on an empathic level: I see an arm rise and I interpret it by running, but not completing, the cognitive motor action that would raise my own arm. On the next level are representational entities called image schemata (see, for example, Feldman 2008, pp. 137–44), which are cognitive structures that represent some kind of relationship we can have involving ourselves and the environment. I may have a containment/container schema, which I understand on a basic embodied level ('in me'/'outside me'), but which I can generalise to other objects through empathy and metaphor. Once again, for me, the precise nature of the neural activity that results in these scripts and schemata is not important. They are schematic concepts that explain some important aspects of the nature and functionality of thought without purporting to be a complete description of the physical mechanism. However, it is worth outlining some of the ideas that are current in this field of study.

Feldman has proposed a further level within the application of embodied cognition in linguistics: the frame, the cognitive representation of a coherent scenario that involves features and values (2008, pp. 145–8). Thus, I might have a 'performance' frame, where the features are performer, activity, venue and audience, and into which I may add the values 'Jane', 'plays guitar', 'park' and 'her friends' to use that frame. Frames can be strung together into longer, more complex scenarios known as scripts. These are a mental equivalent of an instruction manual or flow diagram of various frames, which allows us to understand and navigate frequently encountered activities. Returning to the simple motor actions and the way they may be formed into frames, a collection of motor activities, for example, would move my body from a standing position to a sitting position. This frame would require a sitter and a thing to be sat on as features. In fact, further than this, and bringing us into line with ecological perception, our mental representation of a chair itself would be defined in terms of the affordance of sitting. In general, this theory of embodied cognition and ecological perception defines all nouns in terms of the affordance they offer for literal or metaphorical activity. The further we get from basic level categories like 'chair' towards superordinate categories like 'furniture', the less specific and more schematic the affordances become.

The way these cognitive structures relate to configuration lies in the fact that they are never static. We are constantly checking the appropriateness of these 'idealised cognitive models' (Lakoff 1990, pp. 68–76) against our interpretation of the world and revising where necessary. Thus, when I'm recording a track I may have a model of the song, a model of the process and models for the various people, things and places involved. If I'm working, for example, with a mixing desk I'm unfamiliar with, I will gradually alter my conceptual model of that desk to create something that encompasses the increased level of detail that I come to possess, along with, perhaps, some likes and dislikes. To bring this around to the notion of power relationships again, exercising some level of control over the configuration of other people's cognitive models of the world is to exercise power. Those cognitive models will involve their goals, their expectations, their understanding of a situation, etc.

Porcello has referred to the way in which engineers seek to retain exclusivity in their profession through the development and use of specialised language (2004, pp. 47–9). The vocabulary and correct use of technical language has the dual function of making communication between experts more accurate and efficient and of identifying the user as an expert, acting as a defining characteristic of the members of the expert community. In terms of our theoretical model, the technical language allows the experts to configure and be configured more accurately and efficiently, but it also acts as a defining characteristic that can be associated with the cognitive representations of the various participants to mark them out as expert or non-expert.

Porcello has also pointed to a sharp divide between industry professionals who trained via the 'apprentice' system and those who have progressed through formalised post-secondary education, an observation I am sure anyone involved in the recording industry since about the mid-1990s would corroborate. I think that it is generally perceived on both sides of this divide that the 'old school' of work-based/experiential learning is a more 'authentic' method of acquiring knowledge. However, this may be the result of record companies selecting engineers and producers on the basis of track record rather than qualifications or other measures of perceived technical/artistic knowledge. Here, the detail of the configuration becomes more complex. The record company executives adjust their mental representations of the engineers and producers based on the relatively passive activity of reading or hearing about their track record, and they exercise their power by configuring the engineers and producers to work for them by offering money. The more complicated power interaction involves the tendency among the university-educated professionals to value their own qualifications less than experience in the world of work. Of course, this is logical in many ways, especially if they're not getting work and more experienced professionals are, but what of the cases when the opposite is true? These types of configuration can result in many seemingly illogical power relationships relating to prestige and deference that are only partly associated with the hard facts of a track record. In this instance, I think it is most useful to swap theoretical frameworks again and to return to the idea of different forms of capital.

Types of capital

For me, Bourdieu's (1986) theory of cultural production is problematic because it assumes that competition is the natural and sole motivation. However, I do think that the notion of different types of capital serving to inform social power structures is useful. Those with the economic capital to pay for the production process (let us say a record company) give authority to an agent (let us say a producer) because the producer's social, cultural and symbolic capital endow them with perceived value (the ability to create valuable products). Their social capital will be their position in the industry, their cultural capital will be the perceived expert knowledge they possess and their symbolic capital will be any more ephemeral prestige that may accrue from phenomena such as press coverage or industry gossip. Within the group of participants, particular forms of cultural capital such as instrumental and technical skills and experience will provide them with various levels of authority at various points in the process, which will mean that they are likely to be deferred to. Of course, the problem is that cultural capital doesn't come with the same kind of bank statement as economic capital, and its subjective nature means that the participants may disagree about the hierarchy.

Communication and language

Methods of configuration

If the process of configuration occurs through the alteration of a person's conceptual model of a phenomenon, the next aspect of this process that needs explaining is the various methods through which this can occur. While individuals may alter their own conceptual models based on experience, the most common way for this to happen is through some form of social activity or interaction. These are types of interaction that configure another actor by persuading them to alter some aspect of their conceptual model – either by changing it or adding to it, to make it more complex or nuanced. This can be direct configuration by a co-present actor or indirect configuration through a medium. The types of conceptual models that can be altered may involve the establishment or disestablishment of groupings or roles, the nature of a person's role or the nature of a process, thing or place. Given these definitions, the following is a provisional list of the methods through which one participant may configure another.

1. Suggest or invite the creation or reinforcement of a grouping or role between actors.
2. Reinforce a tentative or ambiguous aspect of the recipient's existing model.
3. Demonstrate – provide an example of activity that conflicts with some aspect of the recipient's model of a process.
4. Provide information that conflicts with some aspect of the recipient's model.
5. Suggest a narrative – by describing an event, person or thing in a way that involves a model of a process that differs from the one the recipient currently holds.
6. Exert physical control – this could be between human actors or could involve the design/physical structure of an object configuring an actor's behaviour or altering some aspect of their model.
7. Contradict some aspect of the recipient's existing model.
8. Give an instruction that causes the recipient to alter some aspect of their existing model.

As I've said, each of these forms of configuration, with the occasional exception of the sixth,[10] involves a social performance. One person engages in an act designed to configure another and the other decides whether to alter their existing mental model accordingly. Of course, the alteration may not be exactly or entirely what the configurer had in mind. That may be because the recipient didn't understand fully what the other had in mind or it may be because they choose to only partially go along with the configuration process.

It should also be remembered that language isn't the only form of communication that can be used in the process of configuration. The following is a provisional list of the possible types of communication:

1. language style of the spoken word;
2. musical sound (e.g. it might demonstrate the tonality or rhythm);
3. sound (timbre);
4. tone of voice;
5. passive/unconscious body language;
6. active gesture or movement;
7. language style of the written word;
8. other visual symbols (e.g. on a computer screen or music notation);
9. moving images.

These modes of communication may be employed in various combinations, consciously or unconsciously, in any of the processes mentioned above.

Talking about sound and talking about music

Of course, a lot of communication and configuration about sound and music in the studio happens through language, and the language of sound engineers and the language of musicians can sometimes not share common ground. Tom Porcello has provided a taxonomy of five categories of ways of talking about sound that he has identified:

1. singing/vocables: mimicry of the timbral and resonance characteristics of the musical sounds with one's voice;

[10] Physical control can work in two different ways. One the one hand, the person who is physically forced to act in a particular way may choose to change their mental model because of the experience that forced activity provides them with. On the other, it may be a case, for example, of wanting someone in a room and pushing them into it: a simple and direct form of configuration, albeit a brutal one.

2. lexical onomatopoesis: words that bear at least a partial acoustic resemblance to the sounds they describe, but which are simultaneously metaphors that more abstractly describe the sounds – words such as 'boomy';
3. 'pure' metaphor: words used to describe timbral characteristics, but which do not bear any acoustic similarity to the sound in question – words such as 'smooth';
4. association: citing other musicians, recordings, sounds, time periods and so forth, in a search for a common frame of reference;
5. evaluation: using value judgements to signify an agreement on sonic goals, on attitudes toward musical technologies and therein, a common ability to work cooperatively.

(2004, pp. 746–7)

Other aspects of communication

There are two further aspects of communication that I want to discuss here. The first relates to the function of the intermediary. In many hierarchical situations of work an intermediary will act to rephrase communication in more appropriate language or a more appropriate level of detail. At the level of the producer, Mike Howlett – a producer as well as an academic – has described this role as a point of nexus between the technicians, the musicians and the record company (2009). This may involve rephrasing communications from one set of participants to another to make them more understandable or more acceptable (or more or less specific), or translating from one mode of conceptualisation to another – for example, from a sonic concept to a performative one. Thus, the engineer might suggest that a sound is too bright and the producer might translate that to the musician as a suggestion to move back from the microphone or play with a rounder tone.

The second aspect refers to a more nuanced feature of Bakhtin's heteroglossia (1982): the notion that individuals negotiate the world through assuming different forms of language in different social situations. We've already mentioned this briefly in relation to the technical language that experts can use to streamline technical communication and to mark themselves out as experts. And in terms of the configuration process, forms of language, turns of phrase and tone of voice can let you speak with multiple voices to help establish who you are talking to and what kind of communication is going on.

9 Performance in the studio

A conflict of interests

'Is that what we did?'

In an interview about producing Miles Davis' album *Bitches Brew* (Davis 1970), Teo Macero said:

I don't think he was aware what really went on in the editing. Because a lot of musicians used to tell me, they would hear this stuff on the radio and they would say, 'Who the hell is that?' And somebody would say, 'Well that was Miles' last record.' The guy says, 'I was on that record. Is that what we did? Is that what we did?' [Laughs.] I mean, some of them wouldn't even recognize the material.[1]

Paul Tingen provides a more explicit account of Macero's creative agency:

Enrico Merlin's research, as well as the 1998 release of the four-CD boxed set *The Complete Bitches Brew Sessions*, have cast important new light on the album's post-production process. They show how Macero did not only use tape editing to glue together large musical sections, as on 'Circle in the Round' or 'In a Silent Way', but extended his scope to editing tiny musical segments to create brand-new musical themes. Courtesy of both approaches, 'Pharaoh's Dance' contains an astonishing seventeen edits. Its famous stop-start opening theme was entirely constructed during postproduction, using repeat loops of 15- and 31-second fragments of tape, while thematic micro-edits occur between 8:53 and 9:00 where a one-second-long fragment appearing at 8:39 is repeated five times.

'I had carte blanche to work with the material,' Macero explained. 'I could move anything around and what I would do is record everything, right from beginning to end, mix it all down and then take all those tapes back to the editing room and listen to them and say: 'This is a good little piece here, this matches with that, put this here,' etc., and then add in all the effects – the electronics, the delays and overlays. [I would] be working it out in the studio and take it back and re-edit it – front to back, back to front and the middle somewhere else and make it into a piece. I was a madman in the engineering room. Right after I'd put it together I'd send it to Miles and ask, "How do you like it?" And he used to say, "That's fine," or "That's OK,"

[1] See: www.youtube.com/watch?v=_UOzvRmEE [accessed 9 March 2014].

> or "I thought you'd do that." He never saw the work that had to be done on those tapes. I'd have to work on those tapes for four or five weeks to make them sound right.' (Tingen 2001a)

And of course the album, with these formal structures that Macero had constructed in the editing room, then became the template for the live performance of these pieces: Macero's edits became the 'work'. This demonstrates Macero's and Davis' understanding of two important issues that characterise the differences between concerts and recordings. First, that the musicians had a way of working that afforded them the right mental space to get the best performances out of them. But second, that the types of performances that this way of working elicited weren't 'right' in some way for release as recordings: they needed more structure and shaping to work with repeated listening as opposed to the one-off experience of the concert. This is one of the forms of conflict of interest that this section's title refers to, but there are others.

Throughout my time as a sound engineer and record producer in the 1980s and 1990s I was aware of the constant negotiation between performance practice and recording practice in decisions about the recording process. There often seemed to be several points of conflict between factors that musicians consider to be conducive to achieving a good performance and those that sound engineers regard as desirable or even necessary for obtaining a recording that meets the technical and aesthetic standards of contemporary recording practice. One underlying problem rests in the principally communal practice of musical performance and the desirability of isolating sound sources from each other in the recording process. The desirability of isolation stems from the use of multiple microphone techniques and the aesthetics of the 'artificial' staging of performances in a virtual environment that was discussed in Chapter 5.

The way these conflicts of interest are resolved is related to the balance of power as far as the symbolic, cultural, social and economic capital of the participants are concerned, but also to the ascription of value or authenticity by the participants and the perceived potential audience (see Chapter 10) – to the forms of creativity and/or technical quality that these interests would supply. In terms of the systems approach to creativity, the musicians and technicians have to reconcile two differing social fields that judge the products of their labour using different criteria. This, though, is a place where Csikszentmihalyi's (1997) notion of a social field and a cultural domain seem to provide too static and compartmentalised a model. There isn't a mechanism in this model for examining the interaction between two or more individuals who have different perceptions of which rules should be applied and how the output will be judged. An ANT model, on the other hand, attempts to model the participants' internal representations of these things and to explore how they aim at and, in some cases, succeed in configuring each other. In any given recording situation, each of the participants will have a different view of what constitutes good, authentic, professional or in some other way appropriate behaviour or practice. They will have different goals relating to that activity and to the eventual recorded output, and they will have different forms and amounts of power to influence the overall running of the process. In short, there is a huge range of potential negotiating positions that can exist in any recording session, and the way the participants interact to configure both the process and the final output is equally complex.

Scripts and goals again

In Chapter 7 I quoted Bob Olhsson as saying 'Sgt. Pepper's is not a recording, Sgt. Pepper's was the solution to the various problems they came up with in the process of producing the record' (Stevenson 2002). This notion of recording as a problem-solving process leads to the twin questions of what are the goals of the process and what are the strategies for achieving them? Of course, each of the participants will have their own set of goals and their own strategy, and hence a potential plan that would afford the achievement of those goals. At whatever level of complexity they may occur, our mental structures involve the connection of perceptual invariants with the affordance of activity. In some very basic instances the term 'activity' needs to be understood in a very general sense. This might, for example, mean an activity that results in the release of dopamine in the brain or the process of digestion. While we think of goals generally in terms of states (e.g. my goal is to change my state from hunger to satiation), the perceptual and cognitive model we're using suggests that the brain's representation of states should be conceived in terms of action and the affordance of action. In these terms, the cognitive model of a goal can be viewed as the action at the end of some previously experienced script, remembering that the script will be for a schematic rather than a specific activity. Matching the affordances of our current situation with some series of scripts that will, according to the associative connections we've made through our experience, allow us to activate the goal script is the planning process for achieving goals. The social performance of collaborative creativity involves the various participants aligning these types of plans and goals in some way. That doesn't mean they have the same goals but it does mean that whatever activity is planned and undertaken stimulates the perception by each individual of affordances that are in accordance with each of their individual plans, the scripts of which they are comprised and the goals they are intended to achieve.

Returning to the example of Miles Davis and Teo Macero, we can use what evidence we have to hypothesise about their personal goals and the way they coincided. In his autobiography, when describing the making of either *In a Silent Way* or *Bitches Brew*, Davis doesn't mention the editing process at all (1990, pp. 286–90). When talking about Macero's involvement in the latter he says: 'I had told Teo Macero . . . to just let the tapes run and get everything we played . . . Just stay in the booth and worry about getting down the sound' (Davis 1990, p. 289). Davis was at this time becoming steeped in the culture of rock music and spent time discussing music with his friend Jimi Hendrix (Davis 1990, pp. 281–3), who had been experimenting with the creative possibilities of the recording process. For the *In a Silent Way* album (Davis 1969), Macero says:

> When we began editing *In a Silent Way* we had two huge stacks of 2" tape, 40-something reels in total. They were recorded over a longer period. It was one of the rare times Miles came to an editing session, because I'd told him, 'This is a big job, you want to get your ass down here.' So Miles said, 'We'll do it together.' And we did. We cut things down to 8½ minutes on one LP side, and 9½ on the other, and then he said to me, 'That's my record.' I said, 'Go to hell!' because it wasn't enough music for an album. So I ended up creating repeats to make it longer. (Tingen 2001b)

This seems to have got Davis thinking about the creative possibilities of recording, because on *Bitches Brew* he records in quite a fragmented way that is obviously designed with the editing process in mind. He says 'recording was a development of the creative process, a living composition' (Davis 1990, p. 289). Both men had, therefore, developed a mental representation of the kind of album and the kind of creative process needed to achieve it. Their individual goals involved an elaboration of their own role from the practice that had emerged out of *In a Silent Way*. Davis had, perhaps also as a result of conversations with Hendrix, decided to explore the creative possibilities of overdubbing onto eight-track but, more importantly, had seen that he could record improvisations in a non-linear manner, stopping and starting, and creating a richer and more carefully thought out set of raw materials for the editing process. Macero, partly as a result of having to extend Davis' edits for *In a Silent Way* with repeats, had developed the idea of creating musical structure through the editing process. Macero (2004), as we've seen, described himself as having 'carte blanche to work on the material' but Ray Moore, the mix and editing engineer he worked with, does describe a few instances when Davis was present and involved in the editing process (Tingen 2001b). Nevertheless, there is obviously substantial creative input from Macero, and the resulting album allowed both men to achieve their goals for both the musical output and for the development of their creative practice.

Frederick Moehn's (2005) description of the changes in recording practice for the annual *Sambas de Enredo* CD that accompanies the Rio de Janeiro Carnival offers another example. In 1999 the producers of the album decided to record the percussion tracks in the Company of Technicians Studio instead of the large circus tent that had been used previously. This involved separating out some of the musicians into isolation booths away from the main room and using headphones. Aside from saving money by employing fewer musicians, this change was instigated by the executive producer and the chief sound engineer 'in order to arrive at a cleaner sound' (Moehn 2005, p. 62). The key driver for this goal of a cleaner sound was itself a change in the broader goal of which audience they were targeting, or perhaps a change in what they perceived the audience wanted from the record. Instead of the rather indistinct sound of a large ensemble that conjured up the atmosphere of the live carnival event, they were aiming to create something that would work on the dance floor – where the rhythmic clarity of the recording would feel right for dancers in a club environment. These changed goals required a changed script, and one that clashed with the notions of performance integrity and group coherence (and differentiation) that were held by the performers in the various samba schools who were competing in the carnival. These performers, in order to achieve their higher goal of creating a recording, had to abandon their goal of creating it in a particular way and go along with the producers.

A contrasting example is described by Beverley Diamond with regard to the Wallace family's recording of their CD *Tzo'kam* (The Wallace Family 2000) in four different studios (2005, p. 123) – the result of their not feeling that the recording process captured the spirit of their performance. In the first studio the drum was in a separate room from the vocals; in the second the singers were separated in different rooms and overdubs were added; in the third they were all in one room with separate microphones; and in the last they performed as they do live but with a single overhead microphone. Russell Wallace performed on and produced the album and describes the changes in terms of seeking a greater comfort level with the performance arrangements, or what Diamond describes as the 'social space of the studio' (2005, p. 126). The choices made are seen as key to getting the right performances from the musicians and as specific to this genre of music. The goals and scripts of the recording engineers in the first three studios were at odds with the goals and scripts of the musicians, but instead of discovering the nature of the problem, the musicians (and the producer) acquiesced and adapted their creative practice to accommodate the technical practice. This illustrates an ideological standpoint that is, perhaps, becoming less prevalent in recent years but is also found in Louise Meintjes' chapter in the same collection (2005): that recording practice, perhaps because of its recourse to science, trumps musical performance practice. Of course, this is also related to the power that different participants have for other reasons, but there can be a sense that the musicians have to accommodate the technology rather than the other way around because the technical practice is scientific and that therefore there is a single, valid way of employing it to produce the 'best' results.

When I was recording jazz albums in London in the late 1980s and early 1990s I took part in many similar negotiations. The musicians had an idea of how they wanted the recording to sound, and typically that required a significant amount of separation; yet they wanted to play in an environment that afforded as much interaction as possible. Factors such as the instrumentation, repertoire and playing styles all contributed to the decision-making process. For example, the studio had a separate isolation booth for drums and a very small booth designed for vocals. The piano was in the main room and was usually screened off from the double bass in the same space. With quartets, the saxophone or trumpet would sometimes perform in the vocal booth and have artificial ambience added. Louder players – and often tenor sax rather than alto players – would frequently dislike the 'feel' of playing in the booth, and we would organise another screened-off area in the main room. Although this usually gave a less satisfactory audio quality, it was accepted as the 'price' of getting the right performance from the player. With quieter drummers the decision was regularly made to leave the door of the isolation booth partly open to improve the line of sight between the drummer and the bass player. In contrast to our previous examples, this represents the continuum of approaches that lies in between the two extremes of either the producer/engineer making all the decisions on technical grounds or the musicians making them on performance grounds. The participants prioritise their sub-goals about how they would like the recording session to proceed and decide upon a strategy and thence a script that reflects this negotiation about the relative importance of different goals.

There is a further complication in that not all the goals that a performer or a technician might have are necessarily going to relate unselfishly to the optimum realisation of whatever recording project they happen to be currently working on. Their notions about their own professional integrity or about the multitudinous ways in which recorded musical sound and performance practice can be seen to be authentic,[2] or goals that relate to their broader professional careers or even that relate to unmusical or unprofessional issues, can all create pressures that influence the recording process and the resulting recorded output. To return to Miles Davis, his heroin addiction resulted in both the creation and destruction of a range of musical relationships that affected the large-scale arc of his musical development, but it must also have affected the day-to-day running of recording sessions by forcing everyone to revise their goals and scripts in relation to his addiction.[3]

People and music

One of the many issues that have emerged out of the development of recording technology is the difference between the many-sided and collaborative process of playing music with other people and the one-sided but nevertheless participatory process of playing along to some music. When musicians are engaged in co-present performance, despite the fact that one person may be leading and the others following or that one may be a soloist to others' accompaniment, there is always an element of mutual attention and accommodation. With the development of overdubbing in recorded music, those who record first don't have the benefit of being able to adjust their performance in response to those who record after, and those who record their part to a pre-recorded backing must follow that lead without any response that might accommodate the dynamic, timbral, rhythmic or tempo inflections they bring to the piece. On the other hand, they have the opportunity to listen to the detail of the performance they are about to play to in advance, and to structure their performance accordingly. Of course, although there is no more inherent advantage or value in either method, a great many forms of value judgement can be ascribed to either. If we are tempted to valorise co-present musical performance as more natural because it predates the other form and involves less technology, it should be remembered that the same argument would suggest that medical practice was better and more natural before the invention of anaesthetics or antibiotics.

[2] See A.F. Moore (2002) for a good summary of ideas about authenticity.

[3] See Davis (1990) for extensive descriptions of how his addiction affected his musical life.

Nevertheless, there tends to be more variation in preference when it comes to performance practice than there is in the use of anaesthetic.

While there are certain generic preferences that may relate to factors such as tradition being favoured over modernity or improvisation and interaction being favoured over adherence to a template of some kind, individual players also choose to engage with recording technology in different ways. In genres where a creative engagement with recording technology is less common, such as classical music and jazz, we still find figures such as Glenn Gould, Leopold Stokowski and Miles Davis using techniques that others in their field characterise as somehow inauthentic. In genres where the opposite is true, such as pop and rock music, we find artists such as the Rolling Stones and the Kings of Leon, who prefer to record in co-present single takes where possible.[4] Once again, I am using examples from opposing ends of a continuum to make the point. While the majority of performers tend to take less extreme standpoints, albeit in relation to the norms of their musical tradition, they are by no means uniform in their preferences. It should, therefore, be borne in mind that conflicts of interest about performance practice in the studio are by no means confined to those between musicians and technicians. They can equally well arise between musicians who have different approaches to how performance practice may need to be altered to accommodate the differing requirements of the concert hall and the recording studio. As we've seen, though, resolving conflicts of interest isn't always about having shared goals. It can be just as much about different participants having different goals that don't conflict.

Before I move away from this idea, there is also the matter of musicians playing along with machines. This may be more commonplace in popular music forms but it certainly also exists in the electroacoustic repertoire of Western art music, among jazz players who have fused jazz with aspects of electronic dance music styles and in world beat styles that do the same with other musical traditions. However, the ubiquitous use of machine-accurate tempi in popular music forms has also led to the interesting phenomenon of pop and rock drummers playing their parts to a click track: an agent-like aspect of technology that not only configures the drummer but, by default, becomes the 'leader' of the entire ensemble. In a recent online conference

[4] Although both bands tended to overdub the lead vocals when they have recorded in this way, and both bands have made recordings using more extensive overdubbing techniques. Nonetheless, their recording practice is unusual in the recent history of rock music in being so grounded in live performance.

Paul Théberge summarised a discussion on the use of click tracks in rhythm section recordings as follows:

> I especially like Anne's characterization [Anne Danielsen in a previous post] of the groove as a set of layers, the click being just one possible layer. For me (and as Anne also suggests) the precision afforded by the click is also a kind of 'feel' – a feel that may be more suited to some genres than others. But what is also interesting to me is the way in which the click itself is, ultimately, a layer that is later removed from the sounding groove and only manifests itself in the structuring impact it has had on other layers.
>
> This places the click within the multi-tracking process as a temporarily sounding, structuring element. The click is not unique in this role – it is a role that's not unlike that of the vocal guide track . . . In most sessions, the guide track is typically removed and replaced by a permanent, more nuanced vocal . . . In case[s] like this, the performance of the rhythm section is, in part, based around the members' response to a musical layer that is not present as part of the final musical texture; and in its turn, the final, sounding vocal may change in response to the layer contributed by the rhythm section (and other players). So perhaps multi-tracking can be thought of as a structuring process that employs both sound (recorded) and silent/silenced (unrecorded) elements.
>
> To some degree, every contributor to a multi-track session works within the realm of the virtual – they can only imagine what the rest of the track will eventually sound like.[5]

This certainly situates the click track in the realm of a non-human agent in actor-network theory (ANT) or as a technology whose design and use configures its human user. To use another example from my experience as a sound engineer, when a drummer was having difficulty getting the right feel when playing to a click track, altering the sound of the click or using a loop of a percussion sample would generally make them play differently. I've also come across drummers with very strong preferences about the timbre of the sounds used, whether and how the first beat of the bar is accentuated by a click and what the subdivision of a click track should be. If we also take into account the active, multi-modal nature of perception and the potential for combined visual and auditory stimuli, there is a multitude of ways in

[5] Taken from a post by Paul Théberge in May 2013 called 'Silent Structuring' in a stream on rhythm sections in the studio in the online conference on Performance in the Studio. Available at: www.artofrecordproduction.com/index.php/people/rhythm-sections [accessed 11 June 2013].

which performance can be influenced and configured by the technologies of machine synchronisation.

Comfort, hearing and atmosphere

The way in which a performer engages with the recording technology is only part of the story. Performers often describe recording sessions in ways that are more reminiscent of rehearsals than of performances: fragmented, repetitive and boring, rather than the comparatively short and intensive experience of the concert performance. If that is the case, what does it do to the way a performer reacts to that intensive energy? Alternatively, performers have also described the debilitating 'red light fear' of knowing that a performance will become fixed by the recording process.[6] In this way, one aspect of the producer's job is to find the right balance for each performer between helping them to relax and thus avoiding this 'red light fear' and generating the kind of excitement and energy they might normally experience in concert, which might help stimulate that special performance.

Getting comfortable

Mike Howlett has described how, when recording Joan Armatrading, they would create an emotionally comfortable space for her in the studio by enclosing her vocal microphone using screens covered with her own fabrics or carpets and creating atmospheric lighting with candles.[7] This idea of creating the impression of a safe environment for a performer in which they can more comfortably express their emotions can also be seen in the way recording studio design has moved from the semi-industrial spaces of the 1950s and 1960s into the much more comfortable and relaxing spaces of the 1970s and 1980s. It can also be seen reflected in the fact that artists and record companies were prepared to spend the money on recording in places such as George Martin's Associated Independent Recording (AIR) studios on the Caribbean island of Montserrat: an idyllic and relaxing environment, but one that required a three thousand mile round trip to fly in spare parts for the recording equipment.

[6] Terence Curran wrote and presented a documentary on this for BBC Radio 4 called *Performing to the Red Light*, which was broadcast in June 2009.
[7] Personal communication with the author, December 2012.

As we've already discussed, there are no fixed rules but musicians often favour working in the same space, at the same time, with good lines of sight for communication and a live acoustic in the space so that they can clearly see and hear the rest of the ensemble and react to them. The technician's desire for separation and isolation in the recording process has developed a practice that works in more or less direct opposition to these preferences. If musicians are playing in the same space and time on a recording, they are often screened off from each other to reduce spillage from one microphone to another. This not only compromises their visual communication but will also reduce their ability to hear the rest of the ensemble clearly. The use of headphones obviously solves this problem, but often at the expense of the musicians' feeling of connection with one another and always by creating a different kind of sound world mediated by microphones.[8] Screens are not always considered to provide a sufficient level of isolation, especially when loud instruments such as kit drums are involved. Musicians are therefore frequently placed in different rooms, making communication less direct, even when glass partitions are used. Multi-track tape recording has extended the possibilities for isolation by allowing musicians to record at different times: this removes the possibility not only of visual communication but also, as we've already discussed, of two-way interaction in the performances. Negotiations between ensuring the comfort of the musicians and creating the right atmosphere for them to stimulate the desired performance on the one hand, and using recording techniques that provide separation on the other, are found in all genres of music and involve many different forms of compromise.

Paul Tingen's (1994) description of the ways in which Daniel Lanois affected the working practices of U2 when producing *The Unforgettable Fire* (1984) and *Achtung Baby* (1991) shows that this negotiation is not confined to genres in which recording is generally restricted to capturing a single live performance. Although Lanois encouraged the band to record as an ensemble, he also extended to other areas of recording practice this desire for getting the right atmosphere so that the musicians could produce the desired performances. The chosen venues were not recording studios at all but a castle and a rented house by the sea in Ireland, into which mobile recording equipment was installed. Lanois was thus prepared from the outset to sacrifice audio quality and ignore the conventions of recording practice in order to achieve the right performances. This extended to the use of amplified monitoring instead of headphones, recording in the control

[8] See A. Williams (2012) for a more detailed discussion of this.

room with the producer and the sound engineer rather than in a separate studio room, and generally allowing the recording process to take second place to the creative processes of composition and performance.

Getting excited

Producers also have to engage in the opposite kind of activity: of encouraging excitement and energy in a performer in what can be the tedious, mundane and even industrial or office-like atmosphere of the studio. An example of this can be seen in the video of producer Bob Rock upbraiding Metallica's guitarist Kirk Hammett by denigrating a solo he's just played and asking: 'Where's the fucking guitar player of the year solo?'[9] Hammett then 'digs deeply' [sic] and plays the solo that ends up on the album, seemingly in response to this taunt. Of course the precise veracity of the story can't be established, and the scene in the video is constructed from a collage of documentary footage from the session, specially filmed retrospective analysis, commentary and a reconstructed performance of the solo mixed with live footage of Hammett playing the solo on tour.

Producer Robin Millar provided a less mediated but no less unverifiable example of his approach to encouraging energy and excitement in a performance in a description he gave in a lecture at the London College of Music in October 2010.[10] Millar described how he would often go into the performance space with the vocalist and would stand next to them, providing vocal encouragement in between the lines as they sang them: generating energy by speaking excitedly into their ear as they performed. Another example is that of Norman Whitfield, one of the Motown producers, on working with Marvin Gaye on 'I Heard it Through the Grapevine' (1969). Whitfield had the arrangement of the track recorded in a key that put it right at the upper end of Gaye's vocal range to force him into the kind of physical exertion that gave his vocal timbre an edge that reinforced the angst-driven sentiments of the song lyric.

Each of these examples, and those in the previous section relating to making the performers feel comfortable, can be understood in terms of one participant attempting to reconfigure another participant's mental representation of, or physical engagement with, the situation in such a way as to alter their performance script.

9 This was the guitar solo on the track 'Unforgiven' on the album *Metallica*; the clip can be found on the Classic Albums DVD (Longfellow 2001)

10 Robin Millar gave a lecture on 'Producing Vocals' in the Making Records lecture series at the London College of Music, University of West London on 28 October 2010.

Being present in the moment

So far in this chapter we've skirted around what is perhaps the most important parameter in the way a musician engages in performance in the studio: what they hear. By its nature, musical performance on the voice or an instrument almost always places the performer in the same or similar physical proximity to and relationship with the sound they produce: if you're playing the violin, it is never on the other side of the room or next to your feet. The way a performer judges their sound has emerged out of this way of hearing it. Listening to your instrument being recorded through a microphone and played back to you through a pair of headphones alters that relationship. Again, that alteration doesn't have to be a negative thing: drummers, for example, often find that the more even balance of frequencies that an overhead microphone provides can be more pleasant than the sound from the drum stool.

Alan Williams (2012) has provided a nuanced account of the different relationships that musicians can develop with headphones. On the one hand, the alteration of their normal acoustic relationship with their instrument can undermine or disrupt their normal process of tonal assessment. This isn't only true when an instrument is mediated through headphones: the same type of disorientation can be caused by acoustic treatment in the studio room. Susan Schmidt-Horning describes how William Savory developed acoustic reflectors for use in Columbia's 30th Street Studios in New York in the 1950s:

> Savory came up with his own design: eight-foot tall parabolic-shaped baffles placed on wheeled tripods so they could be easily repositioned. Savory often put the reflectors behind the musicians so they were unaware of their presence. This gave the recording engineers more control over the sound, and the musicians a better listening environment, but not all were pleased with what they heard. Some of the musicians, 'especially the brass men,' Savory recalled, 'thought it was wonderful . . . it is like having your music under a magnifying glass.' Placing the reflectors close to the musicians produced a more direct rather than reverberant sound; moving them back reduced the intimate presence. But some of the musicians thought it was strange, and one violinist told Savory, 'This is going to make me go home and practice a hell of a lot more. I can hear all my mistakes!' (2012, p. 35)

Alan Williams (2012), however, also describes how particular musicians view the microphone and headphones combination in the same way as the brass men in the Savory example. He quotes a musician who says:

> I feel like I'm a better musician when I'm wearing headphones. I'm able to hear detail in a way that I miss without them. I can correct subtle flaws. But I think

> headphones keep me focused, more at the top of my game because if I'm off, the sound is immediately in my head. It is a really positive pressure. (A. Williams 2012, p. 124)

This goes back to a musician's conceptualisation of their place in a recording and of their sense of ownership or belonging. The more they feel that the recording process is just something that attempts to capture what they really do (i.e. live performance), the less likely they are to engage with and interact with that process. Having said that, there are definitely two sides to the issues surrounding monitoring in the studio. On the one hand, a reduced listening experience that results from either screening or headphones monitoring can be a necessary evil a performer has to put up with in order to allow the types of clarity that modern recording technology can provide. On the other hand, a performer can deliberately utilise a monitoring system (headphones or speakers) to allow themselves to hear through the microphone: to adjust their performance to suit the sound that is being recorded rather than the sound they might otherwise hear in the recording space.

The other aspect of monitoring in the studio is the way it affects communication. We mentioned earlier the problems that can be engendered by the talkback system of communication between a control room and a live room. Isolation rooms and headphones systems force the participants either to move from room to room to speak to each other or to use a talkback microphone, which gives control to the person at the mixing desk (where the button that switches on talkback communication from the microphone on the mixing desk to the headphones system is situated). Musicians often experience a feeling of disempowerment when they finish recording a take and have silence in their headphones while they can see discussion occurring in the control room through the window, then hear the click of the talkback microphone switched on in their headphones followed by: 'That was great, but let's go for another.' The particular forms of configuration that can happen through a musician's interaction with monitoring technology may not be a deliberate consequence of the technology's design, but they can be just as powerful and just as real.

Performing to the edit

Albin Zak, in his book *I Don't Sound Like Nobody*, gives an interesting account of the ways in which the broadcast and recording industry resisted the idea of edited performances (2010, pp. 11–33), typified by Bing Crosby's wishes to produce recorded versions of his hit radio shows rather than do them all live on air. This one example, which marks virtually the start of recording to tape,[11] also illustrates a divide that has characterised the recording industry ever since: between those who look upon the editing together of multiple performances as something akin to cheating and those who see it as a creative activity. In many ways, this also takes us back to the start of this book and the ontological question of whether recorded music should be seen as a different art form from concert performance. If recorded music is simply a pale imitation of concert performance then it follows that the linear, real-time performance of the concert hall is the authentic form musicians should strive for. If it is a different form of art then musicians should explore its technical possibilities: they should embrace the creative potential of the edit in all its forms.

Moving the goalposts

Of course, it isn't as simple as dividing musicians and technicians into pro-edit and anti-edit camps, and it certainly isn't fair to simplify that notional divide solely with reference to what recorded music is or isn't. I'll return to the idea of authenticity in the next chapter in relation to audience perception but, of course, musicians have a notion of what constitutes authentic creative practice, and that varies across history, geography and musical styles – even between different individuals in the same group, making the same album in the same studio. And the factors that affect an individual's attitude and approach to editing go way beyond the question of how they feel it relates to their creative integrity as a musician. There is a multitude of logistical and practical factors, from the general notion of how the fragmentation of a performance affects the quality of their work to the specifics of where there may, or may not, be potential edit points in a particular piece, as well as questions of aesthetics, power structures in the studio, the possible impact on other musicians' performance and even economics.

I started this chapter with a description of the negotiated process through which Miles Davis ceded some of his creative control on *Bitches Brew* (1970) to Teo Macero, cleaning up 'messy' improvisations to create a structured piece that would not only survive repeated listening but also serve as a template for future performances. This process doesn't have to be about

[11] Tape recording technology was introduced to the USA after the war in 1945 by Jack Mullin, who brought an AEG tape machine back from Germany and went into partnership with Ampex and Bing Crosby to develop the technology.

the musician ceding control, however. In a talk at the 2005 Art of Record Production conference, Michael Haas, a record producer for both Sony Classical and Decca, stated:

> Both the pianists Ivo Pogorelich and Andrei Gavrilov, according to their various producers, were notorious for recording only short one or two bar passages at a time, stopping and starting again seamlessly from where they left off. The final edits produced performances that were mechanically beyond remarkable – in fact, they were downright miraculous. Every note was perfectly articulated, every up-beat tempo impossibly fast paced, no note out of place and certainly no clangers. Dynamics were inhumanely [sic] consistent and the articulation at even ppp was crisp and sharp. But, couldn't a person pushing down piano keys with an umbrella, recorded one at a time, and placed in a databank, not have resulted in the same performance, given the correct computer programme? (2005)

Here we have examples of musicians using the editing process to take creative control of their recorded output and a record producer questioning the artistic merit of the process. For Haas, the 'remarkable' and 'miraculous' become 'mechanical' and 'inhuman' and this impossibly perfect articulation becomes a marker of a lack of expression – inhuman rather than super-human. Haas doesn't want the performance on a recording to be any different from the recording in a concert, or, at least, he wants the differences to be marginal. Pogorelich and Gavrilov, on the other hand, obviously saw the recording process as an opportunity to focus in on their technique at a microscopic level and to painstakingly construct their interpretations of these pieces, moment by moment.

I mentioned the question of power relationships and Paul Simon's recording of *Graceland* (1986) provides an interesting example of a songwriter/performer/producer exercising an unusual level of editorial control over the performing musicians he paid to work on the album. Simon's longtime engineer, Roy Halee, has described how Simon wanted to record the South African rhythm section:

> The studio itself was like a garage, and in that regard I thought it could be a problem, especially since we were going to record jam sessions from which songs would be created. As I soon found out, the musicians liked to work very close together, with eye contact to get the feel and the groove going. However, since the songs would be crafted out of these grooves, the instruments had to be isolated so that we could do plenty of editing: repairing parts, pulling out a specific guitar, and so on. We had to have the flexibility to erase. This is where my experience at Columbia came into play. There are ways of setting up a rhythm section and getting good isolation without putting the musicians in separate little booths with headphones . . . Paul is a master

organiser, he's extremely smart, and he was great at determining which section would be nice as a bridge or a chorus or an intro while striking up friendships with the group members with whom he could communicate. (Buskin 2008)

Halee then goes on to describe how:

We recorded everything analogue, so it sounded really good, but without the facility to edit digital I don't think we could have done that project. The first thing I did was take the material to New York and put it on the Sony machine. Then we edited, edited, edited like crazy, put it back on analogue, took it to LA to overdub Linda Ronstadt or whoever, brought it back to New York, put it back on digital and edited some more. We must have done that at least 20 times, and if not for digital we could have ended up with just as many generations of recordings. (Buskin 2008)

In a more labour-intensive way, Simon and Halee are constructing songs from custom-created samples, a technique that a decade later Roni Size was using on his album *New Forms* (1997). Interestingly, Size characterises the choice as, initially, an economic decision:

We were sampling anything that we could get our hands on. You give us a sampler, and what are we going to do? We are going to sample. And at that point in time, we thought we should get real musicians involved – we don't want to get sued for a million and one samples, you know. (Randall 2001)

However, the creative possibilities of that self-imposed restriction to his own creative practice obviously inspired him. While Size was getting Bristol-based jazz musicians to record jam sessions to click tracks or programmed drum beats so that he could sample fragments and create an album of dance music, Portishead had engaged in a similar process on their album *Dummy* (1994), except that they were both the musicians and the samplers. In 2004 Apple released Garageband, a music application that included a library of pre-recorded performance samples called Apple Loops that took this notion of using a collage-based form of creation using the fragmented edits of other musicians' performances as building blocks to another level.[12]

Pride and prejudice

However, alongside this narrative of technological progression, as we have seen from Michael Haas' response to these developments, there was a parallel

12 Although Garageband was by no means the first or even an early technology for the use of loops in composition per se (that goes back to the 1940s and Pierre Schaeffer), it was, along with other software packages like Fruity Loops, a pioneer in the inclusion of a library of loops along with the software.

narrative about musicians' integrity, professional pride and the ideology of concert-hall performance being a more valid art form than creative practice in the studio. That's not to say that a narrative of technological progression isn't ideological. I could just as easily have characterised that as recordists' integrity, professional pride and the ideology of technology as an objective good rather than being driven by the interests of political and economic power.

At the end of this chapter I will discuss the notion of musicians as consumers of production technology: much the same idea as when we discussed producers and sound engineers in the last chapter. Both of these discussions relate to the way production technology and, therefore, the processes of record production have been driven not just by what is possible but by the manufacturers' perception of who was going to buy these products. This meant that for the majority of the twentieth century product innovation was geared towards what the recordists wanted. Technology that achieved their professional aims of better audio quality, even if – as we'll see in the next chapter – quality was a very subjective term, was more likely to sell than technology that served the professional aims of musicians.

Timothy Taylor describes how, in the 1950s, Pierre Boulez and Pierre Schaeffer engaged in an ideological dialogue about the nature and value of different forms of musical activity (2001, pp. 50–60). Boulez denigrated Schaeffer's musique concrète through reference to Lévi-Strauss' (1966) term 'bricolage':

> The bricoleur makes what she needs with the materials at hand, the elements are 'preconstrained'; the scientist, on the other hand, is 'always trying to make his way out of and go beyond the constraints imposed by a particular state of civilisation'. (Taylor 2001, p. 58)

This led Boulez to characterise composers who used this form of creative editing as their artistic practice to be 'as worthless as they are impoverished' (Taylor 2001, p. 51). To bring this argument to bear on the editorial practices of record production, performers are artists (although less so than composers) and editors engage in bricolage. The creation of edited performances is thus seen under this view as a corruption of the performance rather than a creative collaborative activity.

Whether we are talking about Georges Braque and Pablo Picasso's incorporation of collage into their creative practice or Public Enemy's use of sampling in theirs, these forms of bricolage have gradually become a mainstream form of expression throughout the twentieth century. However, wherever they have appeared and in whatever form, they have been both embraced and resisted along ideological grounds that relate to agency, and this is also true of editing in recorded music. But the question of agency is also inflected with the question of value, as we can see in Boulez's argument. If the bricoleur is worthless and impoverished then the scientist and the artist who isn't preconstrained by pre-existing materials must be worthy and enriched. Of course, Boulez doesn't seem concerned that a composer such as Schoenberg might be preconstrained by the material existence of the violin or the piano. Whether through the cultural domain of systems theory or the social construction of technology (SCOT), my argument is that we are all engaged in bricolage to the extent that we are preconstrained by both the material and intellectual culture that we inhabit. The question instead relates to the way that different types of skill afford different types of agency, and that these different types of skill are assigned different forms of value by different individuals and social groupings. Borrowing from Bourdieu again (1993, pp. 43–55), skill in linear performance provides more cultural capital in certain fields of musical activity (e.g. classical, Irish traditional) than in others (e.g. electronic dance music, hip hop). Conversely, skill in the manipulation of audio, and by extension in the editing of other people's musical performance, provides more cultural capital in some fields of musical activity than in others. Moreover, as attitudes towards editing change, skill and experience in non-linear performance – tailoring one's performance practice to the specifics of recorded music – has become a more valued second string to a musician's bow.

Having to choose

A new level of responsibility that came into existence with sound recording, and which has become more complex as the technology has changed, is the evaluation of recorded performance and the decision of what to keep and what to do again. For example, in the 1920s when Louis Armstrong was recording with his Hot Five, takes that included mistakes were sometimes released. Thus, in 'Muskrat Ramble' (1926) Armstrong makes an incorrect harmonic change in the thirteenth bar of his solo; in 'Drop That Sack' (Lil's Hot Shots 1926) he makes errors in the introduction and the ensemble sections, and in 'Once in a While' (1927) Kid Ory on trombone makes a wrong entrance and ends rather abruptly. All these recordings were released in the 1920s, but in 'Don't Jive Me' (1940), where Earl Hines plays the wrong piano chords in the middle section and there is a twenty-three bar chorus, the recording wasn't deemed fit for release in 1928 and was only released in 1940 once Armstrong's status as a performer was firmly established and it could be characterised as part of the archive of his greatness. At this point in recording history and up to the end of the 1940s, the decision was only ever keep it or lose it. There was no option of patching things together.

Once that decision became more multifaceted – which section of which take should be combined with which sections of which other takes – the process took on a different nature. However, editorial decisions don't always lie with musicians. In her PhD thesis, Amy Blier-Carruthers describes how with orchestral recordings very often the edit decisions are made entirely by the producer, enacted from an annotated score by a separate editor, and then the edit is offered to the conductor for comments (which may or may not be acted upon) (2010, pp. 149–53). I'll come back to the notion of power and ceding control over your performance to others in the next section, but before that I want to examine this question of personal evaluation.

Judgement calls and decision-making in the studio are complex phenomena. Musicians will often judge a take by how it felt rather than by how it sounded. The stress of trying something they are unsure of, a moment of indecision or forgetfulness and other factors that may make a player momentarily confused or stressed will often make them feel negative towards a particular take. That negativity is not always reflected in undesirable features of a performance. In fact, performances that are stress-free may, by the same token, prove to be safe and unadventurous. It follows, then, that the performer is not always the right person to be making the judgement call about which takes should be used, at least in the immediate aftermath of the performance. It does, however, require the performer to have a lot of faith in a producer's judgement if they are to allow themselves to be guided about which takes are the ones to use. Either that or the time to disassociate that take from the negativity the performance may have involved, so that they can make judgements based more on the musical output than the sensation of performance.

Producer Malcolm Cecil tells a story with a theme not uncommon among producers in general about the specifics of working with Stevie Wonder on *Innervisions* (1973a):

> Sometimes Stevie would go in there for seventeen, eighteen days, and the more he tried, the worse it got. And at the end of the session you'd turn around and say, 'Hey Stevie, listen to this,' and play him that first take, and he'd say – 'Hey! You kept that? I thought you erased that!' He'd have told you to erase it, but you'd just go to another track – I'm not gonna erase that, that's the track! (Cecil 2004)

Power relationships and authority

Creative control

The complexities of communal creative practice are different in the studio than in the rehearsal room or the concert hall. This is partly because of the different workflow but also because of the different personnel involved. It means that all the protocols for decision-making are different. Most notably, there is this additional layer of decision-making about which performances or parts of these performances should be used. There are also more things that can be done to alter the sound of a player's instrument and their performance and, therefore, potentially more decisions to be made. These kinds of decision about microphone placement and processing are often completely out of the hands of the performer. Geographies of responsibility (Massey 2004) are created in the studio environment that are either entirely outside the expertise of the performer or are things that can happen after they've left the session, with or without their knowledge or permission. Mostly this is considered to be standard practice by both musicians and recordists, and it was certainly not uncommon for session musicians to say to me as they were leaving the studio: 'make me sound good'.

How then do these decisions about creative control get made? As discussed in the last chapter, there is a complex web of delegation of responsibility at work and we are dealing with a creative process that is fundamentally distributed. Obviously, the issue of power relationships and studio politics raised here is not merely a question of aesthetics, determining whose preferences prevail and to what extent. It was only when the Beatles had become a best-selling international commodity that they had enough clout to alter the recording practices at Abbey Road Studios to suit their personal preferences. On the other hand, Louise Meintjes catalogues a sequence of events in the South African recording scene that demonstrates that musicians who, while associating 'liveness' in recordings with their African identity, have also had to compromise with engineers and producers to record what West Nkosi describes as 'piece-piece – every individual plays alone' overdubbed performances (Meintjes 2003, p. 130). The social dynamics of the recording environment offer many potentially fruitful avenues for future study,[13] and some have been alluded to in the previous section, but this aspect of

[13] I have already mentioned the UK Arts and Humanities Research Council network on Performance in the Studio that I recently organised. Details of the case study material and existing and forthcoming publications can be found at: www.artofrecordproduction.com/index.php/ahrc-performance-in-the-studio [accessed 28 July 2013].

negotiating between performance practice and recording practice has a direct and palpable effect on the sonic qualities of the recorded output.

Economics is only one of the factors we have mentioned in relation to the forms of capital and their influence on the power structure, but this is also a point when the question of technology is important. I want to return to the proposition in ANT that non-animate objects can be considered as actors within a network because of the way they configure the actions and thoughts of other, human, actors. If we also return to the example of the Louis Armstrong's Hot Five recordings in the 1920s, both the musicians and the technicians heard the takes only as they were performed. The sound engineers and artist and repertoire (A&R) executives (the job title of record producer is not yet relevant here) would have heard the performance through the speakers in the control room, but everyone had to make an initial assessment based on this first listening as playing back the recoding would destroy it. A week later the technicians, and not usually the musicians, would be played the test pressing to make the final decision. Presumably this kind of editorial power was only afforded to musicians who attracted either great economic capital to the record company or whose symbolic capital had similar value to them.

Once we get into the tape period, when linear editing is possible, these types of technical influence don't disappear. Aside from the performer, the final decision about editing will usually reside with the producer, and yet the practicalities of 'performing' the edit (usually by an engineer) – of offering a multiple choice of possibilities to the producer – can be hugely important in determining the precise microtiming and phrasing of the recorded output. As we noted in the previous chapter, Tim Ingold (2013) has pointed out that the process of 'doing' and the way the tools and materials react to this process of 'doing' mean that there is a complex relationship between intention and result. A producer or musician may ask for take A to be joined to take B on the third beat of bar X, but there isn't a unique way in which that activity can be realised: rather than some edits being right and some being wrong, there will be a continuum of rightness. When they hear a version that sounds acceptable they are likely to move on, but there may still be a way to finesse that edit so that some detail of the microtiming flows better. In fact, Dr. Andrew Bourbon of the London College of Music[14] pointed out that when the Elastic Audio timing correction algorithm in ProTools works, it creates a working version initially that is improved upon when the program 'renders' it and makes the changes permanent.

[14] Personal communication with the author, June 2013.

There's a further aspect to this too. Decisions are not always made by the person or people who are meant to have artistic control. Technicians often make changes and decisions about sound without consultation, adding processing and treatment out of habit or because it is 'good practice'. This can often extend to 'cleaning' up edits and correcting timing. In the recording session for the Arts and Humanities Research Council-funded Performance in the Studio project in December 2012 the engineer, Andrew Bourbon, occasionally made changes to microphone positions during the session after consultation with Mike Howlett, the producer, and occasionally did so without consultation. Of course, Mike and Andrew were continually consulting on the general quality of the sound, but certain geographies of responsibility meant that the delegation of certain decisions was achieved through more of a 'black box' situation. For example: 'How's the bass sound?' rather than: 'I've used microphone X in position A and with pre-amp Y with impedance and gain settings B and C. What do you think?' However, on other occasions they had detailed discussions about the position of the padding inside the bass drum and whether to add a separate microphone on the hi-hat. The fact that a multi-channel, complex recording session involves too many parameters for a single person to hold in their head points not only to the need for the added efficiency of delegated responsibility but also to the need for trust. This is as true for tasks happening within the studio with some 'black box' element to them, where the delegate takes care of the detail and the delegator only assesses the output, as it is for the technology being used. I need to trust the designers and manufacturers of ProTools, the microphones, the audio interfaces, etc. to ensure that the detail is being taken care of effectively and that I only need to assess the output.

Establishing trust

Going back to the ANT model, we can see the establishment of trust as an act of configuration. While we can see trust as something built on reputation, that is only really true in as far as the establishment of trust can be seen as happening before a session. Of course, the issues of capital we have already discussed in relation to the establishment of power are important, but there is another, performative aspect to building trust.

We noted earlier that Bruno Latour (2005) asserted that the social only exists in as much as it is performed. Watching sound engineers, musicians and performers at work is an object lesson in how the creation of trust is both continually negotiated and the result of a permanent and mutual process of configuration. Although the description makes the process sound clinical and manipulative, the goal is to create a sufficiently rich and sympathetic cognitive model of the producer for the artist so that they can relinquish control. The artist needs to feel that they know the producer and that they share common goals in their musical activity. Of course, it can and does happen that production can occur without this trust, but in that case there needs to be an alternative incentive for the artist to cede control or there needs to be a different power relationship between them.

More about configuring each other

When discussing the domain of rules and the field of expert judgement in the systems model there is an aspect of this that reminds me of the classic economic model of perfect competition. Perfect competition is a hypothetical model in which both consumers and producers have complete and instant access to the same information, there are no barriers to new producers entering the market and people's demand for a product is determined by its price. In the systems model of creativity there is a domain of rules and knowledge that either we assume is equally accessible to all practitioners or we have to describe a new and unique domain for each practitioner. The same is true of the social field. Either the output of all practitioners is assumed to be assessed in the same way or we define a separate field for each of them. In my opinion, then, a hypothetical, idealised model such as this is good for general analysis but the messy detail of a specific example is better approached from the ANT/SCOT perspective.

For example, Mike Howlett (2007) has described the process of getting a vocalist in the studio to work line by line, even word by word, on creating a vocal template that they then take away, get accustomed to and use as a guide for a future recorded performance. This gets the performer to focus on every detail, to configure their cognitive model at the level of the fine grain motor activity required to make the right gestural shapes in the right places. By taking it away and using that as a template, the configuration moves to the level of the overarching phrase structure and dynamic shaping once the motor activity is in place.

Democratisation and product design

Playing with yourself

One of the key target markets of the home recording industry has been musicians. Electronic dance music and singer/songwriters are both areas of musical creativity where the recording and production process is more easily transferred to the home studio. That's because they generally don't need to record a co-present ensemble of musicians in an acoustically treated space in the way that, for example, rock bands, jazz groups and classical ensembles do. The essence of the home studio and the recording ideology that has grown up around it is built on individual musical activity. That's not to say that it doesn't allow collective activity, but that isn't the primary focus of the product design. The design process has been tailored to make as much as possible happen at the one-person interface of a PC. Another key aspect in this ideology of democratisation has been that the individual at the interface has the entire creative control of the process at their fingertips.

The notion of democracy obviously comes from the ability of the performing musician to engage in the creative practice of recording without the economic, cultural and logistic barriers to entry that the recording industry afforded in the past. Of course, it requires the musician to define their creativity in terms of recorded output and not just performance. In the majority of popular music and some other genres as well, this isn't a problem. However, classical performers, for example, are generally configured by the culture in which their musical activity develops to see recording as a restrictive activity rather than an enabling one. Amy Blier-Carruthers of the Royal College of Music in London has been working with her students in a project that ran more or less in parallel with the Arts and Humanities Research Council's Performance in the Studio network project. Her work combined a taught module with her research, and the classical performance students had to work with another student, alternating between the roles of performer and producer. The aim, in a similar project to – but with entirely different motivation from – the home recording industry, was to configure performing musicians to understand and start to define their own musical personality in terms of the creative possibilities of recording as well as performance.

More about configuring the user

How then, if at all, does this notion of configuring the user through the design of a product in this area of technology alter when the user is a musician? One obvious impact relates to the target audience. We return to the idea that the designer is configured by their idea of who they are designing for, as well as the overall strategy and organisation of the business they work in. Both Tascam and Fostex, two of the biggest players in the home audio market when it started to develop in the 1970s and 1980s, were manufacturers of domestic hi-fi and speakers before they branched into this area. They were, then, perhaps less focused on the idea of their customers as performing musicians in these initial stages and, unsurprisingly, their products used designs that looked like scaled-down versions of professional recording equipment. They seemed to be aimed more at aspiring sound engineers than at making the process musician friendly. After the onset of Music Instrument Digital Interface (MIDI) in 1983 the technology design was aimed more at musicians, and the impact of this on the recording side of things can be seen in the development of MIDI Machine Control, which allowed musicians to control their recording equipment from their keyboard or a foot pedal. It also became clear that a significant portion of the market for these products was DJs aiming to produce their own dance music. This was reflected in the design of some hardware, but one of the milestones of design that was aimed at the DJ market was Abelton Live, which was developed in 1999.[15]

Probably the biggest long-term influence on musicians as users of recording technology has been the much broader global configuration of people as computer users. As successive generations grew up with the ubiquitous presence of a computer within their households, musicians were configured to feel a much greater sense of potential ownership of any process that required a computer. There was thus a pincer action. On the one hand, musicians were configured to consider themselves as computer users; on the other hand, the digitisation of recorded music afforded the movement of the recording process from tape to hard disc and, therefore, from an unfamiliar technology to a familiar one.

However, we also need to bear in mind the possibility of the antiprogram and the identification of presumptive anomalies. We must take account of the fact that technology is often rejected as well as accepted. Hank Shocklee, one of the production team for Public Enemy, in his keynote speech at the third Art of Record Production conference in Brisbane in 2007, said:

> The one thing that I banned was sequencing . . . and the other thing that I didn't like was quantizing . . . as a human you're never playing exactly all the time so thus your music should have some kind of emotional build up and the emotion comes from you playing something. Even if it's just a sample on a key. Play it down for five minutes because after about three minutes you get a little tired, you know, you start forgetting where you are. Now you're getting this motion happening with your playing . . . the main thing is to create that element of a band. (Shocklee 2007)

[15] Abelton Live was a milestone in music software design because it incorporated features such as beatmatching and crossfading, techniques used widely by DJs, and was designed to be used for live playback/performance as well as music production.

In a musical genre such as hip hop, which is generally considered to be music that was enabled and even partially inspired by the technologies of sequencing and, therefore, quantising, Shocklee's methodology of playing tracks directly off a keyboard onto tape seems very much like a case of anti-production.

The final aspect of this I want to mention is the way musicians are configured in their approach to playing by the sound of recorded music around them. I've written elsewhere (Zagorski-Thomas 2010a) about the way drum performance developed in the last half of the twentieth century in response to changes in both instrument and recording technology. This type of change can be found almost everywhere now. The sound of 'perfection' in recorded music has become an aspirational aesthetic for performers, and the result is that the norms of performance outside the studio have moved towards these levels of consistency and accuracy.

Theoretical interlude 4

The previous theoretical interlude discussed the way our model was going to be applied to the collaborative process of production at the sociological level. One aspect of mass media that is very relevant here is that the production process tends to happen at a relatively micro level in comparison to the macro level of consumption. Although I did have one particularly memorable experience to the contrary when I was in a band during the 1980s, the audience tend to outnumber the performers. Even in the demi-monde of hobby bands and bedroom productions, this is still more true for recorded music. The following two chapters deal with the ways in which audiences, subcultures and the various forms of economic structures involved in the distribution of recorded music influence the production of that music.

In particular the agenda is to connect the sociology of musical sound to the sociology of audiences, subcultures and the economic structures. Our discussion of group behaviour up to this point has dealt with the small scale of groups involved in performance and production, but these two chapters deal with audiences and large-scale organisations. How can we discuss the specifics of configuration when we are discussing many minds? I intend to do this in two ways. The first is through the more general terms of the systems approach to creativity and the second is to discuss the generalities of the process of configuration rather than the specifics of a particular pair or small group of individuals.

Before moving on, I should clarify what I mean by the sociology of musical sound. The rather obvious answer is that it refers to how social groupings engage with and react to the specifics of musical sound rather than, for example, the social activities of musical 'consumption'. How do concepts such as quality, clarity, realism, natural sound, authenticity and heaviness develop? Rather than something that is determined by either the audience or the industry, I will examine these processes as a form of negotiation. I will also argue that they are dynamic, in the sense that the definitions that result from these negotiations are neither homogeneous or static. It should come as no surprise that I treat them as a continuous process of mutual configuration.

10 Aesthetics and consumer influence

How much do audiences hear and do they care?

Natural sound?

Seán Laffey, in his article about the making of the Irish traditional music band Raw Bar Collective's album *Millhouse Measures* (2011), says:

> A theatre, bar and recording studio rolled into one, pints of plain and bottles of powers on one side of the bar, music on the other. Microphone cables going directly into the recording equipment set in the back room. Linked into a Mac Book running ProTools. The plan? Hit the red button, play the tunes and record it as it is, capture the Raw Bar.
>
> So what is this Raw Bar thing? Well, RTÉ [Ireland's national television and radio broadcaster] came up with a workable definition for their TV series of the same name: 'The Raw Bar' is that elusive, pure and indefinable essence of traditional music which offers no easy definition but which is unmistakable when experienced. The key word here is experienced, this is music that happens, it is not overly pre-programmed, nor is it over edited in post-production . . .
>
> That's the essence of the recording they were making that night, it has echoes of what has gone before, when one-take recordings were all that was possible, when the experience of the live music was shared by players and audience alike. Before technology and studio sophistication took the fun and spontaneity out of the music. By the time you read this the album will have been manufactured at Trend Studios in Dublin, the web site www.rawbarcollective.com will be up and running, and a video shot at the live recording will be on YouTube. (Laffey 2011)

A review of the album[1] describes it as 'music recorded without equalization and reverb in an intimate pub setting'. Obviously, the implication is that live music is authentic and that the mediation involved in the recording process renders it inauthentic. The YouTube promotional video[2] is interesting in that it both shows the complicated multiple microphone recording set-up[3]

1 By Earle Hitchner in the *Irish Echo* in April 2011, available at: www.rawbarcollective.com/images/Hitchner_Review_April_6_2011.pdf [accessed 5 July 2013].

2 See: www.youtube.com/watch?v=wE3PKECKRKs [accessed 5 July 2013].

3 I think I can make out seven microphones – close microphones on the flute, fiddle, accordion, bodhran and voice, and a stereo pair pointed towards the audience.

and features a lot of the banter in between tunes (part of the fun and spontaneity?) that has been edited out of the CD recordings. In short, the authenticity comes from the impression, perhaps even a cartoon, of the 'raw bar' rather than a realistic experience. The CD doesn't make you listen to the whole uninterrupted concert from start to finish, including the jokes and the chatter – it provides edited tunes that start without even a count in, and which you can select, skip and shuffle. The recording may be relatively unprocessed, but the balance of seven microphones – with the fine detail of close microphone sound, the audience noise faded in for the applause at the end of each track and the rumble of background noise removed with high pass filters – provides a sonic experience very unlike that of being an audience member in a pub, even such a well-behaved pub audience as this.

The questions of 'liveness' (Auslander 1999) and what it means for a recording to be natural or unnatural are complex phenomena but, in the same way that Allan Moore (A.F. Moore 2002) characterises authenticity, they should be viewed as ascribed attributes rather than something inscribed in the nature of the music. After all, an electronic circuit is no more or less natural than a piano or a violin: they are all complex manufactured artefacts and, as such, we could argue that a bird's nest, a termite mound or a beaver dam is equally artificial (or equally natural). The Raw Bar Collective's website suggests that their approach fosters a 'genuine connection with the listener'[4] – something that aims to bring the experience of the live Irish traditional music session from the pub to the recording. Why, though, is a complex array of microphones – each chosen for the suitability of its transient and frequency response for a particular instrument and situated to capture a particular balance of direct and ambient sound – considered an acceptable form of mediation, when other forms of technology – such as plug-ins or hardware processors that affect the dynamic and frequency content and ambience in similar ways – are considered unacceptable?

Ideological sound

The notion of ideology has been addressed so far in respect to how it affected production and performance decisions; I'm turning now to the way audiences and the gatekeepers of musical taste[5] – Csikszentmihalyi's

[4] See: www.rawbarcollective.com/about/rawbarcollective.html [accessed 5 July 2013].

[5] And by 'gatekeeper' I mean to include as wide a range of taste arbiters and trend setters as possible: those who write or broadcast formal reviews or opinions like radio DJs, journalists and bloggers; those whose choices affect the distribution of music and information about music such as artist and repertoire (A&R) managers, festival bookers and listing guide compilers; and

(1997) social field – reveal their ideological perspective. The idea, like the 'raw bar' sound, that creating a genuine connection with the listener is best done by creating a recording that simulates or emulates the experience of the live performance is something I will return to in the next section. Despite the fact that it appears in a wide range of guises from hi-fi to lo-fi in relation to a wide range of musical styles, it is not the only form of ideological aesthetic that audiences and gatekeepers use to ascribe value to recordings. There is a whole variety of tropes that audiences use to ascribe value to music, musicians and recordings: from modernity to tradition, from familiar to exotic, from classy to trashy and from professional orthodoxy to rebellion. These types of ideological labelling might be looked at from the perspective of semiotics, but the notion that the relationship between the signifier and the signified is purely arbitrary (Saussure 1983) doesn't sit with the model based on ecological perception and embodied cognition.

Although these tropes may be ideological, they are also built on some kind of ecological or embodied metaphorical connection between the sound and the idea. To illustrate this I'm going to look at the example of the album *Introducing Shiyani Ngcobo* (2004). This album, produced by a world music label for Western audiences, is in the musical style Maskanda, which in South Africa has developed into a pop form that often utilises sequenced drums and keyboards as well as the more traditional guitars. Producer Ben Mandelson, in his sleeve notes for the album, writes a commentary that illustrates some of the ideological standpoints that underpin this record; the notes reflect that the album is aimed at world music listeners rather than a local South African audience:

> *Maskanda* has moved from being the music of a kind of dynamic acoustic wandering lone-wolf troubadour to that of a larger ensemble, streamlined and formula-ed by the big studios and a local/pop aesthetic. Drums and rhythm groove programming, electric guitars and bass and more. Nothing wrong with that, if in the right hands . . .
>
> Fantastic – it is a band sound, but not with the template bound, ungiving dimensions of production-line programming. (Dear creative programmers out there, I'm not dissing you; you're artists too. We know what we're discussing here.) . . .
>
> No, we didn't use any preprogrammed grooves (apart from Shiyani's own elastic precision), but we still want some boom and clack on the track. You'll hear the traditional Zulu *isigubhu* drum, brought in from the *ingoma* dance tradition. A drum machine? That tap-tap that pops through on some of the tracks – that's Shiyani's foot. Dave, let's get a mike on Shiyani's foot. (Sleeve notes for Ngcobo 2004)

even the casual and informal opinions of those with influence, from celebrity endorsements down to charismatic kids with a lot of followers on social media.

Mandelson writes with a clear aim of establishing the right form of authenticity for his potential audience. First, there's the implicit statement of difference: of this as exotic music or music of the 'other'. This stems as much from the instrumentation and the mode of production as from anything else, distancing itself from electronic instruments, sampling and sequencing. The adoption of these techniques in the 'local pop aesthetic' that Mandelson rejects reflects the fact that the local South African artists and their audience want the opposite: they want Zulu music that is of the modern world – that is keeping up with the sounds and techniques of contemporary commercial music. This album reflects Mandelson's understanding that a world music audience is looking for something different, something that may groove but that marks out its differences from Western commercial music. However, the distinctions are finer than this. Within the world music market this album distinguishes itself from the world beat sector, which, to put it crudely, seeks to create dance music blended with exotic musical cultures by emphasising its acoustic and traditional elements. It also seeks to reassure listeners that this isn't going to be hard work – it may be traditional but it is also accessible:

> *Maskanda* is traditionally a solo occupation, a one-person multi-voiced skill, which you can hear on several of Shiyani's tracks here. But . . . do we make an album of solo songs, aiming for some kind of ideal, despite the fact that Shiyani has been working in a duet or trio for ages? Or do we go for this full-on ampli-*maskanda*, despite its acoustic heart? And what about the world music listeners (possibly the listeners to this album, to whom isiZulu is at best a learned language), who have to travel music first, lyrics later?
>
> Try to bring out Shiyani's range and depth, without persuading him to be a different kind of Shiyani . . . (Sleeve notes for Ngcobo 2004)

Mandelson's descriptions of the studio sessions are interesting too. On the one hand, despite the fact that drum machines and sequencers are ruled out, the wording hints at the fact that click tracks may well have been part of the process. On the other hand, the potentially inauthentic notion of overdubbing and editing to construct the final tracks is described in ways that suggest that the production process is tailored to the needs of the musicians:

> New boy Thulasizwe takes to the headphones as if he's a hardened old studio sweat . . . Everyone does no-fuss overdubs . . . Things relax: the old starter-pistol of 'Rolling . . . !' is replaced with 'When you are ready, Shiyani, please start.' 'Ah OK.'
>
> Things start to relax more: Shiyani is warming up on the garden-porch sofa with his *igogogo*, the gang is hanging round having outdoor tea and biscuits. Cups chink,

birds squawk, laundry flaps. Sounds wonderful. 'Dave – can we run some mikes into the garden please?'...

This is a good moment. It unlocks the album in a way, and helps us to find a more informal, natural, relaxed – dare I say 'folky' – direction to the recordings that we are making. Looking for the performance, not just the layering. (Sleeve notes for Ngcobo 2004)

I'm certainly not suggesting that these sleeve notes are in any way untrue or cynically constructed. On the contrary, I think they reflect what is possibly a deeper truth about production: that the producer and the artist work best when they are as much part of the fan base as the audience, and where they share the same ideological perspectives as their target listeners. It also reflects the fact that, as we shall explore in a little more detail in the next chapter, the output of a recording team should be examined as a complex web of media outputs, which are part of the complex negotiated process of configuration that goes on between them and the social field. This includes things such as sleeve notes, adverts, interviews and merchandising, etc., as well as any recordings and videos that are released.

In our recent edited collection, *The Art of Record Production* (Zagorski-Thomas and Frith 2012), Simon Frith investigated the way production and producers have been viewed in rock journalism since the late 1960s. One of his points concerned an ideological shift among musicians and journalists:

But Lennon was also using his [1971 Rolling Stone Magazine] interview to explain himself as the genius... and we can read this interview now as the end point of the 1960s ideological shift from pop to rock (which the Beatles embodied), a shift which involved among other things a new understanding of musical creativity in the studio. In the early- to mid-1960s it was the performers who were regarded as uncreative, as malleable voices to which producers, writers, arrangers and engineers gave shape and texture. Rock reversed this hierarchy, re-sited the source of creativity from the producers to the acts they were producing. (Frith 2012)

As his examples show, this often manifested itself in journalists reviewing albums in ways that compare how the music stacks up against their 'authentic' live sound, or that complain about the mechanisation or dehumanisation of a band's music through the production process. My point here, as I hope will be obvious, is simply to demonstrate the ideological nature of these standpoints rather than to pass any judgement about their veracity.

Returning to the question of the connection of these tropes to their musical output or the production processes involved, while the question of value may be socially constructed, the connection of the sonic characteristics to the types of activity that have value ascribed to them has a strong ecological or embodied component. For example, the types of musical sound that are described as mechanical or artificial may have been subject to rhythmic or frequency correction or to dynamic compression or limiting, all of which are processes that reduce the levels of variation and therefore make the activity that generated them seem less human or more mechanical. Nevertheless, there is a still a social process going on. There are no empirical thresholds for the definitions of characteristics like human/mechanical. The social process involves a complex and ongoing process of configuration that produces broad social definitions as a product of the aggregate of multiple individual decisions. So while the signifier (the sonic output) may be causally related to the signified (the activity), the judgement about whether the activity should be valued as authentic is based on socially negotiated criteria – for example, about the desirability of the exotic in comparison to the normal, or about the value of active performance as opposed to direction or instruction.

Opinion forming

The question that remains, of course, is how and why these various ideologies become established. Csikszentmihalyi's (1997) social field, which sets the criteria for judging the creative output of an individual in his systems model, says little about the structures or forces that afford certain individuals or groups greater influence than others in the formation and enforcement of these criteria. Bourdieu's (1986) concepts of fields, habitus and the various forms of capital are often used to describe the ways in which various ideologies gain prominence in different social situations. In our examples we might examine the different types of world music audience as a field in which their respective listening habitus provide a different relationship with dancing. Where there is a habitus of dancing to recorded music, producers and artists with cultural capital in the form of knowledge or understanding that allows them to produce records that make dancing easier, or that otherwise encourage it, will be more valued. Although these concepts, too, are essentially descriptive, by breaking down the world in which these ideologies are constructed into more general analytical categories, they provide a framework for understanding the process through which they emerge. The schematic reduction of these complex messy realities into such categories constitutes a theory of cognition, which combines propositions about the way we construe and form social groupings with those on how we acquire knowledge. The question isn't whether we can actually subdivide (or even define) a group like 'the record-buying public' into discrete groups that can be labelled as fields. The question is whether it is a useful enough artifice to warrant its use. Do numbers of individuals act in a sufficiently homogeneous manner in sufficiently similar circumstances to justify labelling them as a field? And if they do (or at least if that is a sufficiently useful simplification), do the norms of behaviour within that field constitute a sufficiently homogeneous and self-sustaining range of activities to be classified as a habitus?

This is another area where the empirical musicology suggested by Clarke and Cook (2004) can be used to make the subject more rigorous. If the evidence suggests that the definition of a particular field and habitus is a sufficiently useful simplification, can we identify discrete phenomena, either physical or symbolic, that might constitute capital? As Emirbayer and Williams (2005) discuss in relation to the social dynamics of homeless shelters in New York, a large part of the process of analysis that goes on when applying Bourdieu's model lies in the initial stage of determining what should constitute a field and thereafter the notions of habitus and capital that can be identified within it. Once the definitions have been established, understanding the workings of the model becomes less problematic. Indeed, Emirbayer and Williams point to the fact that the protocols used by the professionals involved in homeless shelters or their management (and indeed the study of them) to define and differentiate the types of organisation proved to be wholly inappropriate to their study (2005, pp. 695–9). They quote Bourdieu:

> There is thus a sort of hermeneutic circle: in order to construct the field, one must identify the forms of specific capital that operate within it, and to construct the forms of specific capital one must know the specific logic of the field. (Bourdieu and Wacquant 1992, p. 108)

The point is that a cursory analysis like my example above is likely to be merely the very first step in such a hermeneutic circle. Once such an analysis is compared against the data in such a study the problems in the definitions will become apparent, those problems will suggest potential alternative definitions and the comparative process will start again. How and why a particular ideology might become dominant in a particular field then, more or less, becomes an emergent property of the task of defining the nature of the field and the forms of capital that operate within it.

Another aspect of what Bourdieu calls these 'gaming spaces' (1996, p. 264) – the fields where these ideological conflicts play themselves out – is that one of the invariant and universal properties he suggests they possess is that there is a bipolar opposition between what he calls temporal and spiritual or cultural power. In terms of Bakhtin's heteroglossia (1982), we might return to the notions of centripetal and centrifugal forces – with the former relating to commercial, traditional or otherwise more established forces and the latter relating to the rebellion against them. How well these ideas map onto Bourdieu's polarity between temporal and spiritual is an interesting question, but they certainly reflect the notion of dominant and dominated actors and the characteristic strategies of conservation and subversion that Bourdieu asserts they adopt (Emirbayer and Williams 2005, p. 693). The introduction of the notion of heteroglossia allows for a more nuanced and less polar definition of the 'conflict' and 'gaming' in Bourdieu's model. As stated above, this needs to be examined more thoroughly in each particular example it is applied to, but it seems likely that these kinds of gaming spaces in fields associated with record production can be explored in terms of ideological conflicts between various sorts of binary distinctions: polished and expensive vs. cheap and trashy, natural vs. unnatural, large and epic vs. small and intimate. Once again, the devil is in the detail – in a careful reflection on definitions and the extent to which the actors position themselves as a result of these centripetal and centrifugal forces.

Concert halls and clubs – the norms of audience reception

When looking at audiences and consumer influence on the sound of record production through the prism of Bourdieu, one crucial question is that of the habitus: the norms of activity that drive the creation of an aesthetic of the usual.

Normality and habitus

In the systems model, the social field that judges the outputs of the creative process includes critics, peers and the more general audience. Of course, while critics and peers may develop different criteria for judgement through their familiarity with detail that general audiences are mostly not interested in, they are also steeped in the culture of the audience – the norms of reception and the social aspects and environment of their particular form(s) of musicking. These are the features of a field that form the habitus. What, though, are the mechanisms through which these norms change? How did we get from the point at the start of the twentieth century where the norms of listening were all based around different variations of the concert experience to the broad range in the perception of normality in the staging of recorded music that we find at the start of the twenty-first century?

First we need to think about the way audiences engage with recorded media. On the immediate explicit level, listeners who are not experienced in the audio effect of production will generally only comment on relatively extreme staging effects such as audible delays or unusually prominent reverberation. They will, however, often have something to say about the environmental or social impression that such effects create: intimacy, loneliness, aggression and so forth. There has been very little research in this area in connection with record production, but the ways Gibson (1979) and Clarke (2005) describe our exploratory and proactive modes of perception in their ecological approaches indicate that building an internal understanding of our environment and our position within it is fundamental to the way we perceive the world.

One of the early developmental tests doctors perform on children is the ability not only to hear sound directionally – a physiological test, but to turn towards it – a cognitive test. What, though, is happening when we learn to listen to recorded sound? Children learn very quickly that there is a difference between visual reality and visual representations: they don't mistake photographs for windows and realise that there are no little people inside a television. In most instances the same is true for recorded music: they don't expect there to be small people inside an iPod, a radio or a CD player. However, it is much more intuitive to explain how the two-dimensional nature of a visual representation makes its 'unreal' nature obvious than it is to explain the same for an audio representation. One obvious aspect is the lack of the visual component: if I can hear it happening as if it were right in front of me but I can't see it, it is probably a recording.[6] There is also, however, the limited way that spatial sound can be represented through speakers, which might be seen to be roughly analogous to the way two-dimensional visual projection represents spatial vision in a limited way. As soon as we move in relation to the sound source(s) or visual image, it becomes obvious that it is a representation of a spatial relationship rather than a real one. Once we're outside the stereo or surround-sound 'sweet spot',[7] for example, all the time delays, volume differences and ambient balances that create the representation become distorted, in the same way that perspective, shadow and colour in a picture become distorted when we look at it from an angle.

[6] There are many potential complications here, of course. Can I see an audio system? Can I hear ambience that might suggest that the sound source could be 'real' but out of my line of sight? On the other hand, is it possible that I'm hearing a live performance that is being amplified through a PA system?

[7] The 'sweet spot' in a multi-speaker array is the point where the spatial image is most accurate.

Alongside our ability to tell the difference between the reality of a performance in our presence and an audio representation of one, we also interpret these representations as being more or less realistic in the same way that we might judge the visual representation of a painting. These judgements of realism are partly what we might call 'empirical' and partly subjective. We'll return to the question of audio quality in a moment, but another key factor relates to the question of staging that we examined in Chapter 5. There is a complex set of factors that determines our perception of direction and distance, and yet modern recording techniques have tended to reduce them to two: the relative volume of a signal reaching the right and left ears for direction and the relative balance of direct and ambient sound for distance. This is particularly common in pop music production but is also true of classical, folk and jazz recordings. A famous example is John Culshaw's stereo recordings of Wagner's *Ring Cycle* for Decca in the 1960s (e.g. Wiener Philharmoniker and Solti 1965), where he spread the recorded voices across the stereo image to create a 'theatre in the mind' (Culshaw 1967, p. 19). Although Culshaw developed the idea of stereo imaging in a dynamic way that went further than most in the popular music world,[8] the technical process was simple and relied entirely on the performers moving around static microphones. He certainly embraced the creative possibilities wholeheartedly:

> First there is an obvious improvement in sound *quality*, a sense of spaciousness and a lack of strain . . . Second, there is stereo's ability to covey position in the lateral sense. It differentiates between sounds on the left, sounds in the middle and sounds on the right and should cover all points between the extremities of the two speakers. And when handled properly from the recording end, it can seem to convey that certain sounds are coming from *beyond* the extremities of the speakers . . . Given this possibility to convey position and movement, it was obvious to us from the beginning of stereo that operas would have to be aurally envisaged for the new medium. (Culshaw 1967, p. 23)

As we shall see in the next section on quality, this period was one when the promise of technology to improve lives was reflected in the audio world through the cult of high fidelity and stereo, and Culshaw was someone who believed in and promoted these notions extensively:

> Stereo is therefore a medium to be *used*: it is what you can make of it. At its best, it can bring opera to life in the home in a way that was unimaginable twenty years

[8] By creating a chess board-style grid on the recording stage and mapping out positions and movements (e.g. a4 to c7) on the vocal scores for the singers to follow (Culshaw 1967, p. 24).

ago. The effect is nothing like that of the theatre, for several reasons. The listener at home is not a member of a community, and whether he admits it or not his reactions in private are not the same as his reactions in public. I am not claiming that one environment is better than the other, but simply that they are different, and that therefore the reactions are different. The sound of a good stereo recording played under good conditions in the home will tend to engulf the listener, and may draw him psychologically closer to the characters of the opera than in the theatre. (Culshaw 1967, pp. 23–4)

This, then, provides one of the mechanisms through which the norms of listening changed: the changing technologies that we looked at in Chapter 6. But the benefits of a high-quality stereo system that Culshaw so frequently extols were much less influential than the sound of radio.

Peterson (1995) distinguishes between the 'hard core' and the 'soft shell' in country music and the way it developed throughout the twentieth century. These distinctions are based partly on the original form of listening – or, perhaps more accurately, musicking (Small 1998) – habitus through which their performance conventions evolved: the 'hard core' relating to loud, declamatory musical forms that developed for public, large-scale gatherings and the 'soft shell' relating to the softer, more intimate styles of domestic and parlour music that so strongly influenced certain forms of popular music. Radio broadcasters and, trailing in their wake, popular music recording artists found that they could use microphone technology to transfer this intimate habitus of listening to mass media. Interestingly, this aesthetic of the quiet, intimate parlour performance style didn't transfer to classical music because the dominance of the concert hall was too firmly established as the prestigious platform for performers. Presumably, the performance aesthetic of, for example, solo piano repertoire played in the home by one family member for a few others was more introspective and less declamatory than that of the public piano recital. While the popular and folk versions of that kind of parlour entertainment transferred to the radio and discs from the onset of electrical recording with its more sensitive microphones after 1925, the sound of the homespun or gifted amateur musician was evidently not initially welcome in the classical world. Glenn Gould's 1960s and 1970s Bach recordings (for example, Gould 1963), however, certainly embrace the notion of an intimate sound that has a more domestic rather than a concert-hall aesthetic.

From this, though, we can see that production styles grew slowly out of the norms, the habitus, of audience experience. The large-scale theatrical experience of the opera was eventually afforded, through the development of the requisite technology, the kind of conceptually large-scale staging of

Culshaw's sweeping stereo images. The small-scale parlour music of finger-picked guitar and softly sung voices was equally placed in intimate proximity to our ears through the greater clarity of condenser microphones. But the ways in which these production styles evolved aren't purely about the extent to which the available technology could emulate the habitus of live performance listening in various different musical styles. Pretty early in the twentieth century the radio and, to a lesser extent, the phonograph rivalled live performance as the most common way of experiencing music, and so the habitus also changed in that regard. On top of that, we have, during the 1930s, the development of small public address systems to allow singers to use microphones to be heard above the big bands of the swing era. These are just the starting points of a complex interaction between live, broadcast and recorded music that has helped to shape audience listening expectations in the past century. Once again, the complex process of configuration was not just interactive (i.e. arising from both the affordances of the development of recording technology and the affordances of an existing habitus of listening) but also multi-modal (i.e. radio, live sound and playback technology also influenced the norms of listening to recorded music). All in all, then, although growing out of the world of live performance, there was a more convoluted and distorted lineage to the audience tastes that helped to shape the myriad sounds of modern record production.

Great expectations

We've already mentioned the notion of a hermeneutic circle in relation to Bourdieu, but the idea is also useful in explaining how the way audiences engage with recorded and broadcast representations of performances influences the way they engage with live performance practice and vice versa: the multi-modal process we've just described. The development of a particular habitus of listening – for example in certain forms of extreme heavy metal – is best understood with reference to these multi-modal forms of engagement, but our understanding of these forms can subsequently be better understood with reference to this overarching framework of the habitus – and the circular structure continues. Thus, in our heavy metal example, the trope of 'heaviness' in this field has grown out of different factors from recorded and live performance in particular. In the studio, the process of double tracking, the use of dynamic compression, equalisation, microphone selection and placement, and real or electronic room ambience have all been used in guitar recording to create a greater sense of loudness and density without actually needing to increase the peak amplitude of the signal. On stage, live sound engineers have increased both the overall volume of public address systems and their distribution within the physical space of an auditorium so that there are fewer and less extreme peaks of volume in different parts of the space. Some of the technologies from the studio – such as compression, equalisation and electronic ambience – have transferred to the auditorium as well over the years.

We can track the way audiences have become accustomed to both greater peak amplitudes and greater average amplitudes through live and recorded music in these styles and look at how that has changed expectations about how records should sound.[9] But the issue is more complex than that. The ever-growing 'heaviness' in guitar sounds has also been accompanied by greater strength and clarity in recorded (and live) drum sounds.[10] Dan Turner has described:

> metal guitars as . . . a 'Sonic Wall' that heavily mask other instruments' frequencies, with . . . the use of equalisation necessary to make the drums scale this wall. (2012, pp. 27–8)

Thus, the notion of heaviness is further complicated by the ways the drums and bass interact with the guitars where they share a frequency range, as well as how strong they sound in the frequency range that they don't share. And, of course, the vocals have to be accommodated as well. More than that, the perception of aggression through gesture and timbre, memories of live performances, interviews with the band, the review-style output of various gatekeepers, the video that might accompany it and so forth: these are all potential strands involved in determining 'heaviness'. But that determination, while it may be grounded in certain sonic signifiers that have these embodied and ecological connections, is also partly personal and arbitrary. In the larger scheme of things, an individual's subject-position will give them a unique viewpoint and therefore a unique interpretation, albeit one that may lie in a predictable large sector of viewpoints determined by the generic and universal factors. In terms of ANT, the configuration of each individual's notion of heaviness will be different, but the combination of mass forms of communication (i.e. the members of a listening community

[9] As an interesting aside, the quest for ever louder tracks through compression can also backfire, as we can see from this online *Guardian* report: 'Metallica's ninth studio album, *Death Magnetic*, may be topping the charts, but some fans are signing an online petition that asks the band to re-mix the album and release it again. The problem is the usual one: it has been mixed to sound loud, which has crippled the dynamic range. As one fan says, "Sonically it is barely listenable"' (www.guardian.co.uk/technology/blog/2008/sep/27/digitalmusic [accessed 10 July 2013]).

[10] See my chapter on real and unreal performances (Zagorski-Thomas 2010a) for a more general discussion of the way drum sounds and performances were influenced by changes in recording practice.

will have a lot of shared experience and shared forms of interpretation) will produce enough schematic congruence for us to identify various 'social' definitions of heaviness.

As we can see, the detail of how the habitus of audience expectation is constructed is a complex and tangled set of threads. However, even supposing that an analysis such as this could produce a description rich enough in detail to provide a set of parameters for what kind of sound a particular audience might expect, that's not the way the world works. Record companies, artists and producers do not, unhappily for academics, turn to Bourdieu and fund research projects to examine what their next record should sound like. What, then, are the feedback mechanisms through which these complex habitus have an effect on the production of recorded music?

In Chapter 5 we discussed the idea of functional staging: staging that reflects the use to which the recording is most likely to be put. Here, we examine the ways in which the norms of audience reception help to shape these forms of functional staging. In one regard the connection is obvious: make the recording sound like some form of schematic representation of these norms of audience reception. However, the sound of recorded music has, in turn, affected expectations about the sound of the concert hall. Rock and pop music concerts have come increasingly to provide a hybrid between emulating the sound of the record and providing some tropes of liveness. The balance and make-up of these hybrids is determined, as we shall see, partly by a particular audience's notions of performance authenticity.

Every style in recorded music is the result of a culturally constructed perception of what constitutes authentic recording practice. This perception is based on many different factors, including historical precedent, attitudes to different forms of technology, attitudes to performance practice and the characterisation of auteurship. Differing amounts and types of technological mediation will be considered authentic and acceptable by the different audiences affiliated to different styles of music.

High fidelity and quality

What is good-quality sound?

In 1967 Decca Records (1967) issued a disc called *How to Give Yourself a Stereo Check-Out*, which provided hi-fi enthusiasts with a combination of semi-scientific and entirely subjective tests to assess how well their hi-fi system was performing. One of these tests was about the setting of tone controls:

Most amplifier tone controls affect the extreme high and low frequencies, leaving the mid frequencies relatively unaffected. To help you set these in a position that is correct for your loudspeakers and your own ears, listen carefully to the high-, mid- and low-frequency warble tones recorded in this band. By varying the tone controls until the high and low frequencies sound as loud as the mid frequency, or pilot tone, you will have equalised the frequency response of your amplifier to suit your own listening conditions. (Decca Records 1967)[11]

We saw in earlier chapters how some aspects of the notion of high fidelity developed. Keir Keightley discusses how it was 'part of a significant development in the history of American middle-class culture' (1996, p. 172). The two characteristics Keightley identifies as central to the development of this notion of realism and transparency in recordings are the notion of immersion (related to both volume and spatial audio) and 'an endless search for ever-deeper bass notes and for jet-altitude highs' (1996, p. 152). The marketing of high fidelity by both record companies and record player manufacturers may not have persuaded everybody to buy into some of the extremes of the hobbyists that Keightley describes, but it did lead the social field in a particular direction when it came to judgements of quality. Decca's practical test for assessing at least the volume of your high- and low-frequency response, if not the quality, reflects this schematic approach to quality.

By the time of the 1980s the introduction of digital audio and CDs overcame the limitations of analogue recording and vinyl in terms of hiss, rumble and surface noise, in a way that allowed exaggerated high-frequency content to be included on recordings without the problems of hiss. At the same time, improved speaker and amplifier designs allowed for better reproduction of low frequencies on smaller and cheaper systems. The way high fidelity had been reduced to a schematic representation of the types of thing that should be audible in a good recording is evident in both of these examples.

Clarity

We've encountered the idea that clarity in recording is by no means analogous with fidelity at several points so far. My chief point about this in relation to the record-buying public is that, from a practical perspective rather than a scientific one, greater clarity is associated with greater quality. The fact that 'quality' in this sense might not be about realism is interesting but beside the point. Aside from the distorted exaggerations of high

[11] From a photograph of the sleeve notes at: http://recordbrother.typepad.com/.shared/image.html?/photos/uncategorized/stereo_check_back.jpg [accessed 28 July 2013].

and low frequencies, clarity – the ability to discern the detail of what was happening in the performance – was and is a key marker of quality. The fact that this trope coincided with both the need for more and more expensive equipment and architectural design and greater professional expertise on the part of sound engineers also meant that the semi-public markers of what constituted a good recording – for example, the Grammy for Best Engineered Albums (introduced in 1959) – reflected the same value system. This further entrenched the technological frame in which clarity and audio quality became combined in the notion of high fidelity. As we've seen, this notion of clarity is actually to do with the exaggeration of some features and the reduction or removal of others to create fewer potential ambiguities of interpretation by making the schematic representation of the performance elements more extreme. Thus, for example, the lower frequencies of a guitar sound might be reduced or removed so that they don't clash with a bass sound. Or a clarinet in an orchestral piece might be given a separate spot microphone so that it can be subtly brought up in volume during a particular solo section.

Other qualities

It is often remarked upon in sound-recording circles that the last fifteen years have seen a marked downturn in the quality of the audio products consumers are choosing to buy. Downloadable audio files such as MP3 and AAC utilise lossy data compression codices that create much smaller file sizes but with a loss in audio quality. The difference in this case is that the loss is not in terms of high- or low-frequency range but in terms of the detail in the wave file. In extreme cases the effect is, to me, like an audio form of pixilation. Having said that, the notion that the trade-off between audio quality and portability and convenience is new should be put in the context of vinyl albums and cassettes. Cassettes generally provided a lower audio quality but were a highly popular technology because of their convenience and portability.

Another factor is the increase in personal ear bud- and headphone-based listening, particularly in relatively noisy environments such as trains and buses (Bull 2005). This can be seen as a contributing factor, along with in-car listening, to the 'loudness wars'. This phenomenon involves the changes in mastering practices in the last twenty years or so that have reduced the dynamic range of recorded music. The desirable result of this is that 'quiet' sections in a recording are not so quiet anymore, so they can still be heard in noisy environments. That these changes in the notion of what constitutes a good-quality or desirable recording have affected recording practice is undeniable. The habitus of the record-buying public and how its desire for particular types of audio quality manifests itself permeates seamlessly into the world of production and musical performance because the worlds are in a perpetual state of overlap. The shift in the technological frame from one that lionised high fidelity to one that is centred on convenience and access is, of course, also at the centre of the change in the perceived value of the musical product itself.

Authenticity

The mechanism

As I've already mentioned, my approach to authenticity closely follows that of Allan Moore (A. F. Moore 2002), in as much as I view it as an ascribed attribute of music rather than an inscribed one. That means that it resides in the interpretation by a perceiver – the way the relevant attributes of a piece of music or a performance fit with their conceptual model of what constitutes appropriate creative activity. This, again, relates to the notion of the habitus. In this instance, though, the habitus may not be my personal experience of the norms of musical activity so much as my perception of what they are for the group of which I am an audience member. Although Moore has categorised authenticity as first-, second- and third-person forms relating, in crude terms, to being true to yourself as a performer, true to your audience and true to a tradition, I want to examine the idea in terms of conformity to a conceptual model. Something is authentic if I can match certain features to the cognitive prototype I have constructed, albeit with reference to whichever social activity I have engaged in that has influenced the configuration of this prototype. This may relate to ideas about the correct forms of technology to be used in a particular form of music-making. Thus, Dylan's 1965 adoption of the electric guitar and a rock band accompaniment on *Bringing It All Back Home* (1965) and at the Newport Folk Festival in the same year marked a step over a particular ideological line for some people in the US folk music revival scene. Although there's a lot of controversy about the extent and nature of the criticism, there certainly was a feeling in some quarters that folk music, of which acoustic instruments are an important marker, was a more serious form of expression than commercial popular music. The notion of authenticity in this instance relies on two conditions: first, that an audience member has a mental representation of folk music in which Dylan is a key member and for which acoustic instrumentation is a key characteristic; and second, that their mental representation of rock music must be that it is somehow inferior to folk music and that the move from one world to the other is somehow a betrayal.

Performance authenticity

The bibliographic conventions regarding film require that authorship is assigned to the director, not the scriptwriter or the actors; in recorded music the authorship is assigned to the performers (and/or the composer), not to the producer. Both film-making and recording are communal activities and a large part of any 'leadership' or 'authorship' by either film directors or record producers relates, as we've seen, to the delegation of creative authorship to someone else. Earlier I discussed Lévi-Strauss' (1966) idea of bricolage and the way the twentieth century saw a gradual move towards the acceptance that the editorial manipulation of the work of others could be seen as art. Audiences, however, continue to perceive the 'public face' as the creative agent. While the director may be granted authorship by reviewers and academics, the film-going public often describe films in terms of the actors. Screenplay writers never seem to be granted authorship of films. With recorded music the author is mostly a performer (or ensemble), occasionally a composer. It is rarely a producer, and when it is they are usually perceived as being a composer or co-composer in some way.

The notion of the 'public face' as the creative agent then relates back to what we said earlier about the negativity of a producer having been seen to have interfered with an artist's agency. The 'raw bar' recordings discussed at the start of this chapter can be seen as a reaction against mediated studio recordings, where the performance integrity of the musicians is seen to be compromised by the lack of co-present performance by the musicians and the lack of audience stimulus. In relation to our idea of conformity to a conceptual model, the appropriate mode of performance or habitus for Irish traditional music is seen as the pub session. Rather like the idea of recording classical orchestras in their 'natural habitat', the great European concert halls, the 'raw bar' recording is doing the same thing: identifying the character of a performance style with the place where it normally happens.

In a rather different approach to performance practice, Steve Savage (2008) identifies what he calls the 'it could have happened' approach to editing. Even if it is an entirely 'artificial' (i.e. non-linear) construction, an edited performance in many styles of music needs to sound possible to be acceptable. The 'possible', of course, refers to the idea that although the performance may be a studio construction, it sounds as though someone played it. This may seem like an obvious point, but many solos and vocal performances are cut together from different takes in ways that may be technically impossible to perform. Although the example wasn't included in the written version of his paper, at the conference when he presented it he recounted an incident where Dave Gilmour, the guitarist with Pink Floyd, had edited together a solo on an album in a way that was impossible to play. Years later at a guitar masterclass, a young guitarist told him he'd been trying to work out how it was possible to play that particular jump and had finally worked it out, after which he played the 'impossible' solo. This brings us to the notion of conformity to the conceptual model, in which individual agency is a central characteristic of instrumental performance.

Creative agency

Indeed, the notion that an edited solo is a creative collaboration rather than 'cheating' is anti-intuitive in most forms of musical audience. One exception is in the use of sampling, where the distance between the original performance and its repurposing allows the original performance to be viewed as an artefact rather than a performance that is being hijacked. The idea of studio practice as a valid form of creativity to be seen alongside performance and composition varies a lot from period to period and from style to style. Even in popular music, the image of the producer as a Svengali figure, corrupting the creative purity of the artist with technical shenanigans, is still to be found.

In classical music, the notion of technological mediation as part of the creative process is virtually unknown outside electronic and electroacoustic composition (where it is seen as part of the compositional process). In popular music, from the Beatles and the Beach Boys onwards, artists were seen as having a creative practice that related to the studio as well as a live performance practice. However, audiences do still harbour suspicions about producers who usurp the creative agency of their artists. In fact, artists, producers and record companies develop strategies to illustrate that sufficient creative control has remained with the artist to allay these fears. In 1999 Ed O'Brian, Radiohead's guitarist, wrote an online diary to give fans a narrative through which they could see that this largely electronic album, *Kid A* (2000), was being constructed by them and not through programmers, and in collaboration with the producer, Nigel Godrich:

October 6, 1999: Start working on a band loop called 'fast track' – Thom had a rough arrangement on Cubase last night. Nige and I then do some guitar sounds using my new toy. The first Roland guitar synth, which sounds pretty different. Jonny does a couple of background radio tracks. We then do a bit of editing and pruning. Nige is really into this thing of throwing down random shit and then simply keeping the really good stuff. It is a cool way of writing if only because you end up with things that you couldn't possibly contrive to do. (O'Brian 1999)

Godrich is seen as an enabler here and elsewhere in the diary, providing the framework that encourages the creative agency of the band to emerge. The band members are using the broader notion of creative output I mentioned earlier to ensure that there is sufficient congruence between their own definitions of what constitutes authentic creative practice and the definitions that their audience holds.

Ideology

In the section on high fidelity and quality earlier I mentioned that the practices around the creation of schematic clarity in recordings were not just prized by audiences but had been adopted as markers of professional excellence by the industry as well. These and other tropes of quality have also, in some quarters, come to represent the sound of commercialism as well. One of the drivers of the lo-fi aesthetic in recorded music is as a signifier of the rejection of that form of commercialism, of the money-orientated mainstream of the recording industry. In Chapter 5 we mentioned Darkthrone's album *Transilvanian Hunger* (1994), which deliberately adopted a lo-fi stance to signal the band's rejection of the mainstream commercial market. Of course, not all lo-fi recordings are made because of that specific ideological stance, but it is a marker of rebellion and difference that situates a track outside the commercial norms in some way. Beck's *Loser* (1993) can be considered deliberately lo-fi because of its association with the anti-folk scene in which Beck was involved, but it is also true that he and co-producer Carl Stephenson recorded it in Stephenson's eight-track home studio because they had no financially possible alternative.

Of course, there are albums that embrace the sound of the mainstream through a conformity to these sonic markers of professional excellence. Artists such as Anita Baker, Simply Red, Shania Twain and the Fine Young Cannibals have created polished productions that mark them out as a quality product. The notion of high fidelity is typically a middle-class aspirational concept and the 'expensive' sound of these kinds of production is an extension of that. However, other ideological positions can be expressed through production values that go beyond the notion of adherence to or rebellion against the commercial mainstream. Queen's *A Night at the Opera* (1975) had the phrase 'no synthesisers used in the making of this album' printed on the cover. Whether this was an ideological statement about the validity of synthesisers as a form of musical expression in rock is not entirely clear.[12] It does seem to beg the question of why the 'studio trickery' of 32- to 48-track recording used to multi-track Brian May's guitars and Freddie Mercury's vocals might be authentic but the use of a synthesiser might not. We've already discussed the way Shiyani Ngcobo's (2004) album reflected an ideological position about the 'otherness' of world music, but that is also balanced by the desire of many musicians in these places marked as 'other' by the music industry to create musical products that compete in the same market as Western popular music, rather than as an exotic – and by implication more backwards – alternative. My colleagues Paul Borg and Sara McGuinness at the London College of Music have both recounted instances to me of musicians wanting to use the sound of synthesisers rather than traditional instruments to make their recordings sound more modern. In all these instances, the cognitive model to which the artist or audience wants to conform includes these various characteristics that are key to the definition of category in some way. Whether it is Queen as a guitar-based rock band, world music defined through exotic acoustic instruments, modernity achieved through electronics or clarity as a marker of the commercial mainstream, these signs of authenticity are to do with the ubiquitous cognitive process of categorical inclusion and exclusion as a process of definition. Cars have wheels. If it doesn't have wheels, it is not a real car.

[12] Later statements, after the band started using synthesisers on their albums, suggested that it wasn't an ideological statement but made the point that all the strange textures on the album were guitars and vocals. Whether this is a case of rewriting history after the fact is unclear.

11 The business of record production

Business models

Twinning a chapter on the business of record production with one on audiences and discussing them in terms of reception-based approaches may seem odd. Surely record companies are in the business of production rather than reception or consumption? I would suggest, however, that they lie in some hinterland between production- and reception-based approaches. They are certainly in the business of selling to the record-buying public. But they are also in the business of purchasing the creative services of musicians.

Economics and art

Although audiences might think that the recorded output of musicians is determined by their creative impulses alone, the artists and producers are acutely aware of the way commercial interests influence their decisions. In his book about working as Glenn Gould's producer, Andrew Kazdin says:

> Sometime in 1971, it was felt in Columbia Masterworks that Glenn should record some popular concerto works. After all, it had now been several years since the *Emperor*, and although some Bach concertos intervened, the record company longed for the kind of sales that a disc of some juicy large-orchestra concertos would provide. Gould was amenable, and it was decided to record the Grieg Concerto because of its popularity . . . and the Beethoven Second Concerto because it was the only one of the five that Glen had not recorded in stereo. (1989, pp. 127–8)

This illustrates the influence that record companies exerted on the process of choice of repertoire. It also illustrates the fact that their work, even with classical musicians, is not simply about allowing the artist to fulfil their creative potential or even, as is sometimes hinted at, to direct the creative arc of their career in ways that encourage a stable development. Indeed the Glenn Gould official website goes so far as to say:

> For Columbia, the aura and charisma of the twenty-two-year-old Canadian pianist were no doubt just as important as his unique gifts at the keyboard. He reflected the spirit of the age in an altogether ideal way, a mixture of Jimmy Porter from John

Osborne's 1956 kitchen-sink drama Look Back in Anger and Holden Caulfield, the main character in J.D. Salinger's 1951 novel The Catcher in the Rye: a jeune sauvage in music or, as The New Yorker put it, the 'Marlon Brando of the piano'.[1]

And yet the conventional narrative about an artist is that their vision directs their choices. Despite the acknowledgement that Gould had this film star status, the official website describes everything, including his repertoire choices, in terms of his single artistic agency – the type of mythology we alluded to in Chapter 6:

> Gould was one of the first truly modern classical performers, for whom recording and broadcasting were not adjuncts to the concert hall but separate art forms that represented the future of music. He made scores of albums, steadily expanding his repertoire and developing a professional engineer's command of recording techniques.[2]

So what, then, can we say about the ways economics and the business models of the recording industry have an impact on recorded music and the process of production? Perhaps ironically, given the romantic cult of art and artists as somehow unsullied by business practice, it was only when various types of creative practices became commercial processes that the notion of the artist could emerge – that is, when artists and musicians became specialists who could command an income from their specialism. A profession in art is 'afforded' by money and power precisely because it is a non-essential activity and, thus, an artist requires support from some other members of society if they are to survive. If someone is to dedicate themselves wholeheartedly to the development of a musical (or other artistic) skill, they need to be freed from the need to provide themselves with shelter and sustenance by other means. In early societies, the members of the group who produced food and shelter, if they wanted the benefits of an expert musician, had to be persuaded to provide for them. This remained as true for the 'travelling salesman' troubadour in the thirteenth century, and for Joseph Haydn working as a musical servant to Count Esterhazy in the late eighteenth century, as for a modern recording star like Glenn Gould entering into a contractual agreement with Columbia Masterworks.

The way this affordance of music through money and power works can be understood through a continuum: at one end is the notion of the popular – work for which a large number of people will pay a little; at the other end is the notion of patronage – work for which a single person will pay a larger

[1] See: www.glenngould.com/us/timeline [accessed 19 July 2013].

[2] See: www.glenngould.com/us/biography [accessed 19 July 2013].

sum. This demand-led principle is, however, complicated by the fact that – with commodities such as music – the demand is determined not by need but by taste, in a sector of the world where affluence has transformed virtually all issues of need into issues of taste. My demand for food, a basic need, is transformed in twenty-first-century Britain into a taste-driven demand for different types or brands of food. Whereas it is fairly easy to imagine the circumstances in which my demand for food might revert to a need that can't afford the luxury of taste, the same cannot be said for music, poetry or visual art. I may always decide not to listen to music if I can't find something that I like but I can only do that with food for a limited period of time before I die.

Need-driven demand still drives a lot of economic activity: if I want to make steel I will have a need-driven demand for iron ore. I may be able to buy iron ore from a variety of sources but I can't, for example, substitute copper for iron and still make steel. But that does bring us back to the notion of generic or functional demand, such as the need for food: there is obviously a whole range of foodstuffs that will fulfil that function. Generic or functional demand can stem from needs such as food, drink, heat and shelter, or they can stem from desires such as light, comfort and entertainment. There's obviously a certain amount of overlap here. There's a need for heat if it prevents me from freezing to death, but levels beyond that can be seen as a desire for comfort. When it comes to music, though, no matter how sensitive or romantic I may be, there is no threshold beneath which I will perish for want of a tune. My demand may still be generic or functional: I may want to dance, for example, and in much the way that I need iron ore to make steel, I need music to make dancing happen. I may be able to get music from a variety of sources but I can't, for example, substitute copper for music and still make dancing happen.

The business models in the music industry are structured according to the nature of the demand. The two key factors are taste and function. In questions of taste in recorded music, the primary unit of brand is usually the performer – even in the classical world the audience is more likely to seek out a new Yo-Yo Ma album than a new Thomas Adès composition. Obviously, when the industry revolved around sheet music songs and compositions were the currency, but the world of recording, as we discussed in Chapter 2, placed the performance (or a representation of one) at the centre. Of course there are exceptions but, in some ways, they reinforce the argument. Philip Glass in the world of contemporary art music, for example, is a composer brand, but much of his popularity as a recording artist flows from the Philip Glass Ensemble and his solo piano performances of his own works. Motown, for quite a time, was a stronger brand than its constituent artists, and yet the reasons for this type of label brand coherence often stem from a house band as in Motown and Stax, or a single production team as in PWL or Dr. Dre's productions at Death Row Records. And the marketing of a brand can be based on taste or function (or both). For example, Motown and the Ministry of Sound are both brands that were based on functional demand for dancing. Most artists, though, are marketed on the basis that their audience will develop a much more personal relationship with them and these complexities of taste: of aesthetics, authenticity, of personal and social engagement. There is also an overlap here. Social engagement, the community- and subculture-building aspects of music, are a combination of both functional and taste-driven demand. A label like Two-Tone Records in the UK in the 1980s reflected both a taste for the music and an engagement with the subculture, although not in equal measure for all of their audience.

This idea of branding and the manipulation of, and response to, demand underpins a great deal of the scholarship within popular music studies. Whether considering the way businesses and the musicians they contract to make their records reflect the changing socio-economic and socio-political landscape that surrounds them, or the way they can persuade an audience into demand for products through gatekeepers, trendsetters and marketing experts, popular music studies is often more concerned with the sociology, ideology and economics than with the music. My contention, though – and I see signs of a similar trend gathering momentum in musicology as a whole – is not only that we should be studying how the outputs and processes of musical production are related to these other factors but also that our understanding of both sides of the coin is incomplete and distorted without an understanding of these relationships. My belief is that the connections between the musical gestural shapes (in the broadest sense of the term)[3] and these contextual factors are made explicit through the type of study and analysis I have outlined earlier in this book: how they reflect each other provides a way forward in the interpretation of music and the understanding of the creative process. In particular, in this chapter I want to examine how business models can affect the physical process of production and the sound of recorded music.

[3] I refer to non-human as well as human gestures: to musical morphologies that suggest associations with forms of activity that have inherent ecological or embodied connotations – empathic, associative or metaphorical – that can be related to these wider sociological, ideological and economic factors.

Follow the money

In the film *All the President's Men* (Pakula 1976), Deep Throat, the informant, urges Bob Woodward, the investigative journalist looking into the Watergate scandal, to 'follow the money' as a way to understand the process of corruption that was taking place in the US government under President Nixon. The same invocation could be used to understand the process of record production. Who pays whom, how, when and how much for the processes of production, distribution and promotion? What are the mechanisms through which this all happens? In the previous section we mentioned that art in general, and record production in particular, is afforded by both money and power. It should be noted, however, that in a world such as music there can be a great deal of power in cultural capital, and that is not always in the same hands as the money. In a system where the record companies authorise an artist and repertoire (A&R) executive to be the arbiter of quality (i.e. where they have the cultural capital of being perceived to be able to recognise music that will sell), they are likely to negotiate a different type of production process than if the record company is commissioning the A&R executive to sign an artist who is already in demand for some reason. In the former example, the record company has both the money and the power; in the latter the artist holds more of the power in the form of cultural capital. In general, the more convinced the record company is that the artist (and the producer) will make them money, the more they are likely to spend and the more creative autonomy they are likely to give them. Of course, since the end of the 1960s anything the recording company may spend is recoupable against future income from sales,[4] but if the sales don't cover the costs it is the record company that pays. But not all recordings are paid for by the record company (and then recouped): in some instances the producer or the artist may have financed the production process and bring an already completed recording to the record company. In between these two basic models there may be a variety of hybrid versions: for example, the record company uses the recordings but pays for them to be mixed by someone else. And, of course, whichever party is paying – albeit by loaning the money to the artist as an advance – will feel empowered to exert some creative control over the production process if they feel the need or desire.

Mike Howlett (2009) has described the producer as a nexus between the artist and the record company, but has also discussed the importance of

[4] Thus, bands like the Beatles didn't have to pay for studio time in EMI's Abbey Road Studios, but later contracts provided an 'advance' payment that was designed to cover studio and promotional costs and give the artists something to live on until the income started to come in.

record companies in forging successful creative collaborative relationships. There can be a wide variety of actors involved in this process of negotiating working partnerships in addition to producers and record company executives, from lawyers and managers to the musicians themselves. This process of constructing the networks that are going to undertake the creative collaborative process of production can, therefore, also be seen as another actor network.

More about types of capital

At various points in the history of recording the changing costs of production and distribution have changed the balance of power (or the way it is negotiated) between economic capital and social, symbolic and cultural capital. Thus, in the 1950s with the advent of the cheaper tape-based technologies, the economic barriers to entry were temporarily lowered and there was an increase in the number of smaller entrepreneurial studios, particularly in the USA. This change allowed small independent labels to utilise their cultural capital that related to new musicians, local trends and knowledge of developing musical styles. During the 1960s, as the economic capital required to make records started to climb back up again, the opposite happened and the larger companies started to buy up the smaller players, effectively buying their access to cultural capital. In the latter half of the 1960s and 1970s, the cultural capital the record companies were paying for transferred from those with knowledge about the music (e.g. the smaller labels) to the musicians themselves. This was because the major record companies were once again back in the position where they had confidence in the cultural capital of their own A&R departments – i.e. their ability to recognise marketable talent.

The spread of the semi-professional and home recording technologies in the late 1970s and throughout the 1980s allowed the creation of a two-tier (or even multi-tier) system, initially with the start of the indie/punk scene and then with the development of hip hop and electronic dance music. It was during the 1980s that I went through a seven- or eight-year period when Music Instrument Digital Interface (MIDI) technology was young and I made a living as a freelance MIDI programmer. This relatively short-lived profession spanned the period when few sound engineers or musicians had computer skills and they needed a separate technician with that specific form of cultural capital. The most radical change occurred at the turn of the millennium when the transfer of digital audio to PC systems and the advent of internet distribution developed simultaneously and caused a radical lowering of the economic barriers to entry.

Long Lingo and O'Mahony (2010) have applied the notion of brokerage from business and administration studies to producers. They point out that older theories of brokerage focused on having the idea to put people together and making the connection, but that a more thorough examination of success rates points to the importance of following this up by managing the collaborative process. This kind of analysis offers great potential for the analysis of record company and management involvement in the production process, as well as looking at the role of the producer. Labels such as Chess, Stax, Stiff, Chemical, Mute and so forth could be examined in terms of developing the ideas for musical and technical or production collaborations that bring together different types of capital. The management of these collaborations and the negotiations about the delegation and allocation of power, along with these other factors, can all be examined in terms of the social capital that accrues to those in boundary spanning roles:

> The structural conception of brokerage emphasizes the unique informational benefits that can accrue to those who are structurally central . . . The greater the degree to which an individual can uniquely connect non-redundant sources of information and social contacts, the greater the potential information and control advantages that are likely to accrue to that individual . . . and the more social capital individuals can accrue. (Long Lingo and O'Mahony 2010, p. 49)

The influence of finance on the production process

The root of all evil?

If we are to integrate the business side of the industry into our theoretical models then we also have to theorise the influence of money within ANT. I would suggest that this can be done by thinking of money as a tool, and therefore as a non-human actor in the network. While we might have to think long and hard about the way in which the design(er) of money configures other actors, the way it is used as a tool to configure other actors in the network based upon the affordances it offers seems much more straightforward. Returning to the way the social performance of power is represented within our conceptual model, we encounter the question of presumptive anomalies in the technological frame of money. Obviously, we can choose to try to configure (or not) and to be configured (or not) by money. Are, though, the alternative paradigms we might seek through presumptive anomalies simply the alternative forms of capital? If money is the mechanism through which economic capital works, knowledge is the mechanism through which cultural capital works, the structural/positional advantage of gatekeeping is the mechanism of social capital and culturally constructed prestige is the mechanism of symbolic capital.

In some ways, of course, the budget is one of the primary determinants of the physical shape and extent of the network in the first place. The affordances of money are the budget constraints imposed on pre-production time, on studio time, on the choice of producer and engineer and on hiring session musicians and additional equipment. Although P.J. Harvey is signed to Island Records and can presumably command a reasonable budget for making albums, with her steady and loyal fan base, for *Let England Shake* (2011) she chose a remote church in Dorset for the recording venue. In interview she talks about the search for the right venue and doesn't mention money as a constraint, but her search obviously took place within the limits of a budget:

> I didn't set out that way, to record in the church. I was actually setting out to work in Berlin, as that was a city I was finding quite interesting at the time and wanted to work there. But I went over to Berlin and couldn't find a place that felt right, so I was still looking for places – and then, just coincidentally, the man who runs this church as an arts centre approached me and said if I ever wanted to use it for rehearsing I could, because he liked my music and knew I lived nearby. It wasn't predetermined, but it actually lent itself really well to this record . . . to the nature of the words and the music, it was perfect for it. (Hewitt 2011)

On the other hand, the lack of any clear financial constraints, rather than being a spur to creativity, can have the opposite effect. In 1983 Duran Duran spent three months in a chateau in the south of France achieving virtually nothing, before going to Montserrat, London and Sydney to finally finish the album *Seven and the Ragged Tiger* (1983) with a £250,000 budget. Although the album did make a profit, a lot of expensive unproductive time was wasted. Within this context, record companies are continually having to make budgetary decisions based on potential projected sales, their confidence in the artist and the type of project. In their brokerage capacity they have to set a budget that creates the right balance between giving the creative team space and freedom, and giving them enough rope to hang themselves.

Other financial decisions often have implications for the production process. There is frequently tension between giving an artist time to write and prepare material for a new album, and promoting and touring their previous work. With popular artists there is always a pressure to release something while demand is still high. We've already mentioned Radiohead and *Kid A* (2000), where the band and record company mitigated the effect of Thom Yorke's writer's block through a press campaign and Ed O'Brian's blogging strategy to keep fans in the loop about the progress of the recording.

Changing income streams

How is the changing market for recorded music influencing the way participants in the production process are configured? Of course, the obvious instant response to this is that there's less work and it's less well paid than it used to be, and that producers have to work much harder at marketing themselves to both artists and record companies. Richard Burgess, speaking at the launch of the new edition of his book (2013) at the 2013 Art of Record Production conference in Québec City, said that the types of fee he used to get for producing an album are now the entire budget for the project. On the positive side though, as we've already mentioned, the financial barriers to entry in both the production and distribution sides of the market have been lowered and there are extensive mechanisms for creating small income streams from direct sales without a record company. Another relevant event at the 2013 Art of Record Production conference was a paper by Sheena Hyndman (2013) on the impact of remixes on income streams in the electronic music market. She pointed out that labels seldom paid remixers, and tended to use them as free promotional material for the 'main' mix. Interestingly, her research and the experience of a couple of remixers in the room for the discussion was that remixes tended to act as promotional material for the remixers rather than the original track.

Response to demand

Follow the money again

As we've seen in relation to Richard Burgess' comments, one of the key requirements for making a living as a producer in the current market is to promote oneself to the record companies:

> Reputation is critical, and building one is a matter of taking advantage of the resources and opportunities you have. The more positive recognition your work

receives, the more work will come your way and the more access you may have to major label opportunities, if that is what you want. Major labels gave Danny Saber more work once he had a successful record under his belt. He told me that before that, 'I always had to talk them into why they should use me. Once you have a hit record, you have that to stand on.' Irrespective of that, 'No matter what you did before, it is only going to do them any good if you do good for them' (Burgess 2013, p. 114).

Nothing promotes better than a reputation that stems from a track record. As brokers, record companies are also involved in a business-to-business process as part of their 'bigger picture' business-to-consumer process. The business-to-business element situates record companies as consumers of production services because they have generally outsourced the production of records – to producers. When record companies want a particular sound that is currently popular, it is not only about signing acts but can also be about using 'fashionable' studios, producers and technical personnel. This is not just a recent phenomenon either. In the early 1960s Jerry Wexler at Atlantic Records started to send artists to Stax studios to record after he'd been licensing tracks from the label.

Market distortions

This demand structure, however, points to the social nature of the market and how fuzzy logic and irrationality are important, as well as money and other forms of capital. We referred to the hypothetical notion of perfect competition in Chapter 9 when discussing the systems approach, and I want to return to that now. These forms of ostensibly irrational behaviour do follow an internal logic of their own, but they flow from motivations that lie outside the immediate returns of conventional markets, whether perfect or otherwise. It quite often happens that as a producer becomes successful they become in demand for projects that stylistically they might not be suitable for. Record companies sometimes demonstrate their commitment to certain projects (to the rest of the industry and journalists, rather than to potential customers) with ostentatious displays such as large budgets and the choice of recently successful producers with track records (even if their musical skills might not be right for the project). This, and other practices that are about showing off to, or otherwise communicating with, industry peers are a fascinating glimpse into the anthropology of corporate communities.

If that marks an internal competitive system of the various sorts of capital that exist between record company executives, there is a similar system for producers, engineers and studios. The marketing process for studios involves equipment lists and 'iconic' recordings made in that studio, which are often used to attract engineers. Many of the features may be technical, but there is a broader marketing approach that involves glamour attached to particular pieces of equipment (even if they may not be appropriate for this particular project).

The myth of economics

One of the myths of economics is that all business is motivated by money; this is even less true in the music business. The logic of economics is that capital flows wherever market demand will provide the best return: if my hat-making business starts to make less money, I may transfer my capital to power tools instead. That may be true of the capital invested by banks, but it certainly isn't true of entrepreneurs. For most entrepreneurs, their route into a particular business is: given that this is what I do, how can I make money out of it? How often does the desire to 'make my kind of music' override the basic tenets of economics? While this has been overlooked for the most part in popular music studies, there have been a few instances. Peter Doyle's (2009) 'Working for the Man' looked at figures such as Jack Kapp, Ralph Peer, Milt Gabler and John Hammond. Albin Zak's *I Don't Sound Like Nobody* (2010) deals extensively with the detail of how, in the 1950s, the 'independent record men were more enterprising than their major label counterparts, willing to go out and find performers well off the beaten paths of show business' (Zak 2010, p. 132). And Mike Howlett has discussed how the energy and enthusiasm of what he calls 'entrepreneur producers' such as Chris Blackwell, Richard Branson, Clive Calder and Dave Robinson were so essential in the development of certain currents within popular music history (2009, pp. 24–9).

A similar phenomenon – one in which a business plan is built around a non-business idea – can be found in many concept projects. An aesthetic or otherwise ideological idea is turned into a commercial project. One could say that is the premise of any commercial exploitation of music, but certain projects take this further and form a processual structure on such a foundation, as well as a musical product. For example, Ry Cooder and Nick Gold's *Buena Vista Social Club* (1997) is built on a decidedly pre-communist Cuban aesthetic that involved deciding to use the older Egrem studio in Havana rather than the modern rooms, to reflect the 'character' of the Buena Vista Social Club project.

Demand for what?

The additional chapter Evan Eisenberg wrote for the new edition of his book *The Recording Angel* (2005) is a fantasy about the future production of music. Despite the exciting and exotic technological ideas he weaves into the chapter, there is another basic premise about our musical future: that it will see a return to the domestic self-production of the pre-recording era. We will all make our own music. Obviously, Eisenberg was exploring a specific aspect of music-making – the computer-based home studio – that was still emerging as he was writing. It does, however, raise an intriguing possibility. What if this fundamental shift in the market structure for recorded music leads us to a position where producers and musicians are now the consumers of production and instrument technology, and the majority of recorded music-making becomes an unpaid hobby? In her keynote speech at the eighth Art of Record Production conference, Lori Burns (2013) outlined the production process for Coldplay's *Mylo Xyloto* (2011), not so much in terms of the album but as a multi-media project with the artwork, live show, videos, album and subsequent comic book being developed in a virtually seamless process. It reminded me of a theatrical multi-media event such as *Mamma Mia* or *Stomp*. If recorded music goes down the road of becoming promotional material for live shows or other multi-media projects on the one hand, and a hobbyist industry where the economic end product is the technology that the musicians use rather than the music on the other, what does that mean for the production process?

Control of supply

Owning the means of production

Although we may be witnessing some major shifts in the industry structure, there's still a fairly major recording industry in existence. And although the changing patterns of demand are discussed most often at the moment, there has also been a big shift in the ownership and structure of the means of production. In one way, the concentration of media industries into enormous structures that span music, publishing, film, radio, video and television has pushed change in one direction. The control over the management and timing of the record production process is now only a small component in a larger system involving promoting, touring, videos, the press and an ever-widening potential range of other spin-offs. This means that creative deadlines in the production process are now subject to tighter financial strictures and considerations than ever before. In 1983 during the mixing process for *Seven and the Ragged Tiger* (Duran Duran 1983) in Sydney, the band were given a third and final deadline to deliver the finished masters to the pressing plant in Hayes, West London, because the factory could not be reset before the last possible Christmas release deadline if they missed it. Alex Sadkin and Ian Little, who were co-producing the album with the band, flew the masters back personally and just made the deadline (Buskin 2004).

However, at the same time as these media companies have been broadening their reach over the commissioning, ownership and distribution of recorded music, they have also been shedding their ownership of the means of production. Up to the 1960s, as we saw earlier, the record companies tended to own their own studios and exercise quite a tight control over what happened in them. In many instances in the popular music world, such as Motown, Stax, Goldstar, Muscle Shoals and in the Nashville scene, the labels maintained house bands or pools of particular session musicians. These two factors contributed to the idea of labels having a signature sound. While labels didn't so much shed ownership of their in-house studios in the 1970s and 1980s, they didn't increase their own 'manufacturing potential' by opening new studios to match the increased output of recorded product. Instead, they subcontracted the recording aspect and, in the process, created a much bigger market for independent studios.

This led to a similar shift from the notion of staff producers to freelancers. Thus, for example, staff producers included Mitch Miller at Columbia, Leiber and Stoller at Atlantic, Norman Whitfield at Motown, Walter Legge at EMI and George Martin at Parlophone/EMI. George Martin started his own production company, Associated Independent Recording (AIR), in 1965, but continued to work with the Beatles at EMI. The 1960s was again a turning point, and the major name producers after that are more frequently freelancers. The same rough time period – the middle to the end of the 1960s – also marks a radical change in the manufacture of recording equipment. Although there were independent companies, many of the record companies, large and small, would make or customise their own equipment. This great period of expansion in the market for records, which was encouraging the large companies to outsource more and more of their production activities, saw a similar shift for recording equipment. Right up to the start of the 1970s EMI were installing the same REDD and TG[5] model

[5] REDD was an acronym of Record Engineering Development Department and TG was a contraction of the acronym for The Gramophone Company, the UK company that had merged

desks, built by their own research and development department, in all their studios around the world. That in-house business model started to die out from the 1970s onwards. The basic story was the same: to create a corporate structure that offered the greatest flexibility possible when creating the physical product by making it much more of a freelance, subcontracted operation, while keeping a tight hold over the means of distribution and marketing.

Selling the production process

We've described money as a non-human, configuring actor within the network, and this works on the record company executives as brokers of the collaborative production process too. Their brief, coming through the company board from the shareholders, is to combine the short-term goal of maximising profits with the longer-term goal of maintaining the firm's stability and position, and thereby helping to secure future profitability. This configuring process is the motivation behind the restructuring described in the previous section, and the search for other ways to monetise their assets has, since the 1990s, included selling the production process as well as the musical output.

The mass marketing of star names, whether we go back to the mythologising of royalty at various points in history or the gossip industry that has grown up around film stars and pop stars, involves providing the audience a glimpse into their private lives. Fans of music and film want access to the people as well as to the musical output. This has long been fed by interviews and articles, and more recently by film biographies and television documentaries that deal with the personal lives, motivations and histories of the musicians themselves. At the same time, fans did show interest in certain iconic studios as shrines to the creative output of particular stars. Thus, for example, there are always people being photographed outside Abbey Road Studios in London because of its association with the Beatles, and the old Motown studios in Detroit have been turned into a museum (they moved the majority of commercial production to Los Angeles in 1970).

In 1992 Isis Productions and Eagle Rock Entertainment started to produce a long-running series of documentaries about the making of classic albums,[6]

with Columbia in 1930 to form EMI (Electric and Musical Industries) (Ryan and Keyhew 2006, pp. 14–112).

[6] Forty-four documentaries have been made so far that range from Elvis Presley to Jay-Z, but that tend to focus on US and UK rock from the 1960s, 1970s and 1980s. See: www.eaglerockent.com/search_products.asp?stext=classic%20albums [accessed 30 July 2013].

which combined access to the creative lives of the artists with interviews with sound engineers and producers who worked with them. This interest in the creative practice of the stars is, to a lesser extent, reflected in the 'making of' features on DVD releases of films, in which sound effects, digital visual effects and stunts are often deconstructed. Bands have, since the 1990s, quite regularly used 'home movies', blogs and 'making of' DVDs to bring fans into the studio with them and get them invested in the blood, sweat and tears of the creative process. Metallica's *Some Kind of Monster* (Berlinger and Sinofsky 2004) DVD documentary about the making of *St. Anger* (Metallica 2003), Ed O'Brian's (1999) blog about *Kid A* (Radiohead 2000) and the Kings of Leon's (2008a) online 'home movies' about the making of *Only by the Night* (2008b) are all examples of the production process either being used for marketing or being turned into a physical product itself. And, as we saw in Chapter 6, plug-ins that emulate technology from iconic studios or hardware manufacturers, or that are endorsed by well-known producers or sound engineers, are allowing another aspect of the production process to be directly marketed.

The influence of finance on the role of the producer

Finally, I want to revisit the different roles producers have adopted, and this time to examine them from the perspective of the business models within which they were working. This takes us away from Richard Burgess' categories based on the nature of the producer's working relationship with the artist (Burgess 2013, pp. 7–26) and towards the idea of brokerage (Long Lingo and O'Mahony 2010). I'm going to look at four quite obviously distinct categories of producer role that are based on their economic and managerial relationship with the artist and record company. If and when the participants' ideas about their roles change, so too must their idea of what the process is. Certainly the cultural notion of the recording, like that of the photograph, changed during the twentieth century from that of a 'record' of an event to an output involving its own form of creative practice. With all four of these types of role the industry also sought to maintain the perceived division between commercial and creative decisions.

A&R men as producers

This model relates principally to the period before the 1960s when the producer had virtually complete control over every aspect of the project –

the artist, repertoire, studio, etc. In part it was determined by the nature of popular music at the time, in that artists tended to come as a less complete and more flexible package. For example, a singer would be unlikely to write their own material; a songwriter wouldn't necessarily provide an arrangement and the choice of musicians would therefore relate to whatever arrangement was settled upon. The brokerage activity in these kinds of situations is therefore a lot more complicated and in need of very different skills than it would be with a band that writes and performs its own material. The role in this instance involves quite a modular approach: the brokering process might involve making the various participants aware of each other's work and garnering their agreement to the partnership. However, the work on the arrangement and selection of the musicians would be entrusted to the individuals that the task was delegated to, rather than being a collaborative activity. Examples of this type of producer in the 1950s might be Voyle Gilmore at Capitol Records, Mitch Mitchell at Columbia and Walter Ridley at HMV/EMI in the UK. Production costs were not charged to the artist, as they were seen to be part of the manufacturing costs and therefore the realm of the label. However, the costs of arrangements were often charged to artists because they would want the rights to use them in their live performances as well as on the recordings. This method of production, along with the relatively simple process of recording, meant that recording costs were relatively low and the process was relatively fast once they'd got to the actual studio stage.

Legacy forms of this role still exist within country music in the USA and in the areas of pop where pairing songs and performers is necessary. It can also be found in a more hybrid form within hip hop and RnB, where A&R executives, artist managers and other types of broker might put production teams, rappers and RnB vocalists together for specific projects. In these instances, and in some areas of the pop and dance music markets, the production team will develop a finished backing track either of their own composition or from a given song demo, and the vocalists will then add their own parts, once again either their own composition or from a song demo. In all instances, though, the producer/broker is a kind of creative manager and the partners are likely to work in this modular fashion. The process is quite industrial, with clear roles for the various creative participants and a clear line of management. However, commercial success meant that the record companies gave these producers power over the output. The artists could demand power when they made enough money, but they rarely exerted that power over production rather than musical/arrangement decisions because it wasn't seen as creative practice and, therefore, within their realm.

Staff producers

As the production process (in the manufacturing sense) became more industrial in scale, the recording industry, as all industries were doing at the time, sought to modularise the process so that it could be more effectively managed and the participants could be more specialised, as this was considered to improve efficiency in a large corporation. This, in some instances, simply meant that the A&R men as producers model become more specialised in terms of genre, but it also spawned the staff producer model. The nature of the staff producer's specialism was that they were engaged purely to oversee the creative process in the studio and, like George Martin at Parlophone/EMI, they frequently had practical musical skills.[7] And, in fact, when producers become more specialist, they develop a closer relationship with both the artists and the process.

The fundamental problem with the model of the staff producer was exactly the same as the problem of the staff writer: they almost inevitably started to feel that they weren't receiving sufficient financial rewards for their creative contribution. Leiber and Stoller at Atlantic, George Martin at EMI, Norman Whitfield and Holland–Dozier–Holland at Motown all left to go freelance or to start their own labels. Later examples, such as Mick Stock and Matt Aitkin at PWL in the 1980s, negotiated better financial relationships with their labels precisely because the freelance model that become prominent in popular music in the 1970s set the precedent.

As we've mentioned, artists in the 1960s were not charged for studio time, and as sales and prosperity increased they were allowed more and more freedom to indulge their creativity. This was a clear case of economic capital being prepared to reward cultural capital, because as recording became more expensive it also became more profitable with the larger LP sales from the late 1960s onwards. However, as the different cost structures of putting, for example, the Beatles in the studio for five months and recording a straightforward pop album in a week became more marked, the owners of the economic capital became more concerned with negotiating that employment.

Entrepreneurial producers

I don't want to suggest that there is a simple chronological progression in the development of these types of role as, I hope, the examples I've been citing

[7] Martin was a composer, performer and arranger and, for example, wrote many of the string and orchestral arrangements for the Beatles' records, as well as writing and performing keyboard parts on some of their tracks as well.

will imply. The role of the entrepreneurial producer certainly didn't start with the decline of the staff producer. The small-scale studio and/or label owner is a much older model, which was developing in parallel with the previous two roles. The scale of the economic activity also determined that the business owner couldn't afford either the complexity of the production process or the luxury of paid delegation that could exist in the larger labels. Although a good many of the smaller labels made a living out of local markets, they also caused upset with the majors by breaking national hits. Albin Zak summarises how, in the early 1960s, the singles charts in the USA were, if anything, dominated by independent labels rather than the majors (2010, p. 213). Examples of these kinds of producer are Sam Phillips at Sun Records; Joe Meek, who ran his own RGM[8] studio from his home and licensed his productions to Decca, EMI and Pye; and Phil Spector, who produced for his own label as well as for others. Zak also notes that independent and small-scale producers were now working as a supply industry for the major labels – not merely providing songs for the majors to match to their own signed artists but providing groups with songs and productions ready for development (2010, pp. 204–37). This model of the production company that develops a finished recording and then sells it on to a record label is a model that still remains popular and, in fact, is the major form of production in contemporary electronic dance music.

By the end of the 1960s, this notion of producers as a service industry to the major record companies started to take on a new momentum. As well as independent production companies, as I have mentioned, the record companies increasingly started to subcontract the production process to independent studios and freelance producers. These kinds of service, much like advertising in other industries, were seen as better outsourced to a creative specialist. This is a variation on the notion of increased specialisation to increase efficiency. An appropriate expert is employed temporarily for the specific requirements of each job rather than expecting your employee, the staff producer role, to be able to produce in every style. This model relates to producers such as Alan Parsons, Tony Visconti, Quincy Jones, Dr. Dre and the Neptunes, and has prompted a support infrastructure of producer managers such as Steven Budd. This illustrates the increasing specialisation of the process. The brokerage tasks that involve the financial negotiations are subcontracted by the producer so that they can focus more on the creative side.

[8] Taken from his initials – Robert George Meek. Joe was a nickname.

Artist producers

That focus on the creative side and the greater specialism it reflects is also seen in the rise of the artist producer. Although the following example is about a radio broadcast, Stokowski's reaction illustrates several relevant issues in connection with artist producers:

> When he discovered that the show's engineer controlled the sound levels and mix as it went over the air, the maestro announced 'No-one controls Stokowski's sound but Stokowski!' He insisted that NBC[9] rig up a portable mixing board that could be placed next to him while he conducted . . . Eventually [the engineers] resorted to disconnecting Stokowski's board without informing him. (Milner 2011, pp. 50–76)

Quite rightly, Stokowski identifies the fact that the recording process (or radio broadcast in this instance) has a strong impact on the musical output and wants to engage with its creative possibilities. Milner also describes his work with the recording engineers at RCA Records, moving microphones and adjusting levels to control dynamics and ambience. Both descriptions, however, also mention the problems that Stokowski's limited technical knowledge caused – problems that he just expected the technicians to fix. Of course, the more he worked in the studio, the more he understood; the same is true of all artist producers. Indeed, unlike the supremely confident Stokowski, they generally only gained enough confidence in their abilities after quite a lot of recording experience. As in the Stokowski example, and in accordance with the more general theme that has been running through these four role descriptions, the role of artist producer requires a very specific form of the division of labour. They need either to absorb the reflective editorial role that a producer should provide into their own role or to re-ascribe it to someone else, such as an A&R executive. Also, if the more financial and managerial aspects of the brokerage activity aren't going to be taken on by them, they need to be taken on by someone else – someone who may be their manager or who might take on the role through a more formal title such as executive producer. Examples of this kind of producer might be Stevie Wonder, Marvin Gaye, Mike Oldfield and Prince.

As I say, these four examples of roles are provided not because I think they provide an exhaustive description of the types of roles that exist or have existed. I wouldn't even suggest that they are sufficiently differentiated that there is no overlap. The difference, for example, between a freelance production team and an artist producer is often very unclear. The point is

[9] NBC is the National Broadcasting Company, the US commercial broadcast television and radio network that produced the radio programme in question.

to suggest that among the many ways to think about the producer's role, the financial and managerial structure in which they function is an important one. As we've seen with these four brief descriptions, there is a complex interaction of configuration in these types of networks and the financial and managerial structures are as important in the determination of the production process as the nature of the musical activity is in determining the financial and managerial structure.

Afterword

More on my ideology

The typology of eight categories that I've used in this book can certainly be described as displaying an agenda for studying the way people work in record production, rather than the way the technology works. If I were studying the latter I might create a typology that used technical processes as categories: sound capture, sound storage and editing, dynamic processing, time domain processing, pitch domain processing, timbral domain processing, etc. The reason I haven't done that is because, as I said in Chapter 1, the huge gap I see in courses that study recording arts and music technology is in understanding how they create meaning for listeners. There's plenty of existing work on the technology but it doesn't provide a link with musicology. However, for me, 'creating meaning' frames the question in the wrong way. Record production doesn't create meaning for listeners; neither does music. Listeners engage in the process of interpretation. The meaning is in the people, not in the sound.

The fact that producers and musicians interpret music in much the same way as an otherwise uninvolved listener allows us to build connections between production- and reception-based approaches to musical analysis. That's certainly not to say that I think of music as a way of communicating a message, in the sense that the musician encodes some meaning into the music that the listener must try to decode correctly. I do, however, think that it is possible to suggest a range of psychological reasons for why and how certain people will interpret a particular piece of music in a broadly similar manner and, conversely, for why others won't.

The flip side of that people-focused agenda is the approach to collaborative creative activity and the sociological/ethnomusicological/anthropological side of things. If there is a differentiation to be made between these ideas and the mainstream of ethnomusicology, it is in the focus on how the music is made rather than on how the social interaction happens. Ethnomusicology is more focused on the whys and hows of people getting together to make music. This approach could be characterised as the recording branch of performance studies: the whys and hows of people actually making the music. It is a subtle difference; there's plenty of overlap between ethnomusicology and performance studies and, therefore, with this approach to record production.

If that, hopefully, explains the ideology of how I came at the process of creating a typology, the other big question is whether I have successfully covered the subject matter. I've been thinking about the topic since before the 2005 Art of Record Production conference and, in the seven years since I wrote the article for *Twentieth-Century Music* that was the precursor of this book (Zagorski-Thomas 2007), I have been refining these ideas – gradually changing my mind on some things and developing 'interpretive inflexibility' about others. The more I've thought, the more I've realised that, while I could create some further categories and/or delineate existing ones, it works for me and it seems to make sense to many other people. It is, after all, a schematic representation of an academic subject, not a description of an actual thing. The main criterion for assessment – whether it is a useful typology – is for others to decide.

Am I serious?

When I started work on this book in 2007 the theoretical model that now forms its backbone was much less clear and the typology was the main structuring concept. As the book progressed, the question emerged as to whether this unfolding theoretical substrate that has now become the basis of my approach to musicology should also become the basis of the book. Am I really suggesting that musicology in the more general sense should be based on this theoretical framework?

Well, one thing I am suggesting is that the study of music needs to be based on whatever knowledge from the sciences and humanities we have about musicking. Of course, in the subjects of psychology and sociology, trying to identify which parts of those bodies of knowledge are reliable and likely to stand the test of time is problematic. Whether or not the 'New' musicology of the 1990s was mostly attacking a straw man, it has been part of a shift within the study of history in many disciplines towards the study of complex social systems and the context that surrounded important people and events. And whether that is best accomplished within music using ANT, SCOT and the systems approach to creativity or some other tool from within sociology is less important than the fact the shift has taken place. The important question is: what types of information are being sought within historical musicology, popular music studies, ethnomusicology, performance studies and the study of music theory and analysis?

Historical musicology has, notwithstanding its concentrated focus on a particular canon of composers, engaged with the question of how particular pieces of music came to be produced by particular people in particular circumstances at particular times. When I was taught music in the UK in the 1960s and 1970s, it involved placing a composer in the context of the historical development of a set of musical conventions, almost exclusively discussed in terms of tonality and formal structure. Historical musicology today has broadened this discussion a lot, but the whole thing boils down to looking at a creative system: how people worked, how the techniques and technologies worked, how they varied geographically and over time and how they sat in the wider context of society. Contemporary scholars have widened the net to include a much broader range of information in their studies and, I would argue, this wider net is very well suited to the forms of analysis used in this theoretical framework.

Popular music studies provide an example to illustrate another point that I think is both useful and important about this approach. There has been a historical division in popular music studies between scholars who focus on the social and economic activity through which popular music is produced and consumed, and those who focus on the musical output. As I hope will have become clear as this book progressed, this combination of the ecological perception/embodied cognition approach, with the constructionist approach to the sociology of technology and an expanded version of the systems theory of creativity, provides an opportunity to bridge that divide. There seems at the moment to be a confluence of people looking for ways to bring the music back into popular music studies and people engaging with various aspects of the ecological perception/embodied cognition agenda.

The debate within Stobart's (2008) *The New (Ethno) Musicologies* reflects the changing landscape of music studies in universities. While some of the contributors are arguing that musicology and ethnomusicology are coming closer together, others are arguing that ethnomusicology needs to stand its ground next to anthropology, or maintain its differences in other ways. The connection with anthropology does bring out one of the key issues that I mentioned earlier: do we want to understand music or the social processes through which music is made? Martin Clayton's (2008) contribution to that volume is, in fact, concerned with bringing the sound of music into the heart of ethnomusicology, and likewise draws extensively on ecological perception and embodied cognition.

As I've already, earlier in this Afterword, referred to this musicology of record production as the recording branch of performance studies, there is little to say about how that branch of musicology may be related to this theoretical framework. More difficult though, perhaps, is the study of music theory and analysis. Hopefully the connection with analysis is obvious. Musical analysis only makes sense in terms of understanding how people interpret it or how people created it. The first is obviously at the heart of this approach but the second brings us to another, bigger question.

Is it any use?

In Chapter 2 I posed the question of whether musicology should help us 'do it better' or 'understand it better' and, unsurprisingly, I suggested that it should do both. Having made that assertion, the book is primarily about the latter and certainly has no 'how to' slant. The reasons for this are twofold. First, there are a great many books that already do this in ways that seek to create and enrich the description of good practice in this field.[1] Second, one of the aims of this book is to facilitate the promotion of education in balance with training.

One of the problems with vocational subjects in universities is that courses can simply become training courses for particular forms of technology, process or artistic practice. Of course, it is important for students to learn the rules and conventions of good practice in their field, but the point of a university education is to provide the more general skills that allow problem solving when those rules and conventions are not sufficient to solve a problem at hand. Those problem-solving skills are often couched in terms such as 'lateral thinking' or 'thinking outside the box'. Using the theory of the mind that underpins this book to explain those skills provides a pleasing circularity but is also, hopefully, a useful exercise. These problem-solving skills are based on being able to map features from some schematic representation of the nature of the process or problem in question with similar features in some action script, and then developing a strategy for getting from A to B through a further series of scripts.

Thus, for example, the problem of getting a kick drum sound to 'cut through' a dense texture of bass and guitars can be approached by mapping the notion of 'cutting through' to a variety of ways of thinking about sound. If I think of mixing in static terms I might start by trying to establish a balance between the kick drum and the bass and guitars, such that it is loud enough to be heard. If that isn't working I might try to exaggerate a

[1] Having said that, the literature on how to use the technology far outweighs the literature on how to manage the social situations.

particular frequency in the kick drum sound that isn't present or isn't as loud in the bass and guitar sounds – perhaps a high-frequency clickiness. This is a strategy based on an understanding (although in many cases a tacit rather than explicit understanding) about the nature of perception. Gestalt principles such as continuity will mean that if I can hear one aspect of a sound but another aspect that I expect to be there is obscured (in this instance, I hear the click but the bassier frequencies are masked by the other sounds) my brain will hypothesise the existence of the obscured aspect. If this doesn't work I may utilise a structural metaphor that allows me to think in terms of 'thinning out' the bass and guitar sounds with subtractive equalisation, as well as exaggerating the click of the bass drum. If this also doesn't work I may start thinking of the auditory stream in dynamic rather than static terms. How could I get the bass and guitars to be quieter for those few milliseconds when the kick drum is sounding? That might send me in the direction of techniques such as side chain compression or ducking.

Of course, many of these techniques that sound engineers have been developing over the last half century have now become part of the rules and conventions of good practice and can be learned in the process of training: when A try B. The theoretical knowledge about how sound works and how interpretation works provides a wider range of useful cognitive representations and therefore increases the chances that I can find some kind of feature mapping between a problem and potential solution. The other aspect of this kind of education is to get students used to making those kinds of cognitive leaps. Being able to reconceptualise their problem in different ways will help in the process of finding potential mappings and creating a plan for solving the problem.

To broaden this notion out from record production to musicology in general, this model of applying theoretical knowledge to practical problems is obviously the same, but the question we posed in the previous section was whether this theoretical model can be applied to other aspects of music-making such as performance and composition. This, of course, is reliant on whether we can define creative activity such as composition as problem solving. I believe we can because, just as we can see the choice of how to select a series of words or hand gestures to express ourselves as problem solving, we can view music-making as solving the problem of how a particular atmosphere, narrative or feeling can be expressed in sound. As I discussed in relation to Tim Ingold's (2013) writing about doing as thinking, the nature of the 'thing' we want to express is difficult and sometimes emerges out of the process of doing, so that does make this kind of definition of creativity complicated and potentially problematic. That said, music theory about the practice of performance and composition is generally framed in the form of rules and conventions, albeit ones that are supposed to be continually bent and broken. This same model for encouraging the potential for cross-domain mapping obviously makes sense in this instance as well.

What have I missed?

Of course, I'd like the answer to this question to be 'only the things that I've deliberately chosen to omit for the sake of clarity and brevity'. In short, that my schematic representation of the subject area has been drawn with the nature of cognitive structures in mind. Despite what I'd like, my suspicion is that the reality is more like Ingold's model: that the messy reality of the finished object grew out of the process of writing. The fact that there were many schematic drafts and iterations doesn't diminish the point. If I were to start again and spend another year writing, it would be a different book yet again.

There are two main questions for me. Does the theoretical structure of the book affect what I might have said about the content in the various category chapters? And does the nature of the typology and the divisions it imposes affect what I might have written about any particular topics? In relation to the first question, two issues occur to me. First, that the chapters on cartoons of sound and staging might have included some material on the ways in which these phenomena are produced if they had not been focused on the reception, perception and interpretation of recorded music. This would, though, have taken me down the route of a structure based on what the technology does rather than what the people do. The reception-based approach provides the type of knowledge I think is necessary for the type of problem solving I described earlier, and Chapters 7 and 8 deal with the kinds of ergonomic and practice-based knowledge that could also have been discussed at that earlier stage. Second, the chapter on the development of audio technology might have focused more on the sociology of large-scale political and economic structures if it had been placed after the fourth theoretical interlude, in the same section as the work on audiences and business structures. This did involve a practical compromise decision. It made sense to discuss the way the tools of production developed before the discussion of how they are used. In doing so, I discuss several factors such as the politics and economics of dissemination that might benefit from being discussed in the context of the theoretical framework elaborated in and after the fourth theoretical interlude. I've left readers to engage in that discussion themselves.

In relation to the second question, as to whether the typology imposed any problems, I have only found one generic issue. Certain topics, like the nature of realism or the question of authenticity, have ended up being discussed in a slightly fragmented manner across different categories in the typology. As others have dealt with these topics in a more concentrated manner elsewhere, I have embraced this fragmentation as part of the necessary structure of the book.

Bibliography

Akrich, M. and Latour, B., 1992. A Summary of a Convenient Vocabulary for the Semiotics of Human and Nonhuman Assemblies. In W.E. Bijker and J. Law, eds., *Shaping Technology, Building Society: Studies in Sociotechnical Change.* Cambridge, MA: MIT Press, pp. 259–64.

Arias-Hernandez, R., Kaastra, L.T., Green, T.M. and Fisher, B., 2011. Pair Analytics: Capturing Reasoning Processes in Collaborative Visual Analytics. In 44th Hawaii International Conference on System Sciences (HICSS). Piscataway, NJ: IEEE, pp. 1–10. Available at: http://ieeexplore.ieee.org/xpl/articleDetails.jsp?arnumber=5718616 [accessed 14 February 2014].

Arn, T.D., 1989. Digital Sampling and Signature Sound: Protection under Copyright and Non-Copyright Law. *University of Miami Entertainment & Sports Law Review,* 6(61). Available at: http://heinonline.org/HOL/LandingPage?collection=journals&handle=hein.journals/umelsr6&div=6&id=&page= [accessed 21 July 2013].

Auslander, P., 1999. *Liveness: Performance in a Mediatized Culture.* London: Routledge.

Bakhtin, M.M., 1982. *Dialogic Imagination: Four Essays,* New edn. Austin, TX: University of Texas Press.

Barthes, R., 1977. The Grain of the Voice. In *Image, Music, Text.* New York: Hill and Wang, p. 157.

Bates, E., 2012. What Studios Do. *Journal on the Art of Record Production,* (7). Available at: http://arpjournal.com/2199/what-studios-do/ [accessed 24 July 2013].

Bayley, A., 2011. Ethnographic Research into Contemporary String Quartet Rehearsal. *Ethnomusicology Forum,* 20(3), pp. 385–411.

Benjamin, W., 1969. The Work of Art in the Age of Mechanical Reproduction. In *Illuminations,* ed. H. Arendt; tr. H. Zohn. New York: Schocken, pp. 217–52.

Bennett, S., 2010. Production/Anti Production. Paper presented at the sixth Art of Record Production Conference, Leeds Metropolitan University. Available at: www.academia.edu/attachments/12263326/download_file?st=MTM5NDQ4MTgzNywxMDkuMTUzLjExNy4xNg%3D%3D&ct=MTM5NDQ4MTgzOA%3D%3D [accessed 10 March 2014].

Bennett, S., 2012. Endless Analogue: Situating Vintage Technologies in the Contemporary Recording & Production Workplace. *Journal on the Art of Record*

Production, (7). Available at: http://arpjournal.com/2143/endless-analogue-situating-vintage-technologies-in-the-contemporary-recording-production-workplace/ [accessed 24 July 2013].

Bennett, S., 2014. *Modern Records, Maverick Methods: Technology and Process in Contemporary Record Production.* Ann Arbor, MI: University of Michigan Press.

Bijker, W.E., 1995. *Of Bicycles, Bakelites and Bulbs: Towards a Theory of Sociotechnical Change.* Cambridge, MA: MIT Press.

Blake, A., 2012. Simulating the Ideal Performance: Suvi Raj Grubb and Classical Music Production. In S. Zagorski-Thomas and S. Frith, eds., *The Art of Record Production: an Introductory Reader to a New Academic Field.* Farnham: Ashgate Publishing Limited, pp. 195–206.

Blier-Carruthers, A., 2010. Live Performance – Studio Recording: An Ethnographic and Analytical Study of Sir Charles Mackerras. PhD thesis, King's College London.

Born, G., 2005. On Music Mediation: Ontology, Technology and Mediation. *Twentieth-Century Music*, 2(1), pp. 7–36.

Boss, G., 1998. Sound Perception: from Simple Objects to the Evaluation of Musical Interpretation. In Record Time: an International Conference on Recording and the Record, Jerusalem Music Centre.

Bourdieu, P., 1986. The Forms of Capital. In: J. Richardson, ed. *Handbook of Theory and Research for the Sociology of Education.* New York: Macmillan.

Bourdieu, P., 1993. *The Field of Cultural Production.* New York: Columbia University Press.

Bourdieu, P., 1996. *The State Nobility: Elite Schools in the Field of Power.* Stanford, CA: Stanford University Press.

Bourdieu, P. and Wacquant, L., 1992. *An Invitation to Reflexive Sociology.* Chicago, IL: University of Chicago Press.

Bull, M., 2005. No Dead Air! The iPod and the Culture of Mobile Listening. *Leisure Studies*, 24(4), pp. 343–55.

Burgess, R.J., 2013. *The Art of Music Production*, 4th edn. New York: Oxford University Press.

Burns, L., 2013. The Art of Persuasion: Genre, Discourse and Narrative in the Concept Album Spectacle. Keynote speech at the eighth Art of Record Production Conference, Université Laval, Québec City.

Buskin, R., 2004. Classic Tracks: 'The Reflex'. *Sound On Sound.* Available at: www.soundonsound.com/sos/jul04/articles/classictracks.htm [accessed 24 July 2013].

Buskin, R., 2007. Classic Tracks: The Jam 'Eton Rifles'. *Sound On Sound.* Available at: www.soundonsound.com/sos/mar07/articles/classictracks_0307.htm [accessed 25 February 2014].

Buskin, R., 2008. Classic Tracks: Paul Simon 'You Can Call Me Al'. *Sound On Sound.* Available at: www.soundonsound.com/sos/sep08/articles/classictracks_0908.htm [accessed 14 February 2014].

Cecil, M., 2004. Interview with Malcolm Cecil. *Tape Op*, 44. Available at: http://tapeop.com/interviews/44/malcolm-cecil/ [accessed 14 February 2014].

Chanan, M., 1995. *Repeated Takes: a Short History of Recording and its Effects on Music.* London: Verso Books.

CIA, 2013. People and Society – Sex Ratio. *The World Factbook 2013–14.* Available at: www.cia.gov/library/publications/the-world-factbook/geos/xx.html [accessed 9 March 2014].

Clark, H.H., 1996. *Using Language.* Cambridge: Cambridge University Press.

Clarke, E.F., 2005. *Ways of Listening: an Ecological Approach to the Perception of Musical Meaning.* New York: Oxford University Press.

Clarke, E.F., 2007. The Impact of Recording on Listening. *Twentieth-Century Music*, 4(1), pp. 47–70.

Clarke, E.F. and Cook, N., eds., 2004. *Empirical Musicology: Aims, Methods, Prospects.* Oxford: Oxford University Press.

Clayton, M., 2008. Towards An Ethnomusicology of Sound Experience. In H. Stobart, ed., *The New (Ethno) Musicologies.* Plymouth: Scarecrow Press, pp. 135–69.

Cleveland, B., 2001. *Creative Music Production: Joe Meek's Bold Techniques.* Vallejo, CA: Mix Books.

Collier, G., 1994. The Churchill Report on Jazz Education in America. *Jazz Changes Magazine*, 1(1).

Constant, E.W., 1980. *The Origins of the Turbojet Revolution.* Baltimore, MD: Johns Hopkins University Press.

Cook, N., 2000. *Music: a Very Short Introduction.* Oxford: Oxford Universiy Press.

Csikszentmihalyi, M., 1988. Society, Culture and Person: a Systems View of Creativity. In R. Sternberg, ed., *The Nature of Creativity: Contemporary Psychological Perspectives.* New York: Cambridge University Press, pp. 313–38.

Csikszentmihalyi, M., 1997. *Creativity: Flow and the Psychology of Discovery and Invention.* New York: HarperCollins.

Culshaw, J., 1967. *Ring Resounding.* London: Secker and Warburg.

Cunningham, M., 1999. *Good Vibrations: History of Record Production*, 2nd revised edn. London: Sanctuary Publishing Ltd.

Damasio, A., 2000. *The Feeling of what Happens: Body, Emotion and the Making of Consciousness*, New edn. London: Vintage Books.

Danielsen, A., 2006. *Presence and Pleasure: the Funk Grooves of James Brown and Parliament.* Middletown, CT: Wesleyan University Press.

Davidson, J. and Good, J., 2002. Social and Musical Co-ordination between Members of a String Quartet: an Exploratory Study. *Psychology of Music*, 30(2), pp. 186–201.

Davis, M., 1990. *Miles.* Simon & Schuster.

DeNora, T., 2000. *Music in Everyday Life*, 1st edn. Cambridge: Cambridge University Press.

Diamond, B., 2005. Media as Social Action: Native American Musicians in the Recording Studio. In P.D. Greene and T. Porcello, eds., *Wired For Sound.* Middletown, CT: Wesleyan University Press, pp. 118–37.

Doris, F., 2013. Les Paul: the Legend and the Legacy. Available at: www.frankdoris.com/writing/tas/lespaul.htm [accessed 22 July 2013].

Doyle, P., 2006. *Echo and Reverb: Fabricating Space in Popular Music Recording, 1900–1960.* Middletown, CT: Wesleyan University Press.

Doyle, P., 2009. 'Working for the Man': Figuring the Artist-producer Relationship. Available at: www.digitalpodcast.com/items/7696234 [accessed 5 September 2013].

Edgerton, D., 2006. *The Shock of the Old: Technology and Global History since 1900,* London: Profile Books.

Eisenberg, E., 2005. *The Recording Angel: Explorations in Phonography,* expanded edn. New Haven, CT: Yale University Press.

Emirbayer, M. and Williams, E., 2005. Bourdieu and Social Work. *Social Service Review,* 79(4), pp. 689–725.

Eno, B., 2004. The Studio as Compositional Tool. In C. Cox and D. Warner, eds., *Audio Culture: Readings in Modern Music.* New York and London: Continuum International Publishing Group, pp. 127–30.

Fauconnier, G. and Turner, M., 2003. *The Way We Think: Conceptual Blending and the Mind's Hidden Complexities.* New York: Basic Books.

Feldman, J.A., 2008. *From Molecule to Metaphor: a Neural Theory of Language,* 1st MIT Press paperback edn. Cambridge, MA: MIT Press.

Felton, D., 2012. Top 20 Best Compressor of All Time: 2 – Urei/Universal Audio 1176. *Attack Magazine.* Available at: www.attackmagazine.com/features/top-20-best-hardware-compressors-ever-made/19/ [accessed 25 July 2013].

Fletcher, T., 2005. Recording in the Real World. Paper presented at the first Art of Record Production Conference, University of Westminster, London. Available at: www.artofrecordproduction.com/index.php/arp-conferences/arp-2009/21-arp-conference-archive/arp-2009/110-fletcher-2009 [accessed 10 March 2014].

Frith, S., 1998. *Performing Rites: Evaluating Popular Music,* new edn. Oxford: Oxford University Press.

Frith, S., 2012. The Place of the Producer in the Discourse of Rock. In S. Zagorski-Thomas and S. Frith, eds., *The Art of Record Production: an Introductory Reader to a New Academic Field.* Farnham: Ashgate Publishing Limited, pp. 207–22.

Gell, A., 1998. *Art and Agency.* Oxford: Oxford University Press.

Gibson, J.J., 1979. *The Ecological Approach to Visual Perception.* Hove: Psychology Press.

Gillespie, M., 2007. 'Another Darkchild Classic': Phonographic Forgery and Producer Rodney Jerkins' Sonic Signature. Master's thesis, Université Laval, Québec City. Available at: www.theses.ulaval.ca/2007/24164/24164.pdf [accessed 21 July 2013].

Goffman, E., 1956. *The Presentation of Self in Everyday Life.* Edinburgh: University of Edinburgh, Social Sciences Research Centre.

Gottlieb, G., 2009. *How Does it Sound Now? Legendary Engineers and Vintage Gear.* Boston, MA: Course Technology PTR.

Gould, G., 1966. The Prospects of Recording. *High Fidelity Magazine,* 16(4), pp. 46–63.

Gracyk, T., 1996. *Rhythm and Noise: Aesthetics of Rock.* London: I.B. Tauris.

Grady, J., 1997. Foundations of Meaning: Primary Metaphor and Primary Scenes. PhD thesis, University of California, Berkeley.

Gribbin, J., 2009. *Not Fade Away: the Life and Times of Buddy Holly.* London: Icon Books.

Haas, M., 2005. The Recording Producer as Musicological Filter. Paper presented at the first Art of Record Production Conference, University of Westminster, London. Available at: www.artofrecordproduction.com/index.php/arp-conferences/arp-2005/17-arp-conference-archive/arp-2005/67-haas-2005 [accessed 10 March 2014].

Hall, E.T., 1966. *The Hidden Dimension.* London: Doubleday.

Hammar, P. 1999. John T. Mullin: the Man who put Bing Crosby on Tape. *Mix Magazine Online.* Available at: http://mixonline.com/mag/audio_john_mullin_man/ [accessed 20 July 2013].

Hewitt, B., 2011. 'I Feel Like I've Just Begun': an Interview with PJ Harvey. *The Quietus.* Available at: http://thequietus.com/articles/05520-pj-harvey-interview-let-england-shake [accessed 29 July 2013].

Higgs, R.W., 1974. Sonic Signature Analysis for Arc Furnace Diagnostics and Control. In Ultrasonics Symposium. Piscataway, NJ: IEEE, pp. 653–63. Available at: http://ieeexplore.ieee.org/xpl/mostRecentIssue.jsp?punumber=10274 [accessed 21 July 2013].

Hirsch, E. and Silverstone, R., 2004. *Consuming Technologies: Media and Information in Domestic Spaces.* London: Routledge.

Howlett, M., 2007. Fixing the Volatile – Studio Vocal Performance Techniques. Paper presented at the third Art of Record Production Conference, Queensland University of Technology. Available at: www.artofrecordproduction.com/index.php/arp-conferences/arp-2007/19-arp-conference-archive/arp-2007/123-howlett-2007 [accessed 28 July 2013].

Howlett, M., 2009. The Record Producer as Nexus: Creative Inspiration, Technology and the Recording Industry. PhD thesis, University of Glamorgan, Cardiff.

Hyndman, S., 2013. No Money, Mo' Problems: the Role of the Remix in Restructuring Compensation for Producers of Electronic Dance Music. Paper presentation at the eighth Art of Record Production Conference, Université Laval, Québec City.

Ingold, T., 2013. *Making: Anthropology, Archaeology, Art and Architecture.* London: Routledge.

Iyer, V., 1998. Microstructures of Feel, Macrostructures of Sound: Embodied Cognition in West African and African-American Musics. PhD thesis, University of California, Berkeley. Available at: archive.cnmat.berkeley.edu/People/Vijay/%20THESIS.html [accessed 20 July 2013].

Izhaki, R., 2008. *Mixing Audio: Concepts, Practices and Tools*. Oxford: Focal Press.

Jarrett, M., 2012. The Self-Effacing Producer: Absence Summons Presence. In S. Zagorski-Thomas and S. Frith, eds., *The Art of Record Production: an Introductory Reader to a New Academic Field*. Farnham: Ashgate Publishing Limited, pp. 129–48.

Johnson, M., 1990. *The Body in the Mind: the Bodily Basis of Meaning, Imagination, and Reason*. Chicago, IL: University of Chicago Press.

Johnson, M. and Rohrer, T., 2007. We Are Live Creatures: Embodiment, American Pragmatism, and the Cognitive Organism. In T. Ziemke, J. Zlatev and R.M. Frank, eds., *Body, Language, and Mind*, vol. 1. Berlin: Mouton de Gruyter, pp. 17–54.

Kaastra, L.T., 2008. Systematic Approaches to the Study of Cognition in Western Art Music Performance. PhD thesis, University of British Columbia, Vancouver. Available at: https://circle.ubc.ca/bitstream/handle/2429/678/ubc_2008_spring_kaastra_linda.pdf?sequence=1 [accessed 24 May 2013].

Katz, M., 2004. *Capturing Sound: How Technology Has Changed Music*. Berkeley, CA: University of California Press.

Kazdin, A., 1989. *Glenn Gould at Work: Creative Lying*. New York: E.P. Dutton.

Kealy, E.R., 1979. From Craft to Art: the Case of Sound Mixers and Popular Music. *Work and Occupations*, 6(1), pp. 3–29.

Keep, A., 2005. Does Creative Abuse Drive Developments in Record Production? Paper presented at the first Art of Record Production Conference, University of Westminster, London. Available at: www.artofrecordproduction.com/index.php/arp-conferences/arp-2005/17-arp-conference-archive/arp-2005/72-keep-2005 [accessed 26 July 2013].

Keightley, K., 1996. 'Turn it down!' She Shrieked: Gender, Domestic Space, and High Fidelity, 1948–59. *Popular Music*, 15(2), pp. 149–77.

Kirkley, C., 2011. Music from Saharan Cellphones. *Sahelsounds*. Available at: http://sahelsounds.bandcamp.com/album/music-from-saharan-cellphones [accessed 15 May 2013].

Kuhn, T., 1962. *The Structure of Scientific Revolutions*. Chicago, IL: University of Chicago Press.

Lacasse, S., 2000. 'Listen to My Voice': the Evocative Power of Vocal Staging in Recorded Rock Music and Other Forms of Vocal Expression. PhD thesis, University of Liverpool. Available at: www.mus.ulaval.ca/lacasse/texts/THESIS.pdf [accessed 30 June 2011].

Lacasse, S., 2005. Persona, Emotions and Technology: the Phonographic Staging of the Popular Music Voice. Paper presented at the first Art of Record Production Conference, University of Westminster, London. Available at:

www.artofrecordproduction.com/index.php/arp-conferences/arp-2005/17-arp-conference-archive/arp-2005/74-lacasse-2005 [accessed 14 March 2014].

Laffey, S., 2011. The Essence of Traditional Music. *Folk World*, 45. Available at: www.folkworld.de/45/e/raw.html [accessed 7 May 2013].

Lakoff, G., 1990. *Women, Fire, and Dangerous Things: What Categories Reveal about the Mind*. Chicago, IL: University of Chicago Press.

Lakoff, G. and Johnson, M., 1999. *Philosophy in the Flesh: the Embodied Mind and its Challenge to Western Thought*. New York: Basic Books.

Lakoff, G. and Johnson, M., 2003. *Metaphors We Live By*, 2nd edn. Chicago, IL: University of Chicago Press.

Latour, B., 2005. *Reassembling the Social: an Introduction to Actor-Network-Theory*. New York: Oxford University Press.

Latour, B. and Woolgar, S., 1986. *Laboratory Life: the Construction of Scientific Facts*, 2nd edn. Princeton, NJ: Princeton University Press.

Lawrence, T., 2003. *Love Saves the Day: a History of American Dance Music Culture, 1970–1979*. Durham, NC: Duke University Press.

Les Paul Foundation, 2013. The Les Paul Legacy. Available at: www.lespaulfoundation.org/les-paul-legacy.html [accessed 22 July 2013].

Lévi-Strauss, C., 1966. *The Savage Mind*, Chicago, IL: University of Chicago Press.

Long Lingo, E. and O'Mahony, S., 2010. Nexus Work: Brokerage on Creative Projects. *Administrative Science Quarterly*, 55, pp. 47–81.

Macero, T., 2004. On Creating 'Bitches Brew' with Miles Davis. *Artists House Music*. Available at: www.artistshousemusic.org/videos/teo+macero+on+creating+bitches+brew+with+miles+davis [accessed 31 January 2012].

MacGregor, N., 2010. *A History of the World in 100 Objects*. London: Allen Lane.

Massey, D., 2004. Geographies of Responsibility. *Geografiska Annaler: Series B, Human Geography*, 86(1), pp. 5–18.

McGurk, H. and MacDonald, J., 1976. Hearing Lips and Seeing Voices. *Nature*, 264(5588), pp. 746–8.

McIntyre, P., 2011. *Creativity and Cultural Production: Issues for Media Practice*. Basingstoke: Palgrave Macmillan.

McIntyre, P., 2012. Rethinking Creativity: Record Production and the Systems Model. In S. Zagorski-Thomas and S. Frith, eds., *The Art of Record Production: an Introductory Reader to a New Academic Field*. Farnham: Ashgate Publishing Limited, pp. 149–62.

Mee, C.D. and Daniel, E.D., 1990. *Magnetic Recording Handbook: Technology and Applications*. New York: McGraw-Hill.

Meintjes, L., 2003. *Sound of Africa! Making Music Zulu in a South African Studio*. Durham, NC: Duke University Press.

Meintjes, L., 2005. Reaching 'Overseas': South African Sound Engineers, Technology and Tradition. In P.D. Greene and T. Porcello, eds., *Wired For Sound*. Middletown, CT: Wesleyan University Press, pp. 23–46.

Milner, G., 2011. *Perfecting Sound Forever: the Story of Recorded Music.* London: Granta Publications.

Moehn, F.J., 2005. 'The Disc is Not the Avenue': Schismogenetic Mimesis in Samba Recording. In *Wired For Sound.* Middletown, CT: Wesleyan University Press, pp. 47–83.

Monson, I., 1997. *Saying Something: Jazz Improvisation and Interaction.* Chicago, IL: University of Chicago Press.

Moore, A., 2012. All Buttons In: an Investigation into the Use of the 1176 FET Compressor in Popular Music Production. *Journal on the Art of Record Production,* (6).

Moore, A.F., 1992. *Rock: the Primary Text: Developing a Musicology of Rock,* 2nd edn. Farnham: Ashgate Publishing Limited.

Moore, A.F., 2002. Authenticity as Authentication. *Popular Music,* 21(2), pp. 209–23.

Moore, A.F., 2012a. Beyond a Musicology of Production. In S. Zagorski-Thomas and S. Frith, eds., *The Art of Record Production: an Introductory Reader to a New Academic Field.* Farnham: Ashgate Publishing Limited, pp. 99–112.

Moore, A.F., 2012b. *Song Means: Analysing and Interpreting Recorded Popular Song.* Farnham: Ashgate Publishing Limited.

Moorefield, V., 2005. *The Producer as Composer: Shaping the Sounds of Popular Music: From the Illusion of Reality to the Reality of Illusion.* Cambridge, MA: MIT Press.

Morton, D., 2000. *Off the Record: the Technology and Culture of Sound Recording in America.* New Brunswick, NJ: Rutgers University Press.

Moylan, W., 1992. *The Art of Recording: Understanding and Crafting the Mix.* Oxford: Focal Press.

Mynett, M., 2013. Sounds in Silence: Controlling Ambience and Colouration with a Semi-Anechoic Chamber during Contemporary Metal Music Production. Paper presented at eighth Art of Record Production Conference, Université Laval, Québec City.

Nakamura, J. and Csikszentmihalyi, M., 2009. Flow Theory and Research. In C.R. Snyder and S.J. Lopez, eds., *Handbook of Positive Psychology.* Oxford: Oxford University Press, pp. 195–206.

O'Brian, E., 1999. Ed's Diary. Available at: www.greenplastic.com/coldstorage/articles/edsdiary/ [accessed 28 July 2013].

Oohashi, T. et al., 2000. Inaudible High-Frequency Sounds Affect Brain Activity: Hypersonic Effect. *Journal of Neurophysiology,* 83(6), pp. 3548–58.

Oudshoorn, N. and Pinch, T., eds., 2003. *How Users Matter: the Co-construction of Users and Technology.* Cambridge, MA: MIT Press.

Owsinski, B., 1999. *The Mixing Engineer's Handbook,* 1st edn. Vallejo, CA: MixBooks.

Peterson, R.A., 1995. The Dialectic of Hard-Core and Soft-Shell Country Music. *South Atlantic Quarterly,* 94(1), pp. 273–300.

Peterson, R.A., 1997. *Creating Country Music: Fabricating Authenticity.* Chicago, IL: University of Chicago Press.

Pinch, T. and Bijker, W.E., 1987. The Social Construction of Facts and Artifacts: or How the Sociology of Science and the Sociology of Technology Might Benefit Each Other. In T. Pinch, W.E. Bijker and T.P. Hughes, eds., *The Social Contruction of Technological Systems: New Directions in the Sociology and History of Technology*. Cambridge, MA: MIT Press, pp. 11–44.

Pinch, T., Bijker, W.E. and Hughes, T.P., eds., 2012. *The Social Construction of Technological Systems*, anniversary edn. Cambridge, MA: MIT Press.

Pinch, T. and Trocco, F., 2004. *Analog Days: the Invention and Impact of the Moog Synthesizer*. Cambridge, MA: Harvard University Press.

Porcello, T., 2004. Speaking of Sound: Language and the Professionalization of Sound-Recording Engineers. *Social Studies of Science*, 34(5), pp. 733–58.

Porcello, T., 2005. Music Mediated as Live in Austin: Sound, Technology and Recording Practice. In T. Porcello and P.D. Greene, eds., *Wired for Sound*. Middletown, CT: Wesleyan University Press, pp. 103–17.

Porcello, T. and Greene, P.D., eds., 2004. *Wired for Sound: Engineering and Technologies in Sonic Cultures*. Middletown, CT: Wesleyan University Press.

Randall, M., 2001. Roni Size – Reprazenting Bristol. Interview for Yahoo Music (no longer available online).

Reiss, J.D., 2011. Intelligent Systems for Mixing Multichannel Audio. Paper presented at Seventeenth International Conference on Digital Signal Processing (DSP2011), Corfu, Greece.

Rohrer, T., 2005. Image Schemata in the Brain. In B. Hampe and J. Grady, eds., *From Perception to Meaning: Image Schemas in Cognitive Linguistics*. Berlin: Mouton de Gruyter, pp. 165–96.

Rossing, T.D., Moore, R.F. and Wheeler, P.A., 2001. *The Science of Sound*, 3rd edn. San Fransisco, CA: Addison Wesley.

Ryan, K. and Kehew, B., 2006. *Recording the Beatles*. Houston, TX: Curvebender Publishing.

Saussure, F. de, 1983. *Course in General Linguistics*, eds. C. Bally and A. Sechehaye; tr. A. Harris. Peru, IL: Open Court Publishing Company.

Savage, S., 2005. Lipsmacks, Mouth Noises and Heavy Breathing. Paper presented at the first Art of Record Production Conference, University of Westminster, London. Available at: www.artofrecordproduction.com/index.php/arp-conferences/arp-2005/17-arp-conference-archive/arp-2005/80-savage-2005 [accessed 10 March 2014].

Savage, S., 2008. 'It Could Have Happened' – the Evolution of Music Construction. Paper presented at the fourth Art of Record Production Conference, University of Massachusetts Lowell. Available at: www.artofrecordproduction.com/index.php/arp-conferences/arp-2008/10-arp-conference-archive/170-savage-08 [accessed 28 July 2013].

Schank, R. and Abelson, R., 1977. *Scripts, Plans, Goals and Understanding: an Inquiry into Human Knowledge Structures*. Oxford: Lawrence Erlbaum.

Schmidt-Horning, S., 2012. The Sounds of Space: Studio as Instrument in the Era of High Fidelity. In S. Zagorski-Thomas and S. Frith, eds., *The Art of Record Production: an Introductory Reader to a New Academic Field.* Farnham: Ashgate Publishing Limited, pp. 29–42.

Schonbrun, M., 2013. Early Recording Techniques. Available at: www.netplaces.com/digital-home-recording/recording-basics/early-recording-techniques.htm [accessed 22 July 2013].

Scruton, R., 1999. *The Aesthetics of Music.* Oxford: Clarendon Press.

Sheppard, J., 2003. *Continuum Encyclopedia of Popular Music of the World.* London: Continuum International Publishing Group, Limited.

Shocklee, H., 2007. Keynote Speech. Presented at the third Art of Record Production Conference, Brisbane. Available at: www.artofrecordproduction.com/index.php/arp-resources/8-short-hank-shocklee-2007 [accessed 28 July 2013].

Skea, D., 2001. Rudy Van Gelder in Hackensack: Defining the Jazz Sound in the 1950s. *Current Musicology,* (71–3), pp. 54–76.

Small, C., 1998. *Musicking: the Meanings of Performing and Listening,* 1st edn. Middletown, CT: Wesleyan University Press.

Smalley, D., 1986. Spectromorphology and Structuring Processes. In S. Emmerson, ed., *The Language of Electroacoustic Music.* London: Macmillan, pp. 61–93.

Snow, M., 2013. Reg Presley: 'I Must Learn to Swear More' – a Classic Feature from the Vaults. *The Guardian,* 5 February. Available at: www.theguardian.com/music/2013/feb/05/from-rocks-backpages-troggs-reg-presley [accessed 1 May 2013].

Snyder, R.H., 2003. Sel-Sync and the 'Octopus': How Came to be the First Recorder to Minimize Successive Copying in Overdubs. *ARSC Journal,* 34(2), pp. 209–13.

Stevenson, P., 2002. Bob Olhsson: Looking at Digital Recording. *Tape Op,* 30. Available at: http://tapeop.com/interviews/30/bob-olhsson/ [accessed 24 February 2014].

Stewart, G., 2003. *Rumba on the River: a History of the Popular Music of the Two Congos.* London: Verso Books.

Stobart, H., ed., 2008. *The New (Ethno) Musicologies.* Plymouth: Scarecrow Press.

Stoffregen, T. and Bardy, B., 2001. On Specification and the Senses. *Behavioural and Brain Sciences,* 24, pp. 195–261.

Tagg, P., 2012. *Music's Meanings: a Modern Musicology for Non-musos.* New York and Huddersfield: The Mass Media Music Scholars' Press.

Tallis, R., 2011. *Aping Mankind: Neuromania, Darwinitis and the Misrepresentation of Humanity.* Durham: Acumen Publishing Limited.

Taylor, T.D., 2001. *Strange Sounds: Music, Technology, and Culture,* 1st edn. London: Routledge.

Théberge, P., 1997. *Any Sound you can Imagine: Making Music/Consuming Technology,* 1st edn. Middletown, CT: Wesleyan University Press.

Thornton, S., 1996. *Club Cultures: Music, Media and Subcultural Capital.* Middletown, CT: Wesleyan University Press.

Tingen, P., 1994. Robbie Adams: Recording U2's 'Achtung Baby' and 'Zooropa'. *Sound On Sound.* Available at: www.soundonsound.com/sos/1994_articles/mar94/u2robbieadams.html [accessed 31 January 2012].

Tingen, P., 2001a. Miles Davis and the Making of 'Bitches Brew': Sorcerer's Brew. *Jazz Times.* Available at: www.jazztimes.com/articles/20243-miles-davis-and-the-making-of-bitches-brew-sorcerer-s-brew [accessed 6 November 2013].

Tingen, P., 2001b. The Making of 'In A Silent Way' and 'Bitches Brew'. *Mojo Magazine,* (94). Available at: www.miles-beyond.com/iaswbitchesbrew.htm [accessed 29 August 2013].

Tomaz de Carvalho, A., 2012. The Discourse of Home Recording: Authority of 'Pros' and the Sovereignty of the Big Studios. *Journal on the Art of Record Production,* (7). Available at: http://arpjournal.com/2149/the-discourse-of-home-recording-authority-of-%E2%80%9Cpros%E2%80%9D-and-the-sovereignty-of-the-big-studios/ [accessed 26 July 2013].

Trescott, M.M., 1979. *Dynamos and Virgins Revisited: Women and Technological Change in History: an Anthology.* Plymouth: Scarecrow Press.

Turing, A., 1950. Computing Machinery and Intelligence. *Mind,* 59(236), pp. 433–60.

Turner, D., 2012. *Profiling a Metal Mastermind: the Mixing Techniques of Andy Sneap.* MRes thesis. Cardiff: University of Glamorgan.

Veal, M., 2007. *Dub: Soundscapes and Shattered Songs in Jamaican Reggae.* Middletown, CT: Wesleyan University Press.

Wallach, J., 2005. Engineering Techno-hybrid Grooves in Two Indonesian Sound Studios. In P.D. Greene and T. Porcello, eds., *Wired For Sound.* Middletown, CT: Wesleyan University Press, pp. 138–54.

Walser, R., 1993. *Running with the Devil: Power, Gender and Madness in Heavy Metal Music.* Middletown, CT: Wesleyan University Press.

Williams, A., 2012. 'I'm Not Hearing What You're Hearing' – the Conflict and Connection of Headphone Mixes and Multiple Audioscapes. In S. Zagorski-Thomas and S. Frith, eds., *The Art of Record Production: an Introductory Reader to a New Academic Field.* Farnham: Ashgate Publishing Limited, pp. 113–28.

Williams, S., 2012. Tubby's Dub Style: the Live Art of Record Production. In S. Zagorski-Thomas and S. Frith, eds., *The Art of Record Production: an Introductory Reader to a New Academic Field.* Farnham: Ashgate Publishing Limited, pp. 235–46.

Wishart, T., 1986. Sound Symbols and Landscape. In S. Emmerson, ed., *The Language of Electroacoustic Music.* London: Macmillan, pp. 41–60.

Wolfe, P., 2012. A Studio of One's Own: Music Production, Technology and Gender. *Journal on the Art of Record Production,* (7). Available at: http://arpjournal.com/2156/a-studio-of-one%E2%80%99s-own-music-production-technology-and-gender/ [accessed 24 July 2013].

Woolgar, S., 1991. Configuring the User: the Case of Usability Trials. In J. Law, ed., *The Sociology of Monsters: Essays on Power, Technology and Domination.* London: Routledge, pp. 57–102.

Zagorski-Thomas, S., 2007. The Musicology of Record Production. *Twentieth-Century Music*, 4(2), pp. 189–207.

Zagorski-Thomas, S., 2010a. Real and Unreal Performances. In A. Danielsen, ed., *Rhythm in the Age of Digital Reproduction.* Farnham: Ashgate Publishing Limited, pp. 195–212.

Zagorski-Thomas, S., 2010b. The Stadium in your Bedroom: Functional Staging, Authenticity and the Audience-led Aesthetic in Record Production. *Popular Music*, 29(2).

Zagorski-Thomas, S., 2012a. Musical Meaning and the Musicology of Record Production. *Beitraege zur Popularmusikforschung*, 38.

Zagorski-Thomas, S., 2012b. The US vs the UK Sound: Meaning in Music Production in the 1970s. In S. Zagorski-Thomas & S. Frith, eds., *The Art of Record Production: an Introductory Reader to a New Academic Field.* Farnham: Ashgate Publishing Limited, pp. 57–76.

Zagorski-Thomas, S., 2015. Sonic Cartoons. In M. Hanáček, H. Schulze, and J. Papenburg, eds., *Research Companion to the Sound in Media Culture Network.* Cambridge, MA: MIT Press.

Zagorski-Thomas, S. and Frith, S., eds., 2012. *The Art of Record Production: an Introductory Reader to a New Academic Field*, Farnham: Ashgate Publishing Limited.

Zak, A.J., 2001. *The Poetics of Rock: Cutting Tracks, Making Records.* Berkeley, CA: University of California Press.

Zak, A.J., 2010. *I Don't Sound Like Nobody: Remaking Music in 1950s America.* Ann Arbor, MI: University of Michigan Press.

Zbikowski, L.M., 2009. Music, Language, and Multimodal Metaphor. In C. Forceville and E. Urios-Aparisi, eds., *Multimodal Metaphor.* Berlin: Mouton de Gruyter, pp. 359–81.

Discography

The Beatles, 1966. *Revolver*, Parlophone PCS 7009.

The Beatles, 1967. *Sgt. Pepper's Lonely Hearts Club Band*, Parlophone PCS 7027.

The Beatles, 1968. *The Beatles*, Apple Records PCS 7067/8.

Beck, 1993. *Loser*, Bong Load Records BL5.

Buena Vista Social Club, 1997. *Buena Vista Social Club*, World Circuit WCD050.

The Buggles, 1979. 'Video Killed the Radio Star', Island Records WIP 6524.

Cher, 1998. 'Believe', Warner Bros. Records 9 44576–2.

Coldplay, 2011. *Mylo Xyloto*, Parlophone 087 5532.

Darkthrone, 1994. *Transilvanian Hunger*, Peaceville Vile 43CD.

Davis, M., 1959. *Kind of Blue*, Columbia CS8163.

Davis, M., 1969. *In a Silent Way*, Columbia CS9875.

Davis, M., 1970. *Bitches Brew*, CBS S64010.

Decca Records, 1967. *How to Give Yourself a Stereo Check-Out: Test Recordings*, Decca SKL 4861.

Deep Purple, 1972. *Made in Japan*, Purple Records TPSP351.

Dixie Chicks, 2002. *Home*, Epic EPC509603–2.

Duran Duran, 1983. *Seven and the Ragged Tiger*, EMI EMC1654541.

Dylan, B., 1965. *Bringing It All Back Home*, Columbia CS9128.

Electric Light Orchestra, 1976. 'Telephone Line', United Artists Records UP 36264.

Eminem, 2000. 'The Real Slim Shady', Interscope Records 497 366–2.

Gaye, M., 1969. 'I Heard it Through the Grapevine', Tamla Motown TMG 686.

Gould, G., 1963. *Bach: The Well Tempered Clavier, Book 1, Preludes and Fugues 1–8*, Columbia Masterworks MS6408.

Harvey, P.J., 2011. *Let England Shake*, Island Records 2753189.

Fletcher Henderson and his Orchestra, 1924. 'Naughty Man', Vocalion 14935B.

Houston, W., 1992. 'I Will Always Love You', Arista 74321 12065 7.

The Jam, 1979. 'The Eton Rifles', Polydor 2059 176.

K.C. and the Sunshine Band, 1975. 'That's the Way (I Like it)', RCA Victor PPBO-7018.

Kinch, S., 2006. *A Day in the Life of B19: Tales of the Tower Block*, Dune Records CD014.

King Crimson, 1976. 'Epitaph/21st Century Schizoid Man', Island Records WIP 6274.

Kings of Leon, 2008b. *Only by the Night*, RCA 88697–32712–2.

Led Zeppelin, 1973. *Houses of the Holy*, Atlantic SD 7255.

Lil's Hot Shots, 1926. 'Drop That Sack', Vocalion 1037.
Louis Armstrong and His Hot Five, 1926. 'Muskrat Ramble', Okeh 8300.
Louis Armstrong and His Hot Five, 1927. 'Once in a While', Okeh 8566.
Louis Armstrong and His Hot Five, 1940. 'Don't Jive Me', Columbia 36376.
Metallica, 2003. *St. Anger*, Vertigo 0602498653708.
The Mike Flowers Pops, 1995. 'Wonderwall', London Records LONCD378.
Morissette, A., 1996. 'Ironic', Reprise Records 9362–43700–9.
Ngcobo, S., 2004. *Introducing Shiyani Ngcobo*, World Music Network LC11067.
Oliveros, P., 1997. *Electronic Works 1965/66*, Paradigm Discs PD04.
Portishead, 1994. *Dummy*, Go! Beat 828 522–1.
Prince, 1987. *Sign 'O' the Times*, Paisley Park W 8399.
Public Enemy, 1990. *Fear of a Black Planet*, Def Jam Recordings 314 523 446-2.
Pulp, 1995. 'Common People', Island Records CID 613, 854 329–2.
Queen, 1975. *A Night at the Opera*, EMI EMTC103.
Queen, 1977. 'We Are the Champions/We Will Rock You', EMI 2708.
Radiohead, 2000. *Kid A*, Parlophone LPKIDA1.
The Raw Bar Collective, 2011. *Millhouse Measures*, Dublin: Copperplate RBC001.
Johnnie Ray and the Four Lads, 1951. 'Cry', Okeh 4–6840.
Schaeffer, P., 1948. *Etude aux Chemin de Fer*, Paris: Radiodiffusion-Télévision Française.
Simon, P., 1986. *Graceland*, Warner Bros. Records W1–25447.
Size, R., 1997. *New Forms*, Talkin' Loud 534 933–2.
Skee-Lo, 1995. 'I Wish', Scotti Bros. Records 72392 78032–1.
Smith, P., 1975. *Horses*, Arista ARTY 122.
Spears, B., 2000. 'Oops! . . . I Did It Again', Jive 9250582.
Suede, 1996. *Coming Up*, Nude Records 4851299.
The Tornados, 1962. 'Telstar', Decca 45-F11494.
Turner, I. and T., 1966. 'River Deep, Mountain High', Philles Records 131.
U2, 1984. *The Unforgettable Fire*, Island Records U25.
U2, 1991. *Achtung Baby*, Island Records 212 110.
The Wallace Family, 2000. *Tso'kam*. Red Planet Records.
Wiener Philharmoniker and Solti, G., 1965. *Götterdämmerung*, UK: Decca 414 515–1.
Wonder, S., 1973a. *Innervisions*, Tamla Motown STMA 8011.
Wonder, S., 1973b. 'Living for the City', Tamla T54242F.

Filmography

Berlinger, J. and Sinofsky, B., 2004. *Metallica: Some Kind of Monster*, Radical Media/Third Eye Motion Picture Company.

Gilliam, T., 2009. *The Imaginarium of Dr. Parnassus*, Infinity Features Entertainment.

Kings of Leon, 2008a. *OBTN Home Movies: All 24 Days*, Available at: www.closertokol.com/apps/videos/videos/show/14213289-obtn-home-movies-2008-all-24-days [accessed 21 January 2014].

Longfellow, M., 2001. *Classic Albums: Metallica – Metallica*, Isis Productions/Eagle Rock Entertainment.

Pakula, A.J., 1976. *All the President's Men*, Warner Bros.

Reiner, R., 1984. *This is Spinal Tap*, Embassy Pictures.

Stevens, G., 1936. *Swing Time*, RKO Radio Pictures.

Index